THE SYMPATHETIC CONSUMER

CULTURE
AND
ECONOMIC
LIFE

THE SYMPATHETIC CONSUMER

Moral Critique in Capitalist Culture

TAD SKOTNICKI

STANFORD UNIVERSITY PRESS
Stanford, California

STANFORD UNIVERSITY PRESS
Stanford, California

©2021 by the Board of Trustees of the Leland Stanford Junior University. All rights reserved.

No part of this book may be reproduced or transmitted in any form or by any means, electronic or mechanical, including photocopying and recording, or in any information storage or retrieval system without the prior written permission of Stanford University Press.

Printed in the United States of America on acid-free, archival-quality paper

Library of Congress Cataloging-in-Publication Data

Names: Skotnicki, Tad, author.

Title: The sympathetic consumer : moral critique in capitalist culture / Tad Skotnicki.

Other titles: Culture and economic life.

Description: Stanford, California : Stanford University Press, 2021. | Series: Culture and economic life | Includes bibliographical references and index.

Identifiers: LCCN 2020033193 (print) | LCCN 2020033194 (ebook) | ISBN 9781503614635 (cloth) | ISBN 9781503627734 (paperback) | ISBN 9781503627741 (ebook)

Subjects: LCSH: Consumer movements—United States—History. | Consumer movements—Great Britain—History. | Consumers' leagues—United States—History. | Consumers' leagues—Great Britain—History. | Consumption (Economics)—Moral and ethical aspects—United States—History. | Consumption (Economics)—Moral and ethical aspects—Great Britain—History.

Classification: LCC HC110.C6 S565 2021 (print) | LCC HC110.C6 (ebook) | DDC 306.30941—DC23

LC record available at https://lccn.loc.gov/2020033193

LC ebook record available at https://lccn.loc.gov/2020033194

Cover design: Rob Ehle

Cover images: From *Hull House Maps and Papers*, Florence Kelley, 1895. Graciously provided by the Florence Kelley website at the Northwestern University Library.

Typeset by Kevin Barrett Kane in 10/14 Minion Pro

Table of Contents

Acknowledgments

When I was a teenager, I spent an unhealthy amount of time sprawled out in front of the stereo squinting at liner notes. Years later I find something similar, if perhaps a bit less cryptic, in these sections of books. In that spirit, I offer these remarks.

I began this project in the Department of Sociology at the University of California, San Diego. There I was fortunate to meet Rick Biernacki, who showed me how to seek fundamental questions and, moreover, to learn as much from the answers that I couldn't give as from those that I attempted to give. While always insisting on precision, he nevertheless opened up a space for thinking in a world that often seems to crowd it out. Jeff Haydu always met my flights of fancy with a quick wit, genuine interest, and a keen eye for both ungainly prose and bloated thinking. Kwai Ng helped me discern what I wanted to do and modeled a kind of intellectual patience that I am still trying to learn. Isaac Martin insisted on analytical clarity where I may not have noticed that it was needed. Erika Rappaport risked joining a committee in a foreign discipline at the other end of the Surfliner. But without her insistence on the importance of the consumer co-operatives, among other insights, this would have been a much weaker project. The debts I owe to those already mentioned will be evident in this book, though, like any true debt, I cannot imagine how they could be repaid. I must also thank other faculty and staff in sociology and beyond, who supported me as I wandered into many blind alleys, in particular: Amy Binder, Stan Chodorow, Harvey Goldman, Robert Horwitz, Rebecca Plant, and Stefan Tanaka. I am grateful, also, to the staff within and around the Social Science Building for their support and assistance through my years in San Diego. Finally, the UCSD Sociology Department as well as the Institute for

International, Comparative, and Area Studies underwrote my first trip to the archives in England.

Since then, I stumbled into the Department of Sociology at the University of North Carolina, Greensboro. While they may question many things about me, my colleagues have maintained a catholic vision of sociology and social science—one that makes room for imagination as well as rigor and precision. I am especially indebted to Sarah Daynes, who took it upon herself to ensure that I could find my way in Greensboro. A number of UNCG faculty members have commented on work that appears in or informs this book: Sarah Daynes, Cindy Brooks Dollar, Dan Huebner, Şahan Savaş Karataşli, Şefika Kumral, Zach Levenson, and Ting Wang. I owe an immense debt to Şahan, Şefika, and Zach, who read and commented on the entire manuscript. Their exacting questions invited me to see the work anew. It is a sincere pleasure to work in the same hallway, where I can lob strange queries and half-baked observations only to have them returned to me with greater thought, care, and refinement than they deserve. A Faculty First grant from UNCG funded a second trip to England at a decisive moment in the development of this manuscript.

In general, I am no good at conferences and find them demoralizing. If you ever see me at one and have the interest, consider this an invitation to say hello. But I am grateful to have encountered Michaela DeSoucey, Marc Dixon, Jennifer Jordan, Isaac Reed, Yaniv Ron-El, Lyn Spillman, Sam Stabler, and Fred Wherry along the way. They have, each in their own way, made these professional rituals bearable. In particular, Fred has been extraordinarily supportive from the early stages and has, at decisive points, pushed me to clarify the kind of work that I hoped to produce. At the same time, he also reminded me—repeatedly, since I am a slow learner—that someone, somewhere might have an interest in reading it. Lyn Spillman presented an inspiring vision of what social science could be, one whose distinctness I only recognized belatedly.

In carrying out the research for this book, I received aid from archivists at the Co-operative Archives in Manchester; the Trades Union Congress Library at London Metropolitan University; the London School of Economics Library; the Pusey House in Oxford; the Hull History Centre; the Library of the Society of Friends in London; the Bodleian Library at the University of Oxford; the Kheel Center for Labor-Management Documentation and Archives at Cornell University; as well as the librarians at the University of California, San Diego, and the University of North Carolina, Greensboro. The documents cited in this book can be found in these archives, as well as the Gale Slavery and Anti-Slavery Transnational Archive. I have a special place in my heart for the archivists and staff at the Co-operative Archives. They showed me that time well spent in the archive need not always feel like a wake. Sophie McCulloch graciously tracked down some materials in the Co-operative Archives on my behalf. With characteristic generosity, Rick Biernacki photocopied the records of the Consumers' League of New York City while at the Cornell University Library in Ithaca. My aunt, Peggy Skotnicki, found several news articles about the National Consumers' League in the records of the Buffalo and Erie County Public Library.

Throughout this book's gestation, I have been surrounded by friends I admire; they have informed my thinking and enriched my life. Some have been mentioned above. I shared countless meals and conversations with Gary Lee and Yao-Tai Li. At a semi-weekly theatre of the absurd with pizza and beer, Waqas Butt, Gary Lee, Yao-Tai Li, Corinna Most, David Pinzur, Andrew Somerville, and a rotating cast of fellow travelers created an atmosphere where I felt genuinely at home. Ian Mullins and Natalie Aviles have been fiercely supportive and trusted sources of advice. My ongoing conversations, however intermittent, with Michael Berman, Graham Holt, and BJ Strew always feel like revelations. It was, finally, Kelly Nielsen who suggested that we read *Being and Time* together. Little did either of us know what that would mean. Fortunately, that remains an open question—one that we will continue to explore together.

At Stanford, Marcela Maxfield and the series editors offered some feedback on my initial proposal that helped me clarify how to approach the manuscript. The reviewers for Stanford returned with constructive, discerning reports that encouraged me to write a better book. I hope not to have disappointed them. Many other staff members at Stanford helped bring this manuscript to publication, especially Stephanie Adams, Sunna Juhn, Greta Lindquist, and Emily Smith. Jennifer Gordon's thoughtful copy editing helped me to avert many unforced errors. Allison Brock bravely assisted me in constructing the index.

I also appreciate the thankless work of those behind the scenes. Small portions of Chapter 4 originally appeared in my article "Commodity Fetishism and Consumer Senses: Turn-of-the-Twentieth-Century Consumer Activism in the United States and England" in the *Journal of Historical Sociology*.

My family has encouraged me to pursue the work that resulted in this book, wherever it has taken me. This is a rare privilege. I hope that, even at my most dour, some sense of this cannot be suppressed. All of them insist on loving and supporting me, even if I stubbornly refuse. But perhaps most directly germane to this work, my parents Ted Skotnicki and Laura Vendryes, among countless other things, enabled my obsession with reading from a young age. I spent many hours in the Buffalo Public Library children's section with Peggy Skotnicki. Andy Skotnicki reveled in the enthusiasms of thought and made it seem possible. Gloria Vendryes has been a spirited debating partner and loving grandmother. Though she is no longer with us, I am comforted to know that Helen Skotnicki would have been proud of me. Rachel, John, and Nikolas Kozera have been gracious hosts and confidants. The newest additions to my family never hesitated to embrace me: Judy and Dr. Yiu-Fei Shih, Eddie Shih and Linda Hsu, and Allen Shih and Ina Flores Shih. Though Dr. Shih departed shortly after we met, he ensured that I would be welcome. Judy Shih has shown unparalleled generosity, a kind that can never be earned. That must be said, finally, and with unrivaled force, for Tien-Ann Shih. There are few pleasures more elusive and humbling than thinking with someone who inspires and who, without fail, insists on leading an ethical life. This book is yet another river stone in the path that we are laying together.

1

The Rise of the Sympathetic Consumer

ON APRIL 24, 2015, a UK-based nonprofit organization called Fashion Revolution staged a "social experiment."[1] It documented the experience with a brief video. In the heart of Berlin's Alexanderplatz, a commercial and transport hub, Fashion Revolution placed a vending machine that promised t-shirts for the bargain price of two euros. The vending machine—flaunting an eye-catching, geometrically patterned shell of teal and black—offered row after row of white t-shirts packed in clear plastic with a minimal black and white label and script that read "FashRev." "People want fashion for a bargain," the documentary began, moments before the screen cut to dozens of different people facing the machine, one after another, intrigued by the promise of a cheap t-shirt: Two women, brown shopping bags at their sides, approached cautiously; next, a solitary bearded man with close-cropped hair and a light-brown leather bomber jacket took an interest; then, a pair of young men sidled up to the screen, faces alight as though they couldn't believe their luck. Others gathered around to wait in line or to simply peer over the shoulders of the intrepid bargain hunters. "But would they still buy it," Fashion Revolution asked, "if they knew how it was made?"

Once those at the machine inserted their two euros and selected the desired t-shirt size on the touch screen, a video began to play. "Meet Manisha," the screen read, "one of millions making our cheap clothing for as little as 13 cents an hour each day for 16 hours." The text was superimposed over still images of dignified, predominantly female workers in dingy, crowded factories. While the video played, a camera in the vending machine captured the reactions of prospective buyers as they learned the story behind their bargain-priced t-shirts. One of the women with the brown shopping bags, aghast, covered her mouth. New faces trembled before the vending machine, somber and tense. A mother and father clutched their child. A solitary young woman stood transfixed. After the story of the t-shirt concluded, a question flashed across the screen, "Do you still want to buy this 2€ t-shirt?" More and more new faces appeared in the video. Some laughed nervously. On the vending machine screen, to their left, the prospective buyer could choose to continue with the purchase. To their right, they could choose to donate to Fashion Revolution. As the soundtrack pivoted toward an inspirational crescendo, person after person reached with their right hand—or awkwardly with their left—to select "donate." A father encouraged his little girl to do the honors. Even more new faces, now betraying both relief and purpose, chose to contribute. The documentary concluded: "People care when they know. Help us to remind the world."

Two years after the Rana Plaza garment factory disaster in Bangladesh—a 2013 building collapse that killed 1,134 and injured almost 2,500—Fashion Revolution used this vending machine to make a dramatic point about the origins of fast fashion. The organization spearheads a range of efforts to transform the fashion industry including a social media campaign that encourages consumers to publicly ask brands #whomademyclothes. Workers can reveal themselves to consumers, too, by posting images of themselves holding signs that read "I made your clothes." This campaign draws attention to the laborers behind branded goods and pressures manufacturers to disclose these hidden working conditions. When they see who make their clothes and learn of their working conditions, Fashion Revolution expects that consumers will feel the weight of their responsibility to these invisible laborers.

Just over a century earlier, with less technical flare, a group of reform-minded women in the National Consumers' League took on a very similar problem. In 1904, the league told of the "Travesty of Christmas."[2] "For thousands of men, women and children," a member wrote, "the holiday season has come to mean chiefly weariness due to excessive work, followed often by illness and still oftener by an enforced holiday without pay, a bitter inversion of the order of holiday cheer." A veritable "army of workers"—from employees in the stores and delivery boys in streets to laborers in factories and in tenements—exposed themselves to "bitter hardships," moral turpitude, illness, and even death. But the perpetrators of these "Christmas cruelties" were not greedy manufacturers or heartless shop owners. "These things occur," the league continued, "not because employers are deliberately cruel, but because they must meet the demands of their customers or fail. The customers cause the suffering, faintly hinted at in this brief sketch, not because they are deliberately cruel, but because they are thoughtless." It was the task of the National Consumers' League to build a thoughtful consuming public, one that took to heart the conditions of those laboring to manufacture, sell, and distribute goods.

If people became thoughtful consumers, league members argued, this would spur changes in the production process. In that spirit, the NCL developed a label for goods "made under clean and healthful conditions." Any articles bearing the label—typically, though not exclusively, textiles—were "authorized after investigation." League members were directly involved in the investigation of working conditions in industries from mining and farm-working to tenement homework and department stores. Further, the league publicized these findings to educate and organize the public as consumers. As with Fashion Revolution, the National Consumers' League hoped that, upon learning about the hidden costs of their goods, consumers would feel their responsibility to those harmed and shop accordingly.

Nearly one century before the National Consumers' League, in 1792, the abolitionist movement was in bloom. Agitators and visionaries penned pamphlets and poems to advance the abolitionist cause. One such pamphlet began with a verse from the Apostle James: "Pure religion and undefiled before God and the Father is this, To visit the fatherless and widows in their affliction, and to keep himself unspotted from the world." The pamphlet picked up where the Letter of James left off: "Now, if many thousands are made fatherless and widows, by the grievous oppression of our fellow creatures in the sugar colonies, and by the trade to Africa for negroes, to supply the place of those who are worn out, or destroyed by excessive labour and cruel treatment, is not the produce of such labour polluted with blood?"[3] The anonymous author insisted that the rum and sugar produced by enslaved people were polluted, spiritually and physically, and that it was the duty of all Christians to refrain from the "purchase and use" of slave-made goods.[4] The author presented slave-made rum and sugar in terms of the goods' origins and consumers' responsibility for them: "[I]t must be admitted that the consumers are supporters of those iniquitous proceedings; and without them the slave-trade, with its lamentable consequences, must soon cease."[5] To fend off arguments against this anti-sugar campaign, the author appealed to the law and scripture, which confirmed the consumer's responsibility. Lest the individual consumer lose heart at her diminutive contribution to the cause of the oppressed Africans, the author concluded, "Let not any be discouraged by looking at the little that is in their power to do; but rather be concerned to be found faithful in that little, leaving the event to Him who hath begun powerfully to plead the cause of the greatly oppressed people; and is able, as he hath promised, to carry on the work of their deliverance, to the praise of his own great name."[6] The British imperial consumer of slave-grown sugar, too, was charged with the responsibility of ethical purchasing.

The Sympathetic Consumer

Across different eras of capitalist development, these activists urged people to sympathize with distant, hidden laborers via the goods that linked them. There is, here, an interlaced pattern of interpretations of the lived world and the social conditions upon which this lived world rests that I call the sympathetic consumer. The sympathetic consumer points to a cultural pattern of ideas, practices, and conditions specific to a capitalist social order—one where the exchange of commodities obscures the labor behind it and turns labor into a mere means of commodity production. This book explores several interpretive features of the sympathetic consumer and demonstrates what renders them coherent—in relation to one another and to the social conditions upon which they depend.

These interpretative features appear in activists' campaigns to encourage ethical purchasing. One appears in activists' *visions* of the consumer as the central figure in a capitalist system. When the abolitionists' rallied consumers to the cause of the enslaved Africans and the National Consumers' League blamed thoughtless consumers for "Christmas cruelties," they placed the consumer at the heart of a network of production, distribution, and exchange. This systemic centrality had important ramifications. Crucially, these activists viewed it as the consumer's responsibility to sympathize with invisible laborers. Another interpretive feature appears in activists' *practical* efforts to cultivate consumer sympathy. Consider the abolitionists' vivid descriptions of sugar plantations, the National Consumers' League label, or the dramatic video in the Fashion Revolution vending machine. These "ways of seeing" invited consumers to imagine and look into those otherwise invisible labor conditions. Having access to such ways of seeing, these activists hoped, would encourage consumers to "feel with" those laborers and purchase with them in mind. A third interpretive feature appears in the *assumptions* that structured activists' moral arguments as to why people should be ethical consumers. Their chains of reasoning, like the National Consumers' League argument about "Christmas cruelties," tracked the links that joined producers to consumers. The coherence of their moral case and activism depended, in other words, on the image and organization of a capitalist system.

To investigate the sympathetic consumer, this book focuses on the abolitionist movement in the late eighteenth century and consumer movements at the turn of the twentieth century (the National Consumers' League, the Co-operative Wholesale Society, and the Women's Co-operative Guild). Arising at crucial junctures in merchant and industrial capitalism, respectively, these movements laid a template for subsequent consumer activists—from boycotts and selective purchasing to ethical product labeling and product exhibitions. Yet the sympathetic consumer is not merely a matter of antiquarian interest, as the opening pages make clear. Thus, the book concludes with a discussion of recent fair trade campaigns and related market-based advocacy. It is, after all, this kind of contemporary consumer activism that people deride as a distinctive outgrowth of late twentieth century neoliberal capitalism. But we need not narrate these contemporary developments in consumer activism as a clean break with the past. Rather, we can tell them as a story of recurrence.[7]

What accounts for the recurrence of the sympathetic consumer across different capitalist regimes? My answer to that question is rather simple: These activists were all trying to make sense of commodity-exchange. More precisely, they wrestled with curiously depersonalized[8] goods in exchange—that is, goods that conceal the conditions of their making and exchangeability. For all of their differences, the abolitionists, National Consumers' League, and Fashion Revolution sought to expose the hidden conditions of production to consumers— the slavery and the sweatshops and the suffering within them. In sum, these structurally similar experiences of commodity-exchange correlate with remarkably similar interpretations, wherein consumption matters in terms of the labor behind consumer goods.

To explain, the book revisits an important, oft-misunderstood notion of Karl Marx's: commodity fetishism. Commodity fetishism allows us to understand how people make sense of commodity-exchange and the social conditions out of which it emerges (e.g., the commodity-form and depersonalized labor, especially). According to Marx, capitalist commodity-exchange is at once banal and strange. The work of the abolitionists, National Consumers' League, Fashion Revolution, and many others reveals a common interpretation of commodity-exchange as a contradictory unity of banality and strangeness. In this way, commodity fetishism—interpretations that depend on the appearance of commodity-exchange in a capitalist social order—can account for the recurrence of the sympathetic consumer, from an era of steam power, colonial empires, and gunpowder to one of fossil fuels, nation-states, and nuclear weapons.

Before inquiring into this pattern, though, I have invoked several important concepts that demand further discussion: sympathy, capitalism, culture, and commodity fetishism. Discussing them will clarify what it means to claim that the sympathetic consumer is a feature of a capitalist social order.

Feeling For, Feeling With

In these campaigns, the activists invited consumers to imagine the people, places, and things that made ordinary, everyday commodities possible. Abolitionists lamented those "made fatherless and widowed" by a devilish slave system. The National Consumers' League evoked bedraggled delivery boys and fatigued shop girls in a disorganized world of industrial mass production. Fashion Revolution portrayed Manisha, one of "millions" exploited in the production of fast fashion. In virtue of their connection through circuits of production, distribution, and exchange, consumers were offered the chance to "feel with," not just for, invisible workers all along the supply chain. This *feeling with*," or sympathy, resonated through the process of commodity-exchange. By looking through commodity-exchange to the labor behind it, consumers could make inferences about these hidden workers' feelings and thoughts—whether sorrow, dignity, outrage, or others. The phrase "sympathetic consumer," therefore, suggests both the conditions of exchange through which sympathy develops and the consumer's efforts to "feel with" these workers.

It is common to associate sympathy with specific emotions, especially pity. These consumer activists certainly expressed and sought to cultivate pity for distant laborers. But I use "sympathy" in a broader sense—one that encompasses yet also transcends mere pity. This usage can be traced through the Scottish Enlightenment—especially David Hume and Adam Smith—and has been helpfully elaborated as a materialist account of sympathy by contemporary anthropologists Danilyn Rutherford and Catherine Fennell. A materialist account of sympathy "tracks the intricate pathways through which encounters with objects and others give rise to feelings and thoughts."[9] These "feelings and thoughts" involve inferences about the feelings and thoughts of others. In this way, these feelings and thoughts are shared in the sympathizer's imagination. Asked to consider the "grievous oppression" visited upon enslaved Africans in the sugar colonies, the British consumer of sugar could imagine what *they* would feel if *they* were enslaved, fatherless, widowed, or otherwise oppressed. This is what I mean by sympathy. It is a practical and imaginative act of feeling with others. To feel with others is, in effect, to imagine that those with whom you feel are in some sense like you. Without this imagined likeness, sympathy would be impossible.

Though it may seem anodyne, sympathy also reveals the workings of power. Whether in the construction of colonial empires or modern states, sympathy has abetted projects of power, domination, and governance.[10] To rule in unknown lands, for instance, colonial state-builders needed to sympathize with potential imperial subjects. This enabled would-be colonists to foster some compliance among native populations upon whom, in many other respects, their survival depended.[11] The sympathetic consumer is no exception to such patterns. However scrupulous and thoughtful these activists may have been, they were dedicated to mobilizing people as consumers on behalf of workers. As a result, their attentions were biased toward the sympathies that consumers could extend through commodity-exchange to laborers and laboring conditions. While consumers were asked to identify with the workers through commodity-exchange, the workers themselves remained largely mute, or were ventriloquized by the activists. Many—though not all—of these activists were unconcerned with the reverse question: whether unseen workers sympathized with consumers. In the consumer activist's imagination, we will see, power traveled from consumers to producers.

Those who study sympathy or emotions know well that such phenomena are not simply natural or instinctive; people also cultivate, manage, and strategize with emotions.[12] Catherine Fennell reminds us that "*feeling with* does not emerge easily or spontaneously."[13] Consumer activists recognized this. They gave people the tools through which they could sympathize with distant laborers. What was the National Consumers' League label, if not a tool that would enable consumers to feel with workers? Activists wanted to evoke and harness sympathetic emotions—sorrow, yearning, pity, even rage—in the service of popular movements for change. But it is important to recall that the sympathetic consumer indicates an aspiration more than an achievement. By no means did these activists always succeed. Moreover, I must stress that I do not write as an advocate for the sympathetic consumer. Nor do I seek to simply dismiss sympathetic consumption. Rather, I describe the emergence of this cultural pattern, trace its form, and adduce several arguments about how it develops within a capitalist social order. Ultimately, I explore how these activists sought to make sympathy reverberate from consumers to producers through the process of exchange. These efforts illuminate something about culture and capitalism that may, in turn, help to clarify the limitations and possibilities of sympathetic consumption.

In Search of a Capitalist Culture

Since Weber sought the Protestant origins of a capitalist spirit and Horkheimer and Adorno inveighed against the degradation of thought in a world of mass culture, the desire to describe a distinctly capitalist culture has fractured and dissipated into more specialized pursuits.[14] There has been plenty of excellent work on the cultures of the market or commercial culture or moralized markets by historians, sociologists, anthropologists, and economists.[15] My concerns are at once more specific and broader than these approaches. Though we may sometimes forget this, capitalism doesn't own markets or commerce; these are social forms that accompany human civilization writ large. To speak, then, of a market culture or moral markets suggests a generic sociological concern with the ways that markets arise through, create, and depend upon particular ways of understanding the world. One could investigate efforts to free markets from their social moorings or to re-attach markets to these social moorings through government regulation, popular movements, and other forms of resistance to market liberalization.[16] Or one could, for instance, investigate the coexistence of capitalist and non-capitalist market cultures in booksellers who feel queasy about the demands of running a cutthroat business.[17] Such investigations often stop short of demonstrating connections between these market cultures and capitalism as a system. Through this investigation of the sympathetic consumer, I explore a distinct pattern in a culture that refers, directly, to features of a capitalist social order. This pattern is not a feature of market cultures in general, but of a specifically capitalist one.

The search for a capitalist culture is broader, in effect, because it traces the recurrence of cultural patterns like the sympathetic consumer across distinct historical periods and areas. The abolitionists, the National Consumers' League, and Fashion Revolution interpreted and organized around the consumer in very similar ways; I want to account for these similarities. In studies of market cultures, there is a tendency to identify the new, the different, and the plural—not the similar.[18] For example, Viviana Zelizer traces how, at the turn of the twentieth century, a new understanding of childhood emerged in the United States through a shift in the emotional value of children.[19] Richard Biernacki exposes the distinct cultural idioms around labor that manifested in Great Britain and Germany throughout early periods of industrialization.[20] Of late, the notion that we should discuss "cultures of capitalism" has become more or less axiomatic—to speak of a capitalist culture, in the singular, seems to trample over great empirical diversity.[21] While we have much to learn from these approaches, it strikes me as no less important to investigate how similar patterns may manifest across longer timespans and space. The search for a capitalist culture, I argue, allows us to discover similarities without effacing differences across places and over time.

This phrase, "capitalist culture," invokes two concepts that have been sufficiently fraught as to render their union intimidating, at best, and hopelessly incoherent, at worst. It may recall the bad old days, where culture appears to merely reflect or follow the economy. As such, one may worry that the phrase consigns this work to the dustbin of history, where fiery materialists and dreamy idealists are locked in a struggle to the death. There is, at least on this score, good news. Not only is it possible to speak of a capitalist culture, but we can do so in a way that doesn't simply rehash a profound but suffocating debate.

What is capitalism?

The book covers several distinct periods in the historical development of capitalism—an era of mercantilism and colonial empires, an era of industry and mass production, and, finally, a present of hyper-financialization and speculation. Thus, it is important to establish what makes them capitalist.

One tendency is to consider capitalism—in any of its phases of development—as a mere economic system. This narrow definition of capitalism has facilitated exemplary works of political economy that enrich our understanding of trends in productivity, wages, profits, wealth, markets, monetary policy, finance, trade, and states—all surely fundamental to any adequate account of a capitalist society.[22] These works have been complemented by studies of the relations between aspects of a capitalist economic system and social or cultural life—the social relations, beliefs, practices, and institutions that exist "outside" of the economy, even as they allow that the relationship between economy and culture may run both ways.[23] Within such a framework, the shift from the abolitionist pamphlet to the digital vending machine indexes a whole series of transformations in economic life—technological, productive, and organizational—that could shape or be shaped by social or cultural life and vice versa. One might approach the matter of defining capitalism, then, by detailing the unique or essential features of an economic system along with, in some cases, associated political or regulatory institutions.

But another tendency, one that proceeds through Marx, is to approach capitalism as an entire social order. This order includes the social relations, beliefs, practices, and institutions that evolve within and through the more familiar economic and political features of a capitalist society. One might speak of the bourgeois family, or the distinction between the public and private sphere, or nationalism as belonging to a capitalist social order.[24] Rather than segregate capitalism and society or culture into separate spheres, they treat them as a whole. Within this framework, the shift from pamphlet to the digital vending machine indexes not just economic changes but a shift in the nature of public discussion and debate and the role of consumerism in capitalist society. Approached in this manner, these cultural shifts do not refer to something "outside" or potentially independent of the economy; rather, the relations between culture and the economy are internal and mutually dependent.[25] For some time, this broader approach to capitalism was kept alive in world-systems analysis and in Marxist traditions, though in the last decade or so others have taken up it up as well.[26] In these traditions, one would approach capitalism not only in terms of essential economic and political features, but also the social and cultural features that evolve through them.

I use the term "capitalism" and various cognates in this more holistic sense to refer to a social order organized around historically specific systemic tendencies and social relations.[27] Even now, hundreds of years on, a capitalist social order does not simply arrive readymade. It entails the ongoing work of producing and making sense of these distinct relations, tendencies, and associated phenomena. But what kinds of tendencies, relations, and phenomena are distinctly capitalist? I describe several principal features of a capitalist social order. In and of themselves, none of these features suffices as a definition of capitalism. But they can sensitize us to the ways that systemic tendencies appear in the course of ordinary life. After all, some of these tendencies and phenomena have bedeviled consumer activists repeatedly over the last three centuries—from slave-grown sugar in eighteenth-century England and Christmas cruelties in turn-of-the-twentieth-century United States to the two-euro t-shirt in Berlin.

First, capitalist societies revolve around the commodity-form—wealth is produced and distributed by means of commodification.[28] Consumers in search of the two-euro t-shirt or sugar in colonial Great Britain could assume that those goods were produced for sale on the market, that is, as commodities. Those who brought the goods to market, in other words, were not simply selling off excess produce cultivated for personal consumption. In commodity-exchange, when consumers give money over for goods, the labor behind the goods appears necessarily as depersonalized and abstract (see "Commodity Fetishism and the Sympathetic Consumer"). There is, further, a distinct tendency to produce commodities by means of other commodities. The commodities purchased in the consumer marketplace are just the tip of iceberg. The entire circuit of t-shirt production, distribution, exchange, and consumption, for instance, tends toward commodification: the cultivation and refinement of raw materials; the sourcing of machinery, land, and other materials used in manufacture; the labor required to assemble the t-shirt; the design of the product, the packaging, and the transport and distribution of the t-shirt; the marketing, its sale, and even disposal. The consumer at the vending machine in Berlin or even in a marketplace in colonial England sees but a moment in an intricate pattern of commodification, where labor appears as nothing more than a measure of equal value.[29]

Second, capitalist societies are characterized by the imperative to grow or accumulate profits. If profits don't grow—if sugar or t-shirts yield losses—then those particular ventures will either disappear or be taken over by someone who will turn a profit.[30] As Max Weber and Werner Sombart recognized over a century ago, this imperative has implications that run well beyond the economy, narrowly construed; people feel compelled to work, save, and reinvest, or enticed to spend lavishly.[31] To cast this growth imperative as merely economic, then, would miss the anxieties, drives, and passions on which it depends. This imperative to grow, further, yields systemic patterns of expansion and contraction, where crises of growth—producing too much, producing too little, stagnant returns, and so forth—roil markets, states, and entire world orders.[32]

Third, there is a tendency toward a basic class division between the great majority of people who must make ends meet by entering the labor market and a much smaller minority who live on the interest or surplus that results from their ownership of wealth-producing assets.[33] This class division applies, empirically, only inconsistently across the period under study—particularly in the British empire of the eighteenth and early nineteenth centuries. The abolitionists were obviously concerned with chattel slavery, a form of labor that—in some accounts—is fundamentally incompatible with a capitalist social order. I do not attempt to resolve that deep historical debate here.[34] But it is uncontroversial to identify the eighteenth century as a period of development in a capitalist social order. Many enslaved people were forced to cultivate cash crops that were intended for sale within colonial empires and beyond. This is not wage labor, of course, but that merely shows that the class division is a tendency within—not a necessary condition for—a capitalist social order.

Fourth, capitalist societies grant private individuals the rights to control wealth-producing property. These rights entail the ability to own, buy, and sell private property. Not only do these property rights secure the control of wealth-producing assets like land, technology, and labor, but they also secure individual rights to personal assets and possessions. These rights often rest upon a legal and political system that elaborates, facilitates, and protects ownership.[35] Not only are there legal protections on sugar and t-shirts—those wanting sugar in colonial London or t-shirts in Berlin cannot simply take them without repercussions—but people often reveal their consciousness of these laws explicitly. To build the case against sugar consumption, an abolitionist wrote, "He that receives or buys goods, knowing them to be stolen, is deemed an encourager of theft; and, as such, punishable by the law. Yet goods stolen privately; is [sic] simply a fraud, in property; unattended with the aggravating circumstances of oppression and bloodshed."[36] A sense of individual property rights evolves with and through the law. Many people think of private, wealth-producing property and personal property as the same thing. This way of thinking, too, is bound up with the legal and political organization of property rights.

Fifth, these direct institutions for producing and distributing wealth also rely on other means of producing, ensuring, or extracting wealth—means that aren't always recognized as "economic." There is plenty of uncompensated, unrecognized, and coerced labor that lies behind straightforward wealth-producing activities—the gendered "second shift" within families, for instance, plays an important role in reproducing the workforce.[37] By providing health care or social insurance, the state can "de-commodify" essential services, thus diminishing labor unrest and shoring up the production of wealth.[38] Further, racial and ethnic status hierarchies, colonial and imperial expansion, and war-making—all of which have been fundamental to the development of capitalism to this day—enable the ongoing expropriation of wealth. The slave trade, for instance, upon which the immensely profitable sugar colonies depended, siphoned wealth from the peoples of Africa, India, the Americas, and the Caribbean into the British Isles and Europe.[39] More recently, employers who employ workers from vulnerable communities—non-citizens, persecuted minorities—can use these vulnerabilities and status hierarchies to drive down wages and extract unpaid labor.[40]

These tendencies draw attention to several principal features of a capitalist social order and suggest how we might locate them in everyday life. In this book, I will focus especially on the commodity-form, exchange, and depersonalized labor. Of course, the world and, by extension, capitalism have changed dramatically since the eighteenth century. It is, after all, these changes that make the recurrence of the sympathetic consumer such a fascinating issue. By examining how people have made sense of the commodity-form, however, we may arrive at more precise accounts of what has and what hasn't changed.

What is culture?

"If we purchase and use that which is produced by oppression," our anonymous abolitionist observed, "we contribute to the gain of the oppressor." When, the author continued, aware of these oppressive circumstances, we purchase and use those products, "we knowingly receive the price of blood, and contribute in the most effectual way to uphold the oppressor."[41] Here we have an interpretation of the consumer's role in the slave trade and slavery. Even the unknowing consumer of slave-made sugar upholds the oppressor. Those who "knowingly receive" slave-made sugar are, in this account, distinctly guilty. All contribute to the continued oppression of their fellow humans. This short passage draws our attention to an essential matter of culture: interpretation. When social scientists study culture, they may focus on abstract knowledge, beliefs, and ideologies; they may focus on practices, performances, and habits; they may focus on cognitive schemas, norms, and codes; they may focus on experiences, meaning-making, and understandings; and they may focus on the customs, materials, and products that play into or result from these varied aspects of social life.[42] What these approaches all share, in spite of the distinct modes of study and analysis with which they are associated, is a concern with interpretation and sense-making.

When I use the word "culture," I refer to ways that people make sense of or interpret their world. The abolitionist pamphlet joined producers, both "oppressors and oppressed," and consumers via a commodity—sugar. The Fashion Revolution vending machine proposed a similar connection between the producers and consumers of t-shirts. Both interpreted the meaning of consumption in terms of production. I am interested in these interpretations—their formal structure, how the activists developed them, the conditions upon which they depend, and their consequences. It is through layers of such interpretations—evident in various notions of culture—that we come to know the world.[43]

As I see it, these interpretations matter for two main reasons. First, they are necessary to any account of a social phenomenon.[44] In truth, any account of a social phenomenon—from consumer activism to coming of age rituals—requires that the analyst consider how people interpret the world, however rudimentary that consideration may be. Consumer activists' interpretations of commodity-exchange also make sense of a whole constellation of social practices—investigating and publicizing the conditions of labor, encouraging people not to buy tainted goods, forming organizations dedicated to these purposes, and other consequences that may follow therefrom.[45] Without the notion of the sympathetic consumer or something like it, in other words, the things that these activists did would be difficult to understand. Whether the associated interpretations cause these forms of activism, as force applied to a ball causes it to roll, is not the only important question. Rather, we should also ask: Are these interpretations necessary for the relevant social phenomena to make sense and, if so, why? It is my task to demonstrate that these interpretations manifest in this activism *and* render aspects of this activism coherent.

Second, these interpretations can, like a prism, disclose other features of the social world—whether these features are directly given to the senses or not. The Fashion Revolution's two-euro t-shirt experiment—like the National Consumers' League labeling campaign and the abolitionist anti-sugar campaign—makes a very simple point: The commodities around us do not simply reveal the conditions that made them possible. For that reason, these activists must find ways to make those conditions and those laborers visible to consumers. In these forms of consumer activism, the depersonalized nature of commodities gives activists a reason to seek out the world that makes the commodity possible. When these activists draw attention to depersonalized goods, they tacitly indicate the conditions that make this interpretation possible. Thus, depersonalized goods become a lens through which they bring unperceived but necessary institutions and processes like exploited or expropriated labor, elaborated supply chains, and price competition into the foreground. In this way, we can see how certain interpretations that are critical to the sympathetic consumer bear the imprints of the world out of which they arise, even as that world hides so much from the consumer's view.

To study the sympathetic consumer, therefore, is to study the ways that people interpret the world of capitalist commodity-exchange. The relevant interpretations will manifest in people's visions, practices, and assumptions. And while there may be more to the study of culture than interpretation, there is certainly no study of culture without such a concern.

Toward a capitalist culture

Now I can venture a definition of a capitalist culture: interpretations that depend on the tendencies, social relations, and phenomena central to a capitalist social order. By depend, I mean two things. First, specific interpretations make sense and take the forms that they do because of the way in which capitalist phenomena appear to people in their everyday lives.[46] Second, these phenomena themselves refer to conditions in the social order (specific practices, institutions, and organizations) that make their appearances possible. Accordingly, the sympathetic consumer coheres via reference to specific, observable features of the capitalist social order within which it arises. It is important to note that not all interpretations will depend on a capitalist social order. To claim, justly, that an interpretation depends on a capitalist social order, one must demonstrate that some principal tendencies, social relations, or phenomena (e.g., like those bound up with the sympathetic consumer via commodity fetishism, as I show in this book) are necessary for the interpretation to make sense.[47] Because of this, patterns like the sympathetic consumer may seem to be nothing more than mechanical effects of that same social order—simple consequences of a world that requires people to literally buy in. It is more appropriate, I think, to conceive of them as patterns of interpretations along with their social conditions of possibility, where the former appears both as a condition and as a consequence of the latter.

This definition requires several important but technical clarifications. First, a capitalist culture need not be localized or regional; it can develop wherever these capitalist phenomena appear. However, the uneven and varied historical development of capitalism would lead us to anticipate historical and regional variation.[48] Where a capitalist culture does appear, then, we should expect it to bear distinct features of the places and times under study. Note, further, that this description does not entail any specific causal claims about the source of the patterns that comprise a capitalist culture. They need not issue from cabals of elites shuttered away in boardrooms or from institutions that inculcate specific beliefs like schools, churches, families, and so forth—though that is possible.[49] It is also entirely possible that elements of a capitalist culture could arise "spontaneously"—through people's efforts to make sense of the world in which they find themselves with the tools they have available.[50] Finally, the patterns that make up a capitalist culture need not serve strictly functional and ideological purposes. That is, they need not shore up the workings of a capitalist social order though, again, they certainly could do so. These are all empirical questions that can only be adjudicated once we have adequately documented and synthesized aspects of a capitalist culture.

I use the phrase "capitalist culture," not capitalist cultures, advisedly. My interest is to identify patterns of interpretations and social conditions that become native to a capitalist social order.[51] But it does not follow that these patterns will be unchanging or fixed. Many have observed that a capitalist social order is relentlessly dynamic.[52] This dynamism, though, has a predictable or repetitive character. In other words, capitalism is a historical social order that operates according to a predictable logic of imperative growth.[53] The initial sketches of consumer activism, for instance, reveal this blend of dynamism and predictability. From the late eighteenth century onward, the appeals to consumers gain a certain kind of technological sophistication—from the pamphlet to the label to the vending machine with a touch screen. The nature of the work changes. The beliefs of the activists change. Many other things change. Nevertheless, these activists each arrive at similar interpretations of commodity-exchange: The consumer relates, sympathetically, to the producer by means of the commodity. This basic pattern of the sympathetic consumer persists as it evolves. To study a capitalist culture, then, is to seek out those patterns that recur across centuries of capitalist development. It is not just the search for one damn novelty after another.[54]

One last wrinkle. This book investigates a single pattern—the sympathetic consumer—in what I presume is a collection of such patterns—a capitalist culture. There is much more to capitalism than commodity-exchange. And there are certainly more ways to make sense of commodity-exchange than the particular gloss provided by consumer activists. Consequently, I see no reason why a capitalist culture would need to be logically coherent. It is certainly possible that distinct patterns could form a semi-coherent structure—where they jointly reinforce principal features of a capitalist social order. For example, one's experiences as a consumer and wage worker may reinforce the sense that life is and must be a competition between individuals in a marketplace.[55] In such instances, a capitalist culture would look more like ideology. But it may also be the case that one's experiences in the labor market or workforce or the home may nurture anti- or post-capitalist patterns—ones that arise within a capitalist social order but nevertheless point beyond it.[56] It is possible that, as a whole, a capitalist culture coheres empirically, but only sometimes ideologically or logically. These are all matters for further study, not speculation. This work contributes to such a project.

Commodity Fetishism and the Sympathetic Consumer

If the sympathetic consumer depends on a capitalist social order, how, exactly, would we establish this? What phenomena could reveal the sympathetic consumer to be a feature of a capitalist culture? We can find the answer through an analysis of a weird, wonderful idea: commodity fetishism. The trouble with commodity fetishism, though, is its infamous opacity. By and large, social scientists—even those who make it their business to study culture and economic life—have made almost no explicit use of commodity fetishism in their work. Even research on directly related issues, such as labor and local food or national food politics or commodification, tends to avoid it.[57] I suspect that many see commodity fetishism as an antiquated, vaguely mystical, and deterministic notion that leads into an intellectual cul-de-sac. Marx himself repeatedly tells of the commodity's great mysteries. Commodity fetishism is a mysterious circumstance, he notes, where "the definite social relation between men . . . assumes . . . the fantastic form of a relation between things."[58] But the concept can, I argue, help us understand much about the development of the sympathetic consumer.

When people have sought to understand commodity fetishism, several themes predominate. Many describe it as an error made by consumers, as something to be corrected. Thus, in a wholly typical reference, Sharon Zukin writes of "unmasking the commodity fetish."[59] Joel Stillerman refers to commodity fetishism as a "confusion" and "superstition."[60] If it is an error, confusion, or superstition, the fetish prevents us from seeing what we could otherwise see. More subtly, Julie Guthman reads commodity fetishism as "the necessary masking of the social relations under which commodities are produced."[61] It is a "misapprehension" or a masking of reality.[62] Fetishists misunderstand or err in their interpretation of the world. The world, further, may simply induce such a misunderstanding.[63]

The account of commodity fetishism as a delusion is close kin to these themes of error and illusion. Here the fetish is associated mainly with fantasy and vice. "I confess," writes anthropologist Elizabeth Chin, "I am a commodity fetishist. eBay has been, for months, my not-so-secret-vice."[64] Commodity fetishism is, in this version, associated with the intoxicating power of goods. Thus, Chin seeks to disarm Marx's harsh critique by embracing the label "commodity fetishist." The very phrase "commodity fetishist" suggests there is something wrong with the person who loves goods. Not only is that person deluded, but he is superficial or inauthentic.[65] By this measure, the commodity fetishist can't see that there is more to life than what he can buy. Thus, in some readings, commodity fetishism becomes indistinguishable from consumerism.

In general, commodity fetishism gets cast in psychological terms (cognitive error, delusion, intoxication) or ideological terms (misapprehension, masking, false consciousness).[66] It is, moreover, presented as largely pacifying. If such readings were wholly accurate, the idea would place the analyst in a bind. By invoking commodity fetishism, one would necessarily claim that consumers are little more than dullards and useful idiots. While these readings may be plausible—especially given Marx's own cryptic turns of phrase—I think they miss something important that, in turn, undercuts their usefulness. By reading Marx alongside an essay from a turn-of-the-twentieth-century consumer activist, I offer a more precise and, ultimately, more helpful formulation. When we recognize commodity-exchange as a contradictory unity of banality and strangeness, we will see that commodity fetishism encompasses two distinct features of capitalist exchange characterized by depersonalized goods—interpretations *in* exchange and interpretations *of* exchange.

Further, this account addresses a longstanding concern among those who study consumption, culture, and economic life: how the conditions of commodity production relate to the meaning or significance of consumption. The tendency has been to stress the myriad ways that a consumer's immediate social context and relations, not the hidden abodes of production, inform her interpretations of consumption. Thus, researchers have prioritized affective ties, strategies of status distinction, group identity, self-making, and sites of consumption in their accounts of how people make sense of consumption.[67] Consumption means something to people, in other words, because of the ways that people dream with or imagine themselves through goods; the ways that these goods help them relate to their friends, family, and foes; the ways that they allow people to participate in the life of ethnic, religious, national, or sub-cultural groups; and the places where or contexts within which they purchase goods. These aspects of a consumer's social context, they argue, can account for the meanings of goods—to grasp such meanings, no attention to commodity production is necessary. Yet if this were true, the recurrence of the sympathetic consumer over three centuries, across such widely varying social contexts, would be puzzling indeed. A proper account of commodity fetishism will reveal, along with recent work on food,[68] the ways that the sites and character of production can creep into and condition what consumption means to people. This allows us to appreciate how labor's absence gives consumers' cause to ponder its whereabouts and build it into their interpretations of consumption.

The banality of the commodity fetish

Marx begins his discussion of commodity fetishism with a knotty observation: The commodity appears "extremely obvious," but it is, in fact, "very strange."[69] About thirty years later, a co-operator named Katy made a similar observation. In 1892, the Women's Co-operative Guild—a group of working-class British consumer activists—hosted an essay competition on shopping. As women were often charged with household provisioning, the essay prompt asked co-operative women to reflect on how to shop and why it mattered. Katy's prize-winning essay, "Shopping," was published in the movement's central publication, *the Co-operative News*. She began, "It does seem strange, when we think of it, how lightly and thoughtlessly we go out shopping, how easily we let the money slip through our fingers, money that has cost thought and toil and weariness."[70] The thoughtlessness highlights, with Marx, the banality of shopping. To Katy, the strangeness of shopping manifests first in ease of spending—in the way that money, which results from the shopper's own toils, perhaps also that of her spouse's, slips through her fingers.[71]

"There is an old saying," she continued, "'If a man would thrive he must ask his wife.' It is quite certain a man would never thrive who had a wife that was careless in spending money."[72] Katy brought this folksy, self-deprecating wisdom to all manner of shopping dilemmas and offered counsel to the beleaguered shopper. After providing tips for purchasing food and clothing, she turned her attention to the allure of the bargain. "Some of these 'bargains,' when examined," she warned, "prove 'sells' instead. I have not patience to read about those 'enormous sacrifices,' 'under cost price,' 'absolute clearance,' and 'bankrupt stocks' that are placed so temptingly before us. They are but traps to catch the unwary."[73] The consumer, as Katy tells it, finds herself beset by cajoling shop owners, by her own whimsy, and by the allure of the goods themselves. Ensnared in these traps, the consumer loses touch with some important questions. Her essay, then, is ultimately a call to reflect on what consumers miss and why.

Marx and Katy begin in a very similar place; they identify something both obvious and strange about exchange in a capitalist society. Marx describes the mysteries that result when an object "emerges as a commodity."[74] Katy observes the strange thoughtlessness of shopping. But these observations share something significant: This strangeness, whatever it is, only surfaces belatedly. Marx writes that "[the commodity's] analysis brings out that it is a very strange thing."[75] Katy finds it strange, "when we think of it." Both insist that commodities do not appear strange as we acquire them. When we exchange money for commodities, everything about it is "extremely obvious," "trivial," "light," and "easy."[76] It is the opposite of strange. In fact, these experiences of purchase are so obvious and trivial that it may be easy to overlook the way Katy's opening statement blends two exchanges seamlessly: a person's labor power for money and the money for some other commodity.

This raises two important questions: What is this strangeness? And why does this strangeness only appear upon reflection?[77] Those who think of commodity fetishism simply as delusion or error miss the familiar, decidedly boring appearance and experience of exchange. Bewitched by the mystery, perhaps, we overlook the banal.

The strangeness of the commodity fetish

Marx identifies the strangeness of the commodity fetish in the situation where the products of human labor "appear as autonomous figures with a life of their own, which enter into relations both with each other and with the human race."[78] Upon reflection, exchange in a capitalist social order makes commodities into living beings and laboring humans into mere means—gelatinous masses of depersonalized labor that make commodity-exchange possible. Moreover, the human characteristics of labor—its organization, distribution, power, ingenuity, and creativity—seem to belong to the goods themselves.

These goods, which are "the products of men's hands," take on lives of their own as commodities.[79] In exchange, when we trade money for goods, we value commodities in relation to other commodities. It is as if their worth derives only from qualities inherent in commodities themselves. A two-euro t-shirt and a two-euro candy bar and a two-euro coffee all express the same value—no matter how different those objects and associated labors may be.[80] But when we reflect on this exchange, we can recognize that we have assumed away the distinct contributions of the labor that made it possible. In commodity-exchange, we behave in a way that we do not otherwise believe—as if commodity-exchange is strictly independent of the labor process, and labor is nothing but a mere means of commodity-exchange.[81] Thus, commodity-exchange makes a mockery of our ability to reason our way through our actions.

Where Marx analyzes the social order submerged in commodity-exchange, Katy offers practical guidance. "To do shopping well," she advises, "we need forethought, decision, order, and self-denial."[82] She encourages readers to make lists, estimate costs, and seek out higher quality goods. For Katy, the strangeness lies in the ways that shopping short-circuits people's ability to reason. "In shopping for [produce]," she admits, "we cannot always keep to what we have planned before we set out." All manner of shopping circumstances—the infernal desire for bargains, the vagaries of supply, the range of available goods, the general paucity of information—all of these, especially the desire for bargains, contravene the ability to reason. And when Katy looks into these bargains, she argues that they come from one of two places: "Either the trader must put a very heavy profit on at first to cover all loss when the reduction comes, or the things must have been bought in such a cheap market that no labour employed on them can have been properly paid."[83] These unreasoning pressures derive from the conditions upon which exchange rests.

But this strange unreason goes even deeper; it subverts a person's values and beliefs. In the essay, Katy imagines a person, one not committed to the communal ideals of the co-operative movement, who learned about these unsavory sources of bargains. "What does it matter," she speculates, "if some one did have to pay more, so long as we get a bargain?" Katy acknowledges that committed co-operative readers might "scorn" such sentiments. But despite their scorn, "we may *act* as if we held them, just for want of thought and looking into things."[84] For Katy, then, the world around us elicits this strange unreason, which manifests not necessarily in our thoughts, but in our purchases. Just as in Marx's account, the structure of capitalist commodity-exchange, upon reflection, betrays a certain strangeness. Moreover, just like Marx, this strangeness manifests in a tension between what people say or think and what they do or experience.

Banality and strangeness as interpretations of depersonalized goods

Why does this strangeness only become evident upon reflection? This is not a simple error or delusion.[85] In fact, the answer is entirely the opposite, and it directs us to apparent features of a capitalist system. Not error, but banality explains why this strangeness arises belatedly. "Reflection on the forms of human life," writes Marx, "hence also scientific analysis of those forms, takes a course directly opposite to their real development."[86] In a well-established capitalist social order, exchanging money for commodities *is* trivial and obvious. In a sense, we barely notice the process because we take commodity-exchange for granted: "[T]he forms which stamp products as commodities . . . already possess the fixed quality of natural forms of social life . . . for *in his eyes* [the one who seeks to give an account of this] they are immutable."[87] Only upon reflection can we appreciate that which we take for granted *in* the act of exchange. Marx shows this when he rewrites ordinary, everyday commodity-exchange in the language of political economy: "If I state that coats or boots stand in a relation to linen because the latter is the universal incarnation of abstract human labor, the absurdity of the statement is self-evident. Nevertheless, when the producers of coats and boots bring these commodities into a relation with linen, or with gold or silver . . . as the universal equivalent, the relation between their own private labour and the collective labour of society appears to them in exactly this absurd form."[88]

When we exchange goods for money, we interpret those goods as anonymous. In the above passage, Marx describes the depersonalization of goods and labor in a capitalist social order. This depersonalization is bound to an interpretation: We cannot see, nor could we ever see, the form of labor that we nevertheless presume *in* each and every act of exchange.[89] Where a capitalist social order obtains, we are all commodity fetishists—including those of us who think we aren't. In one sense, then, commodity fetishism describes an accurate interpretation of consumer goods and the labor that makes them possible as anonymous *in* the act of exchange. In exchange, these goods do not and, in fact, cannot reveal the labor upon which they depend. There is, in other words, an interpretation of commodity-exchange as banal.

Like Marx, Katy notices the strangeness that creeps into our reflections on shopping. "If we could only have a 'magic mirror,'" she laments, "that would show us the beginning and the end of 'bargains' and cheap goods, which look so attractive, we should need no more arguments."[90] With such a magic mirror, we could "see the little suits, braided and trimmed so nicely, turned about in dark, unwholesome rooms where 'sweated' Jews are crowded, we should not care so much to see them on our little ones."[91] She continues, "We should perhaps begin to dimly perceive a little of what is involved in 'bargains,' and I think we should see very clearly that it is our duty to encourage and give our support to those who will pay fair wages to those poor workers, and who are striving to better their condition."[92] To Katy, the banality of commodity-exchange makes fools and hypocrites of us all. Thus, it explains why we recognize the strangeness of commodity-exchange only after the fact.

But Katy's discussion of the magic mirror also reveals where she and Marx part ways. In her rueful wish for a magic mirror, she writes as if it were possible to see through the depersonalization of goods—that is, to unmask the fetish, as those who write about such things often say. She concludes with the hope that, as her strategies for seeing through depersonalized goods "touch all shopping," they could be "safely followed by all."[93] For Marx, the banal anonymity of commodity-exchange derived from the nature and organization of a capitalist social order itself. Were one to see into the conditions where "'sweated' Jews were crowded," or enslaved Africans cultivated sugar cane, this would not unmask the fetish. Only the transformation of a capitalist social order could accomplish this unmasking.

Yet in a capitalist social order, commodities aren't just trivial and obvious—they are also mysterious and strange. Marx and Katy alike find these mysteries in reflection. It is here, too, that we can locate the delusions associated with commodity fetishism. When people—whether imperious political economists or ordinary consumers and laborers—reflect on commodity-exchange and interpret it only as banal or natural, then Marx would judge them delusional and Katy would judge them "thoughtless." These interpretations *of* exchange make up the second crucial feature of commodity fetishism. It appears in the sense that people make of commodity-exchange when they stop and think about it. Marx lambasts liberal political economists as credulous and deluded for taking commodity-exchange at face value. But are all such interpretations *of* commodity-exchange similarly delusional?

This is where the differences between Marx and Katy matter. In her desire for magic mirrors, Katy both takes commodity-exchange for granted and calls it into question. Thus, she distinguishes herself from liberal political economists in some ways, while working within the very same limits in others. Marx was not, however, primarily concerned with apparent variation in interpretations *of* exchange. Unlike the interpretations *in* exchange, which admit little variation, these interpretations *of* exchange—which occur upon reflection—admit much greater variety. Given this, the social scientist concerned that commodity fetishism acts like a theoretical straitjacket can breathe easily. There is plenty of room for varying interpretations *of* exchange, and no need to begin by denouncing everyone as delusional.

To sum up, commodity fetishism comprises two distinct, but related interpretations tied to a capitalist social order: the practical interpretation of goods as anonymous *in* exchange and the interpretations *of* commodity-exchange as natural. Throughout the book I will demonstrate how these interpretations *in* and *of* exchange inform the development of the sympathetic consumer. From the t-shirts Fashion Revolution dangled before passersby in Berlin's Alexanderplatz to the sugar sold in markets in imperial London, consumer activists have repeatedly made such interpretations. These activists imagine, interpret, and seek to transform a capitalist social order by means of commodity-exchange. It seems that the secret of the commodity fetish hides in plain sight. Recognizing this will help to specify how the sympathetic consumer depends on a capitalist social order.

Cases, Data, and Comparisons

To study the sympathetic consumer, I rely on primary source archival research into movements in two historical eras—the late eighteenth century and the turn of the twentieth century. The most pioneering and elaborate instances of consumer activism in these periods emerged in the heart of the colonial British empire and the United States. The abolitionists first formulated the grammar of the sympathetic consumer, while a mélange of late nineteenth century consumer activists expanded the lexicon. The materials they left behind supply evidence of the ways that abolitionists and turn-of-the-twentieth-century activists conceived of and organized around consumers. Moreover, these groups vary in ways that underscore this study's social scientific and historical stakes: class, gender, nation, and organization.

The abolitionist movement gained momentum in the British empire during the 1780s. This popular movement included a campaign against the consumption of sugar and rum from the West Indian colonies. Driven by a dedicated core of activists, historians estimate that at least several hundred thousand Britons participated in the abolitionist movement.[94] The anti-sugar campaign initiated a form of humanitarian consumer activism oriented toward the lives of distant strangers. While many core activists were businessmen, dissenting clerics, and intellectuals, the movement drew participants from across social classes—including industrialists and some laborers—and involved noteworthy, observable contributions of women and free Blacks. The abolitionists formed antislavery organizations, the most influential of which was the Society for Effecting the Abolition of the Slave Trade. They researched and published tracts on the history and horrors of slavery and strategies for its cessation. They published poetry, literature, artwork, and other creative means for promoting the abolitionist cause. The movement ebbed and flowed during the period upon which I focus most extensively from the 1780s through the 1830s. Although my focus is on abolitionists in the British empire, I also refer, where relevant, to abolitionists in the United States and beyond. This activism resulted in a trove of pamphlets, letters, journals, advertisements, meeting minutes, and newspapers, which serve as the basis for my account.

By the turn of the twentieth century, several groups placed the consumer at the heart of their activism: the Co-operative Wholesale Society, the Women's Co-operative Guild, and the National Consumers' League. Founded in 1863 as a way for British working men to pool their resources and buy goods in bulk, the Co-operative Wholesale Society identified itself as a working-class consumer movement by the 1880s. The Co-operative Women's Guild emerged in the 1880s to stake out an active role for women in the male-dominated co-operative movement. I examine in detail these two wings of the British co-operative movement, which claimed over 3 million members by the beginning of the First World War. Although ostensibly sharing a commitment to consumers' co-operation, these groups had distinct organizational structures, memberships, and purposes.

Across the Atlantic in the United States, the National Consumers' League was founded in 1899. The organization was dedicated to creating an enlightened shopping public and protecting vulnerable working people, particularly immigrant women and children. At its progressive-era peak, the NCL claimed just under 16,000 dues-paying members, but its influence extended well beyond this dedicated core of activists into the law, state, and social life of the United States. While the Women's Co-operative Guild and the Co-operative Wholesale Society were in close, if sometimes fraught, conversation, the

National Consumers' League remained almost entirely aloof from the co-operatives and vice versa. As with the abolitionists, I constructed my analysis on the basis of a wide range of archival materials including newspapers, annual reports, propaganda and advertisements, meeting minutes and conference proceedings, internal memos, photographs, and other ephemera.

Rationale

There are several important reasons to study these activists. First, they bring the developments associated with the sympathetic consumer into the most dramatic relief. The abolitionists pioneered this humanitarian consumer activism, while turn-of-the-twentieth-century activists built entire movements around it. These activists possessed a missionary zeal to spread consumer sympathy far and wide. As such, they needed to build the consumer activist infrastructure themselves and to justify their work before a doubting public. This provides an unparalleled opportunity to see not only the development of their visions and practices, but also of the explicit arguments they made in favor of this activism. That I emphasize pioneering activists who make up relatively small percentages of the population may suggest something further about the dynamics of a capitalist culture. The elements that comprise it need not have a popular mandate, at least initially. Even if they do arise in relation to common phenomena within a capitalist social order, the interpretations of these phenomena may require public advocacy to gain traction.

Second, these activists tried to make sense of the moral stakes of private consumption. As such, they have a lot to tell us about interpretations as systemic phenomena. Where others might not dwell on the relations between consumers and producers—who, after all, seeks to trace an obscure commodity chain every time he goes to the market and decides to buy something?—these activists make such connections explicit. Like those involved with the Fashion Revolution t-shirt or the National Consumers' League label, these are the kind of people who aren't afraid to pose uncomfortable questions to other consumers—where did your t-shirt come from? why do you want to buy these things? don't you have obligations to those who produced these goods? These questions are instructive to those of us who seek to understand patterns of interpretations and the social conditions that make them possible. By questioning how people work out or avoid moral interpretations of personal consumption, these activists invite others to examine their everyday lives in terms of system dynamics. Accordingly, to study their reflections on consumption is to see how their moral interpretations relate to the comprehensive social systems in which they formulate these questions.

Third, these activists vary in ways that those who study consumption, culture, and economic life have often treated as decisive: class, gender, and nation. Given that consumer activism, especially humanitarian consumer activism, has been understood as a project of the leisured classes, their differing class and gender compositions can reveal how and when these backgrounds decisively shaped their activism. Co-operatives tended to find members among the stable working classes, with men and women largely segregated into distinct organizations. The National Consumers' League, by contrast, was driven by upper-class women. The abolitionists drew upon a stable core of bourgeois men and women, with a broad popular base that included workers, artisans, industrialists, and others. The national differences, especially at the turn of the twentieth century, permit me to examine the extent to which national cultures shaped this consumer activism.

These activists developed distinct organizational forms, too. The abolitionists were far less formally organized than later activists. They were building a network of abolitionist sympathizers who were oriented toward pressuring Parliament to outlaw the slave trade. Still, they encouraged the formation of antislavery groups across Great Britain, hosted talks, and presented petitions and reports to Parliament. In the 1820s, the abolitionists began to adopt and publish constitutions, form official societies, and take on more formal organizational characteristics. By the turn of the twentieth century, the co-operatives and the National Consumers' League had adopted federated organizational structures, with local chapters and national and regional conferences, and had developed official leadership. But while the Co-operative Wholesale Society managed stores and were a business as well as a movement, the National Consumers' League and the Women's Co-operative Guild were not businesses. Consequently, their organizational purposes differed in important ways. Taken together, these differences present questions about variation in accordance with common sociological concerns—social class, gender, nation, and organizational structure.

The historical differences between abolitionists and turn-of-the-twentieth-century activists bear further mention as well. While many historians, and some sociologists, have taken an interest in these groups of consumer activists, they have remained either within national borders or within single historical eras. Further, historians have, not without cause, treated abolitionists' consumer activism as largely incidental.[95] Consequently, this comparative historical design occasions a different approach to what some may see as familiar, individually distinct movements. Though as historian Lawrence Glickman has observed, there is a "relative absence of memory and myth" among consumer activists and the broader public.[96] As such, many remain unfamiliar with this oddly familiar history.

The abolitionist movement surfaced within a period of declining mercantile capitalism and nascent liberal industrial capitalism. In this period, the colonial world powers like Great Britain and France battled for commercial supremacy through efforts to control the Atlantic system of maritime trade—including, of course, the traffic in enslaved Africans. These empires relied heavily on the use of slave labor to produce cash crops like sugar, rum, cotton, coffee, and indigo for the colonial metropoles and beyond.[97] Within the British empire, some consumer goods, like sugar, made their way into the lives of all manner of residents from workers to royals—but more luxurious goods, like household wares, circulated primarily within the rising bourgeoisie and nobility.[98] These colonial empires did not just rely on settlers and slave production of commodities; they also began to build a national economy and state. The British taxed colonial revenues and other war-making enterprises, which they were able to transfer into investment in domestic enterprise.[99] This was an era of expanding large-scale domestic industry and manufacture in cotton and pottery, including magnates like Josiah Wedgwood, who, incidentally, contributed to the abolitionist movement.[100] The ideology of free trade, too, began its ascent during this period—perhaps most notably, Adam Smith's *The Wealth of Nations* was published in 1776.[101] Thus, this period of capitalist development—in the colonial metropole—entailed more expansive commodity production, a strong national state, and more opportunities for mass consumption. It also relied on slave labor in the colonies and mercantile trade to generate wealth, in addition to the inchoate reliance on wage laborers within England.

By the turn of the twentieth century, the still-potent British empire had begun its slow decline, while the United States was in ascendance. The liberal, industrial capitalism of the nineteenth century was beginning to give way to welfare or state-managed capitalism, with more robust social provisions and regulations, the rise of the modern corporation, and growing opportunities for mass consumption. These consumer activists participated in the reform movements that resulted in state agencies—food and health regulators, laws and boards regulating wages and hours worked—and regulations.[102] Large-scale industrial and machine production accelerated in the second half of the nineteenth century, which accompanied more elaborate supply chains both nationally and globally. With immigration, urbanization, and mass production, the purchase of staple goods escalated, though widespread mass consumption would not develop until after the Second World War.[103] Department stores offered a spectacular experience of shopping and augured that rise of unprecedented mass consumerism. The modern, hierarchical corporation—especially the monopolistic trust—developed in the United States and was exported to the United Kingdom and beyond.[104] On the flip side, trade union and labor militancy escalated throughout the 1890s and early 1900s in many countries. This was all accompanied by a rethinking of social life and the relations between state, society, and economy; many were concerned with "the social question"—with efforts to regulate the disorder that accompanied great social inequalities, unhealthy living, mass immigration, and poor working conditions.[105] With the legal abolition of chattel slavery in the last half of the nineteenth century by the United States (1865), Cuba (1886), and Brazil (1888), turn-of-the-twentieth-century consumer activists looked out on a greatly transformed landscape of capitalist development.

To the extent, then, that the sympathetic consumer appears amid such historical and sociological variations, it is not arbitrary or accidental. Obviously, the present book can do nothing more than establish the basic form of the sympathetic consumer and recommend that its features be fleshed out, clarified, or jettisoned with further research. But to establish these patterns requires careful interpretation of activists' projects. It is only through the historical details of their activism that we can appreciate the structure, development, and consequences of the sympathetic consumer as well as the capitalist culture in which it participates.

Looking Ahead

In this book, I seek to understand the conditions across three centuries that made the rise of the sympathetic consumer possible. To this end, the book does two things. First, I offer a comparative historical study of consumer activism in the late eighteenth, early twentieth, and early twenty-first centuries. The sympathetic consumer, I conclude, depends on a capitalist social order for its coherence. Confronted with depersonalized goods in commodity-exchange, these activists arrived at a common understanding of the relationship between consumers, producers, and commodities. Second, these historical comparisons establish a framework through which researchers can investigate what constitutes a capitalist culture by focusing on the ways that people interpret phenomena essential to capitalism. I model this approach by tracing the relevance of commodity fetishism, which manifests *in* commodity-exchange and the interpretations that people make *of* it, to these instances of consumer activism.

There is much about these consumer activists that I don't address. Given the public-facing nature of their activism, I make no arguments about the intentions or genuineness of these activists. Nor do I offer any definitive account of why these specific people took up the cause of sympathetic consumption and not others. On the basis of the historical record, I can offer only some informed judgments. What matters, here, are the recurring patterns of interpretations and their social conditions of possibility, evident in what these activists said and did. To unearth some secret motives that dictate these interpretations and conditions would require tools that I cannot rightly claim to possess. Moreover, while my sources confirm obvious differences across and even within these groups of consumer activists, I do not dwell on these differences. This is not because I think them irrelevant, but simply because these differences have been well-documented elsewhere. I am convinced that there is still much to learn from their similarities.

One issue that I would like to address, but do not yet have sufficient evidence to discuss well, is the matter of race and the sympathetic consumer. It is clear that the sympathetic consumer often stood out in contrast to enslaved Africans or "sweated Jews" or Italians in tenements. The workers were sometimes depicted in racial caricatures both outrageous and subtle. I have little doubt that the racialized history and dynamics of a capitalist social order inform the development of the sympathetic consumer.[106] Though turn-of-the-twentieth-century activists did advocate on behalf of non-white workers, there were few records of non-white members. Overall, it is not clear whether these racialized developments are specific to commodity-exchange or bound up with other aspects of social life. It is possible that the sympathetic consumer may be an essentially racialized figure—a kind of white savior. It is also possible that these efforts to cultivate sympathy for unseen laborers by means of the commodity rely on the distance, both physical and cultural, between consumers and laborers. And it is this distance, then, that could create a space for various well-established fantasies of difference to shape the sympathetic consumer over time. Either way, this book does not answer that question or the others above—but not for lack of interest.

Given that my argument depends on a great deal of historical detail, knowing something of the path beforehand will aid in following the argumentative thread. The next four chapters present the sympathetic consumer as it develops vis-à-vis commodity fetishism in several parts—visions, practices, and moral assumptions. To introduce activists' visions in their historical context, I discuss the abolitionists in Chapter 2 and the turn-of-the-twentieth-century activists in Chapter 3. Through historical narrative and close readings of propaganda, these chapters illustrate that activists envisioned the consumer as central to a network of production, distribution, and exchange. They insisted, further, on the need for consumers to sympathize with invisible workers through commodities. These visions are interpretations *of* commodity-exchange that attempt to challenge interpretations *in* commodity-exchange. Chapter 4 reveals how these consumer activists grappled directly with depersonalized goods. They forged ways of seeing into the obscured realm of production, which would entice consumers to feel with oppressed workers and act accordingly. In these tactics we can see how interpretations *in* commodity-exchange informed their interpretations *of* commodity-exchange. This exposes, further, the paradoxical way that commodity fetishism can invite activism, not merely defuse it. Chapter 5 reconstructs the assumptions implicit to moral arguments for the sympathetic consumer. These assumptions track the character and organization of capitalist markets and supply chains via interpretations *of* commodity-exchange as natural. Thus, the specific circumstances upon which commodity fetishism depends—expanding commodification and the consumer's connection to the producer via the marketplace—decisively shaped activists' moral justifications for consumer activism.

Having established that these aspects of the sympathetic consumer depend on a capitalist social order, Chapter 6 takes a hard look at the differences between some of these activists. When faced with challenges from labor and business, turn-of-the-twentieth-century activists took paths that reflected class, gender, nation, and organizational differences. These differences show that the sympathetic consumer orients but does not strictly determine what people do and how they do it. This clarifies what it means for the sympathetic consumer to appear as a condition and as a consequence of a capitalist social order. Finally, in Chapter 7 I conclude with some observations about the sympathetic consumer in the present. These observations suggest comparative questions to ask about the sympathetic consumer and the workings of a capitalist culture. But they also invite us to reflect on the character of the interpretations of the world that we make as we lead our lives.

2

Abolitionist Visions

"It is now generally admitted, that the slave-trade is a violation of all the rights of men . . . That the labour of slaves in the islands is so oppressive and their treatment and accommodation so bad, as to occasion the death of many thousands annually: And

That the sugar and rum raised in the West-Indian islands are cultivated and prepared by this oppressed people, and publickly sold in this country as such. These being established facts, does it not behove all professors of Christianity well to consider how far they encourage the oppressors, by purchasing their commodities, thus defiled with blood?"

Considerations Addressed to Professors of Christianity of Every Denomination, on the Impropriety of Consuming West-India Sugar and Rum, as Produced by the Oppressive Labour of Slaves, 1792, p. 3

BY THE END OF 1792, dozens of pamphlets, speeches, and newspapers told of a popular mobilization against slavery that incorporated consumer activism—abstention from West Indian sugar. Although the rhetoric has aged, the demand is familiar: Consumers, as supporters of "iniquitous proceedings,"[1] could refrain from purchasing commodities in the service of a greater social good. The abolitionists proposed a role for sympathetic consumers, who purportedly occupied a central node in this mercantile brand of capitalism. Who were these abolitionists and where did this popular movement come from? What did the abolitionists accomplish? How did they conceive of the consumer? And what role did this consumer activism play in the abolitionist movement? It turns out that, from the perspective of many in the late eighteenth century, the surprise would not simply have been that abolitionists pioneered a form of consumer activism; it would have been just as surprising that a substantial antislavery movement emerged at all. That one could claim antislavery sentiment as "generally admitted" highlights a dramatic ideological transformation in British and European colonial history. To understand these pioneers of sympathetic consumption, then, we must know something of the world from which this antislavery sentiment emerged.

When abolitionists asked consumers to sympathize with enslaved people in the West Indies, abolitionists placed the consumer at the center of a system of imperial production, distribution, and exchange.[2] Such a vision, furthermore, reveals an interpretation *of* commodity-exchange that both assumes and challenges interpretations *in* commodity-exchange. In this way, commodity fetishism is crucial to the vision of the sympathetic consumer.

The Historical Crucible of Abolitionism

While slavery had advocates and detractors throughout human history, the late eighteenth century was a watershed moment for British attitudes toward slavery. Antislavery opinions gained traction beyond the "eccentrics" and "fanatics" at the periphery of polite society.[3] Masses of British people were exposed to antislavery ideas and, further, were called upon to voice their displeasure with the slave system. A robust public debate placed the slave interests and their advocates on the defensive, at least rhetorically, in a way that was without precedent. What had appeared to many people as an immovable, if unsavory, bulwark for British imperial supremacy suddenly become a political, though not necessarily an economic, weakness. Why?

Obstacles to abolition

There were, as many historians and fellow travelers have documented, serious obstacles to the popular embrace of antislavery opinion and abolition. For one, the tide of historical opinion and practice rested with slavery. Throughout human history, all manner of forced labor and enslavement had been the rule rather than the exception—even if the systems of chattel slavery since the fifteenth century were novel in terms of their commercial intensity and racial hierarchies.[4] In the sixteenth century Bartolomé de las Casas, one of the pioneers of modern humanitarian advocacy, condemned indigenous exploitation in Spanish colonial *encomiendas* and mines; yet his initial solution—one that he eventually renounced—was to import Africans as slave laborers instead.[5]

In eighteenth century Great Britain, even those discomfited by the treatment of other humans as personal property—chattel slavery—struggled to discern alternatives that would preserve British imperial power. After all, slavery
could yield great profits for colonial empires, especially in the production of
what would become staple agricultural cash crops like sugar.[6] As such, the slave
trade was a boon to the British empire and its beneficiaries. Owing to slave
plantations in the Caribbean, between 1710 and the 1770s per annum sugar
consumption in England vaulted from 6 pounds per capita to over 23 pounds,
which reflected a transformation in the diets of ordinary Britons in the colonial
metropole.[7] The treaties of Utrecht (1713–1715), which concluded the War of
Spanish Succession in Europe, granted the British control over the slave trade
into Spanish and British colonial holdings in America;[8] this bolstered the rapid
growth of British commerce, such that the British empire would become the
preeminent world maritime and commercial power by the time the abolitionist movement effloresced in the 1780s and 90s. Thus, the developing imperial
supremacy of Great Britain, along with the access to more and more consumer
goods in the metropole, appeared to rest on the transatlantic slave trade. To
challenge the propriety of slavery or the slave trade, then, contradicted both
longstanding sensibilities and the apparent commercial and geopolitical interests of the British empire.

The ethnocentric and racial ideologies that evolved through colonial slavery
further stood in the way of widespread antislavery sentiment. Slavery in the
European colonies did not begin as a fully formed racial caste system, though
racial and ethnic prejudices were surely present. One could justify colonial
slavery because of the colonized peoples' non-Christian beliefs or foreign-
ness, without a fully formed rationale of permanent racial hierarchy.[9] In the
fifteenth and early sixteenth centuries, the first plantations in the Caribbean
included "free workers, native tied labourers, those of mixed Spanish and native descent, immigrants from the [Spanish] peninsula, and Berber or black
African slaves."[10] Early English colonies in North America included "white in-
dentured servants and Irish, Scottish, and Native American prisoners of war
condemned to lifetimes of servitude" in addition to African servants.[11] But as
plantations proved increasingly dangerous for the laborers and lucrative for
the colonists, European labor sources began to dry up. Moreover, colonies like
Virginia began to codify white racial superiority in the law during the final
third of the seventeenth century. They passed strict anti-miscegenation laws
and other formal restrictions on the rights of free Blacks, while also importing

unprecedented numbers of Africans as slaves.[12] From that period on, the slave plantations in English colonies contributed to a racial caste system, wherein Black Africans were judged to be uniquely degraded and therefore fitted for slavery—while native peoples were often characterized as savage obstacles to the imperial project.[13]

Yet these obstacles to the popular spread of antislavery ideology did not snuff out antislavery sentiment and incipient efforts to organize such sentiment entirely. Disparate, moderately organized antislavery opinions can be discerned throughout the period of chattel slavery's early rise—from the fifteenth century through the middle of the seventeenth. While Christianity most often accommodated slavery throughout its history, there is also no denying the role that Christian organizations and thought played in the persistence of antislavery projects.[14] In the sixteenth century, the Spanish empire produced a network of indigenous advocates including Bartolomé de las Casas, whose histories of the West Indies chronicled the atrocities committed against the indigenous people. Las Casas, who had arrived in Hispaniola in the early 1500s as a settler and plantation owner, eventually gave up his rights as an *encomendero*—that is, the right to control the products of the *encomienda*—and freed any enslaved people associated with his *encomienda.* He became a Dominican friar and helped to form an advocacy network that defended the rights of indigenous people in the courts of Spanish King Ferdinand, the Holy Roman Emperor Charles V, and Pope Paul III.[15] This advocacy resulted in some commitments from the Crown to respect the rights of indigenous people, though the Spanish imperatives to raise money for ongoing imperial wars and expansion tended to smother these rhetorical gains. Within orders of Catholic clergy—such as the Dominicans, Jesuits, Capuchins, and others—these indigenous and sometimes antislavery advocates pressed the issue, with very limited observable success into the end of the seventeenth century.

As the center of global imperial power shifted toward the British empire in the eighteenth century, these antislavery efforts found a home among the Quakers. The Quakers were a dissenting Christian sect that emerged in the wake of the English civil wars; they emphasized that Christ's divine revelation was immediately given to all in experience, with no need for priests or other intermediaries. To hear that revelation, Quakers excised the baroque clutter and chatter of English religion and public life. Quaker ceremonies were austere, with participants often sitting in silence until they heard the spirit and were moved to speak—not in tongues, but carefully and clearly. As such, Quakers were, by English standards, eccentrics who dressed and spoke plainly, refused to use pagan names for days and months, and renounced the use of formal titles and honorifics.[16] They also engaged in a largely intra-Quaker debate about the morality of slavery from the late seventeenth century until taking that debate public at the end of the eighteenth century.[17] But it is also important to appreciate that Quakers did not simply withdraw from public life. Quakers also excelled in business. Many leading members of the ascendant bourgeoisie belonged to the faith. Thus, many exemplified a version of the Protestant work ethic and flourished in this world of merchant capitalism.

To little public fanfare, Quakers in Philadelphia published statements in 1713 and 1727, politely reminding other Quakers that the slave trade was neither "commendable nor allowed."[18] Some devoted Quakers pressed the issue beyond pleasantries. At the 1738 yearly meeting of Quakers in Philadelphia, the radical gadfly Benjamin Lay shocked the attendees when he took his turn on the floor and bellowed, "Thus shall God shed the blood of those who enslave their fellow creatures." Lay, who stood no higher than four and a half feet, brandished a sword. He then impaled a hollowed-out book filled with a bladder of red pokeberry juice over his head, let the "blood" flow down his body, and then sprayed this blood on the slave-holders present.[19] His apocalyptic performances earned him denunciations from the Quaker community. Other Quakers were less aggressive in their antislavery advocacy. John Woolman deemed slave-holding an obstacle to salvation and implored his fellow Quakers to renounce this sin for their own sake as well as the enslaved.[20] Yet in the first half of the eighteenth century, the concerns of Lay, Woolman, and others remained contested as well as contained within particular Quaker societies. The Quakers' dissenting traditions and eccentricity seemed to work against the development of broader antislavery sentiment.

Shifting tides
On the other hand, throughout the eighteenth century several events and trends redounded to the antislavery cause—from intellectual trends and public tragedies to economic instability in the Caribbean and the war for American independence.

Intellectual trends toward rational social philosophies separated claims about social order and function from theological claims about sin, redemption, and divine will. To make the philosophical argument for slavery on these terms, one needed to consider social interest, utility, and order in themselves—not with recourse to scripture. Further, the concurrent rise of an ethic of benevolence or sympathy stressed the role of sentiment and human feeling in thought and judgment.[21] In 1759, Adam Smith's *Theory of Moral Sentiments* introduced the spectator with a natural tendency to care for and respond to the fortunes and misfortunes of others.[22] Around that same time, the catastrophic Lisbon earthquake loomed large in European popular imaginations. The event was widely represented and circulated via wood carvings and etchings, which allowed distant strangers to participate, emotionally, in the earthquake in the years that followed.[23] Such imaginative participation could extend the sympathies of distant strangers to the people of Lisbon, even if they would never come across those affected personally. These intellectual trends were useful to the spread of antislavery opinion, which required people to sympathize with distant strangers.

But the most significant developments, at least for British abolitionism, were twofold: the conflicts in the American colonies that culminated in the political founding of the United States and the economic instability of the Caribbean sugar colonies during those conflicts. The Caribbean islands under British control were largely given over to the production of sugar as a cash crop. Consequently, the islands depended on imports of food and staple goods, many of them from the American mainland, to sustain the lives of enslaved people and settlers alike. Historian Selwyn Carrington noted that, during the 1770s,

> [T]he British West Indies received from the mainland colonies approximately one third of their dried fish; almost all of their pickled fish; seven eighths of their oats; almost three quarters of their corn; nearly all of their peas, beans, butter, cheese and onions; half of their flour; quarter of their rice; five sixths of their pine, oak, and cedar boards; over half of their slaves; nearly all of their hoops; most of their horses, sheep, hogs, and poultry; and almost all of their soap and candles.[24]

The American Revolution disrupted these trading patterns and, in the process, revealed the dependence of the sugar colonies on provisions and trade with others in North America—not just England and Europe. Naval warfare between the British and American colonists resulted in famine and inflation in the Caribbean. In turn, this increased the costs of sugar production at a time when the British lost access to the colonial market in America, and the Americans began to trade with the French colony in St. Domingue (now Haiti). This bolstered the market position of French sugar, cacao, cotton, and indigo at the expense of the British.[25] These disruptions, while by no means sounding a death knell to the profitability of British sugar plantations, illustrated their volatility.[26] As a result of the American revolution, slavery and the slave trade could appear as more of an imperial liability than it had earlier in the century.

The American Revolution also cleared the way for a broader antislavery politics. Whereas many critiques of slavery and imperial policy issued from members of marginal religious groups like the Quakers, in the American Revolution and its aftermath a wide range of colonists and members of polite British society challenged the morality of the British empire. They denounced British tyranny, from levying excessive taxes and the housing of British soldiers to the usurpation of colonial governance and legal authority.[27] Christopher Brown details how American colonists and British loyalists both employed antislavery rhetoric to gain the political upper hand as tensions escalated. They cast slavery as a matter of public concern and a stain on the British empire. Moreover, the British military freed enslaved people during the war. This established a precedent of using state action to abrogate slavery and the slave trade. Finally, the war opened up profound doubts about the morality of British imperial rule. And while many people may have had no qualms about the morality of empire as such, more and more were willing to critique the manner in which Britain ruled abroad.[28] There were also critiques of the British empire informed by experience of colonial rule in India.[29] At the same time, the American Revolution continued to popularize a discourse about egalitarian and democratic rights. While many tried to construe universalist notions of rights narrowly, these ideas proved difficult to contain.[30] These geopolitical and intellectual developments nurtured antislavery ideas and popular movements.

To announce, as in that abolitionist pamphlet from 1792, that the "slave-trade is a [generally admitted] violation of all the rights of men" reflects these currents and trends in imperial slavery since the sixteenth century. Even though the writer, like many abolitionists before, exaggerated the force of public sentiment, it was true that there was a dedicated and popular antislavery opinion. By the 1780s, abolitionists were simultaneously swimming against the grand historical tides and contributing to an unprecedented swell of antislavery opinion. In the crucible of these historical forces, it behooves us to consider what this popular abolitionist social movement looked like and what this movement accomplished. Once the features and influence of the abolitionist movement have been established, we will be in a better position to appreciate the ideal of the sympathetic consumer in the abolitionist campaigns.

Abolition as a Popular Movement

When antislavery opinion and the popular movement for abolition gained strength in the 1780s, the movement had several noteworthy features. For one, the core of abolitionist advocacy shifted from colonial America to metropolitan Great Britain. For another, this advocacy looked, in important ways, like a contemporary social movement—the kind of transregional, national, and even transnational mobilization of activism via a shared repertoire of tactics that we see today. Finally, it developed in fits and starts, and, therefore, it is difficult to ascertain exactly what effect the abolitionist movement had. Thus, we need to clarify what, exactly, the abolitionist movement accomplished and what it didn't.

From colonial America to metropolitan Britain

Throughout the eighteenth century, the most vocal and dedicated antislavery advocates resided in colonial America. In addition to the aforementioned Benjamin Lay and John Woolman, there was a robust and growing network of antislavery advocates in the middle of the eighteenth century. These included Benjamin Franklin, who published antislavery tracts—among them the untutored writings of Benjamin Lay. Another Benjamin—Benjamin Rush—published an antislavery tract in 1773 and, despite his virulent racism, denounced slavery and the slave trade throughout his life. John Churchman, another Quaker, identified slave-holding as the sin responsible for leading the colonists into the Seven Years' War with the French and Indians, beginning in 1756.[31] However, the most significant of these figures to the abolitionist movement was the schoolteacher and Quaker convert Anthony Benezet.

Benezet documented and denounced the slave trade in a manner consonant with his most obvious predecessor Bartolomé de las Casas, the priest who advocated on behalf of indigenous people in the Spanish empire. Like many others, Benezet insisted that slavery was inconsistent with Christian teachings. But he laid the groundwork for more enduring forms of advocacy than mere appeals to the consciences of particular slave-holders. A French-born Protestant who discovered Quakerism when living in London, Benezet moved to Philadelphia in 1731. There he taught at several schools and began to offer classes for enslaved Blacks. In 1770, he founded the Negro School at Philadelphia, and several years later he founded one of the first antislavery societies, the Society for the Relief of Free Negroes Unlawfully Held in Bondage.[32] Throughout that time, he researched and published antislavery tracts about the calamitous history of the slave trade and the degradation of enslaved Africans. In one such pamphlet, published in 1767, he called slavers and their benefactors to account:

> How dreadful then is this slave-trade, whereby so many thousands of our fellow creatures, free by nature, endued with the same rational faculties, and called to be heirs of the same salvation with us, lose their lives, and are, truly and properly speaking, murdered every year! For it is not necessary, in order to convict a man of murder, to make it appear that he had an *intention* to commit murder. Whoever does, by unjust force or violence, deprive another of his liberty, and, while he hath him in his power, continues so to oppress him by cruel treatment, as eventually to occasion his death, is actually guilty of murder. It is enough to make a thoughtful person tremble, to think what a load of guilt lies upon our nation on this account; and that the blood of thousands of poor innocent creatures, murdered every year in the prosecution of this wicked trade, cries aloud to Heaven for vengeance.[33]

When he condemned the "nation" writ large, Benezet assigned responsibility for slavery to the policies and practices of the British empire—not merely to slave-holders and slave-traders. Thus, he treated slavery as a political problem, not only a religious one.

To address this problem, in the 1760s and 70s Benezet and his fellow reformers began to organize abolitionist sentiment across the Atlantic. Their goal was to appeal to political authorities directly both in the American colonies as well as in Great Britain.[34] Benezet asked a contact in London to distribute some of his early pamphlets as well as publish information in newspapers and local bulletins. The pamphlets were distributed to members of Parliament to little fanfare and effect.[35] Benezet persisted with his London contacts and, in addition to circulating information about the slave trade, he promoted antislavery petitions in legislatures throughout the colonies and in metropolitan England. Crucially, he sought not only Quaker allies but members of other religious confessions such as Methodists and Anglicans. In so doing, he forged a friendship with a man who would become a persistent antislavery advocate in the years to come—the English scholar and musician Granville Sharp. These exchanges helped them to devise a political strategy that entailed the popular dissemination of information and displays of popular support for abolition to legislative bodies and to the royalty. However, official petitions for the abolition of the slave trade did not materialize in England until the 1780s.

While these transatlantic efforts in the 1760s and 70s neither set the public aflame with antislavery sentiment nor deterred the slave trade, they codified a template upon which abolitionists could build as the movement grew. It was in the context of the American Revolution, then, that the efforts to organize abolitionist sentiment shifted from the colonies to the imperial metropole. In the newly developing American republic, the internal abolitionist discussion shifted, unsuccessfully, to the status of slavery in the Constitution and within the nation.[36] In England, as mentioned above, the colonial revolt unsettled the profitability of slavery and the critique of slavery challenged the moral and political legitimacy of the British empire. Following debates with colonial Americans, slavery became a target precisely because one could plausibly argue that it undermined the legitimacy of British imperial rule.

Structure and character of the early abolitionist movement

When the movement emerged in the 1780s, abolitionists developed a common repertoire of contention that circulated throughout England and the British empire.[37] Unlike many of their contemporaries, the abolitionists took up national and imperial issues, not just local ones. They did so with strategies and tactics that were adapted and adopted across many different localities in England and beyond. Further, these strategies and tactics often relied on and expressed the will of the participants directly. These features clue us into something important about the context within which the sympathetic consumer emerged: Charles Tilly identified the origins of what we now call social movements in England between the 1750s and the 1830s. In the midst of a consolidating national state and an industrial capitalist economy, popular movements, including abolition, helped to usher in distinct forms of public politics. Thus, by tracing abolition in light of these broad tendencies, we can appreciate that the sympathetic consumer emerged along with the popular social movement—a tradition that paved the way for many others including turn-of-the-twentieth-century consumer activists.

Historically, popular contention addressed local issues associated with abuse, maltreatment, and moral affronts perpetrated by shopkeepers, landholders, and other local residents. By contrast, abolition addressed an imperial matter—not just one for enslaved people, slave-owners, and governors in the West Indies; or weavers and industrialists in the north of England; or bankers in London; and so forth.

Abolitionists' pursued strategies that were designed to create a groundswell of popular support for abolition. Above all else, the abolitionist movement aimed to make the slave trade and, by the 1820s, slavery itself illegal in the British empire. This popular support would either compel parliamentarians to address the slavery issue or, as we will see, circumvent Parliament to apply pressure on slave-holders and slave-traders through the market. To carry out this immense task, they employed many tactics that were portable throughout Great Britain and beyond. In 1787, they established the Society for Effecting the Abolition of the Slave Trade, a core group that promoted the abolitionist cause. This group and their growing network of allies appealed to authorities, especially political and religious ones, to eliminate the slave trade. The activism involved popular petitions submitted to legislators as well as other leaders like King George III or the Duchess of York. They established political alliances throughout the British empire and beyond. For instance, the French Société des Amis des Noirs arose in communication with members of British abolitionist societies. Free Blacks and formerly enslaved Africans such as Olaudah Equiano, Ignatius Sancho, and Phillis Wheatley circulated narratives, gave speeches, and wrote poetry that both testified to the horrors of slavery and underscored how it squandered human potential.

The broader transnational or imperial network of antislavery advocates circulated information about the hellish nature of the slave trade and slavery. This included publishing thousands of pamphlets, writing letters to local periodicals, holding public meetings and lectures, founding reading groups, and circulating literature, poetry, and visual art associated with the abolitionist movement. The fiery, precocious deacon Thomas Clarkson tirelessly campaigned for abolition like a community organizer *avant la lettre*. He traveled throughout the British Isles with a trunk of antislavery paraphernalia in tow, giving lectures and hosting meetings to build local committees of antislavery sentiment. Finally, and perhaps most crucially for my purposes, abolitionists encouraged abstention from slave-produced sugar and rum. They did so to build popular awareness and sympathy for enslaved people and to leverage pressure on slave-holders and traders via the market. Later, they encouraged people to replace slave-produced sugar with that produced by free laborers.[38] All of these strategies could be adopted and pursued by abolitionist supporters throughout the British Isles and the empire; they did not depend on locality.

The most prominent abolitionist tactic—the petition—asked participants to voice their will directly to Parliament. They submitted hundreds of these petitions to Parliament in the first several years of public antislavery mobilization from 1787 to 1793. Petitions were available to sign in specific municipalities for a period of time, say, several weeks to a month. During this time, antislavery advocates might post announcements about the petition and how eligible citizens—that is, men—could subscribe in newspapers or in other public forums. When one signed on to a petition, one in effect appealed directly to political authorities. Rather than delegate a local authority to speak on their behalf, the petition spoke with many voices of the male residents of Manchester or Bristol or London and so forth.

The participants in this early phase of popular abolition represented a variety of backgrounds. The leadership hailed disproportionately from the rising bourgeois classes. There were many Quaker businesspeople, industrialists, pastors, lawyers, and some parliamentarians. As the activist core expanded beyond Quakers to include Methodists, Anglicans, and others, they continued to rely on educated clergy, lawyers, and reform-minded businesspeople. Some have wondered why the relatively well-to-do abolitionist leadership rarely compared the harsh conditions of colonial slavery to the "satanic mills" of industrial production in England.[39] These accounts have argued that the abolitionist leaders were ideologically blind to the struggles and suffering of much more local industrial laborers. When we look beyond the leaders of the movement, however, it appears that workers sometimes made exactly these connections. A letter to a Manchester newspaper encouraging abstention from slave sugar noted, "[L]abour is the most unequivocal kind of property; the labour of the negroes has not only been unpaid for, but has cost multitudes of them their lives and liberties."[40]

There are further reasons to understand the movement as a cross-class one. For one, the scale of popular mobilization and the regions in which abolitionists mobilized suggest substantial participation by working people. From existing antislavery petitions in the 1790s, historian Seymour Drescher extrapolated that artisans and miners may have been solid sources of support.[41] It has been demonstrated that workers both signed on to and actively campaigned on behalf of antislavery in cities like Manchester—in the heart of England's industrial revolution.[42] In the early phases of popular abolition, historians estimate that hundreds of thousands of Britons participated in the movement to end the slave trade in some way. The 1820s movement to abolish slavery throughout the British empire involved over 1 million people.[43] Thus, while the movement certainly relied on bourgeois leadership, it was also a popular social movement that enjoyed support across social classes.

Women also played a significant role in abolitionism, particularly though not exclusively women from bourgeois classes.[44] While women were unable to sign petitions and discouraged from taking explicitly public roles, they forged other ways to participate significantly in the movement from the very beginning. Martha Gurney, for instance, owned a bookshop in London and published dozens of antislavery and radical tracts, including the most popular pamphlet of the eighteenth century on the consumption of sugar by William Fox.[45] The campaign against the consumption of sugar created a distinct opportunity for women to influence abolition. As the sympathetic sex with authority over domestic affairs, women could model these feminine virtues by encouraging abstention from the consumption of morally and physically tainted slave sugar.[46] By the 1820s, women had begun to form "ladies antislavery societies" throughout the British Isles. These societies focused on disseminating information about the continuing evils of slavery and the paths to abolition. Many of these women's antislavery societies insisted that abolitionists should seek immediate abolition, while many predominantly male organizations cautioned against such radicalism. Convinced that women had a responsibility to marshal their unique capacity for sympathy, women in these societies stimulated the radical turn toward immediate abolition that gained power on both sides of the Atlantic in the 1820s and 30s.[47]

While the abolitionist movement involved mass participation from whites in Great Britain and, later, in Europe and the United States, Black resistance to slavery, within the colonies and even within England, also contributed to the development of abolitionism.[48] There were, as I mentioned, formerly enslaved, popular figures such as Olaudah Equiano, Ignatius Sancho, and Phillis Wheatley who advocated against slavery in public and private. But in the decades leading up to the abolitionist social movement of the 1780s and 90s, enslaved Africans on English land used the law to petition for their freedom. With the aid of Granville Sharp and others, people of African descent put slavery on trial, which culminated in the 1772 *Somerset* decision. This decision was, at the time, interpreted as outlawing slavery in England—not, of course, in the colonies.[49] But other contributions to abolition in the 1780s and 90s came from outside of the colonial metropole. Atlantic travelers and laborers, including formerly enslaved people, contributed to what historians Peter Linebaugh and

Marcus Rediker called the "Revolutionary Atlantic." Their revolutionary notions of freedom and equality challenged the abolitionist movement to advance
stronger accounts of rights. In 1791, the slave insurrection in St. Domingue
had indirect effects on abolition. While there seems to be little indication that it
unsettled the public debate around slavery in England, it disrupted the French
sugar trade, which actually undermined the abolitionist campaign against slave
sugar. By the 1820s, slave revolts developed in relation to abolitionist activism in the metropole.[50] While the abolitionist movement within England did
not involve massive, direct Black participation, it is clear that abolitionism was
shaped by Black resistance and participation in England and abroad.

Thus, the abolitionist movement was a popular movement—especially
within England. It employed a wide range of tactics, including the campaign to
abstain from West Indian sugar, that were deployed throughout England and
even replicated by abolitionists outside of the British empire. The primary object of this early campaign was, however, a legal one: to abolish the slave trade.
The movement also depended on the efforts of a wide array of people, especially bourgeois reformers, artisans, and miners as well as women and those
less visible figures that struggled against bondage.

What abolition accomplished (and what it didn't)

The impact of abolition has been a matter of some contention. We should
avoid either overstating its achievements or diminishing its accomplishments.
Moreover, in looking back at abolition from the present, we must refrain from
projecting goals, virtues, and accomplishments onto the abolitionist movement that flatter our assumptions about what abolition must mean. It might
be comforting to imagine the abolitionists as a stubborn, heroic minority of
egalitarians who, through their will and craft, eradicated chattel slavery. But
the historical record should caution us against overrating the abolitionists' motives or singular achievements, significant though the latter may have been. To
clarify, we can track the effects of the abolitionist movement in two phases: the
1780s and 90s and the 1820s and 30s.[51]

Like many popular movements since, the first phase of the abolitionist movement helped to amplify and secure a cultural shift in attitudes toward slavery.
This is, perhaps, its most enduring achievement. The movement marshaled
public opinion in the campaign against slavery and, in the process, helped to
shift the tides of popular opinion in the British empire against slavery as an institution.[52] They did so by redefining the slave trade and, in the end, slavery, as

fundamentally immoral. Of course, such advocacy no more abolished slavery than civil rights movements ended racism or anticolonial movements eradicated the influence of former colonial powers. The British empire did not officially end the slave trade until 1807, nearly fifteen years after the first wave of popular abolition began to dissipate, and some form of chattel slavery persisted in the British empire until 1838. But in their campaigns against slavery and the slave trade, including the wildly popular campaign against the purchase and use of sugar, abolitionists brought the hideousness of slavery home to the metropole.

The abolitionists certainly forced the public conversation and, in particular, pestered Parliament to formally address the slave trade. But despite coming up for a vote in the House of Commons—a project at first taken up cautiously by William Wilberforce, a member of Parliament representing Yorkshire— the motions to outlaw the slave trade failed until 1807. The king supported the slave trade, especially because the West Indies remained significant to the imperial economy, and shifts in the colonial islands threatened to unsettle financiers and consumers in the metropole.[53] Moreover, in the wake of the 1791 insurrection in St. Domingue, France lost its major source of Caribbean sugar. Thus, British colonial sugar found eager buyers in France, which offset any declines in domestic consumption that may have resulted from the abolitionist campaign.[54] At the same time, tensions between monarchical Britain and revolutionary France pulled the rug out from underneath the radicalism of the abolitionist movement. Only after the Haitian insurrection concluded in 1804 were the abolitionists able to make any headway with the British imperial government. In a British climate fearful of mass agitation, abolitionists were not able to recreate the popular politics of the early 1790s. But, strategically, they sought to drum up abolitionist sentiment to pressure members of Parliament within their constituencies prior to the 1807 vote that finally abolished the slave trade within the British empire.[55] Slavery, however, remained. It also remained profitable, or at least harbored the potential to profit for the empire.[56]

While we cannot claim that abolitionists ended the slave trade in this first wave of activism, it is fair to assert that they developed an influential recipe for challenging existing authorities and advocating on behalf of distant strangers: The pioneering use of the petition; the methods of fundraising for abolitionist projects (some dubious, like the fervent colonization societies dedicated to sending formerly enslaved Africans back to Africa); the organizing premises of mass education and circulation of information; the popular abstention from sugar; the formation of advocacy groups in many different localities—these tools were accessible to later iterations of the abolitionist movement as well as movements concerned with other issues.[57]

In that first wave of popular agitation, many abolitionists insisted that ending the slave trade would lead ineluctably, if gradually, to the demise of slavery. They reasoned that life in the colonies was so harsh and plantation owners so cruel because the latter were able to rely on the transatlantic slave trade to replenish the stock of enslaved workers. But the decade after the abolition of the slave trade exposed this vision to be little more than fancy. There was no obvious decline in colonial slavery or any amelioration of slave conditions. After the British vote, even the United States outlawed the slave trade, content that slave populations in the American south, especially, were robust enough that they could grow without regular external imports of newly enslaved people from Africa.

As abolitionists struggled to regain momentum in a British climate hostile to radicalism and as revolts continued in the Caribbean, women pushed for immediate abolition; antislavery societies, both men's and women's, spread throughout the 1820s.[58] Abolitionist activism followed the patterns evident in the first wave of abolitionism: local organization, propaganda campaigns, petitions delivered to Parliament. Again, this activism included a popular campaign against the consumption of sugar and, this time, cotton as well. Moreover, abolitionists advocated the purchase of sugar and cotton produced by free labor to replace the slave-made goods.[59]

While the campaign against slavery within the colonial metropole intensified, so did resistance within the colonies. Enslaved people in Barbados (1816), Demerara (1823, now Guyana), and Jamaica (1831) plotted under the cover of churches and launched insurrections against colonial planters and authorities.[60] These were but the largest and most resonant instances of slave rebellion in the colonial metropole after the rebellion in St. Domingue. Abolitionists argued that the British should expect ongoing revolts as long as the slave system persisted. Faced with slave insurrections and popular pressure from abolitionists, Parliament finally passed an emancipation act in 1833. In addition to compensating slave-holders for the loss of chattel slaves, the act preserved a system of "apprenticeship," which consigned former slaves to their masters for a fixed portion of the working day. But ongoing disobedience within the colonies as well as abolitionist agitation ensured that the apprenticeship system was eliminated in 1838.[61]

Ultimately, the abolitionist movement contributed to the erosion of chattel slavery's legitimacy as a means of securing imperial profits and control. It certainly did not eliminate slavery on its own. The intransigence of the colonial planters, declining sugar prices, slave revolts, the search for more docile labor forces, and a shifting political climate in England all rendered Parliament sensitive to the resurgent abolitionist pressure.[62] Abolitionists' bequeathed both a substantive popular revulsion to slavery as well as a method of seeking to address moral and political issues. These latter contributions are of special interest to me. After all, one of their persistent campaigns asked consumers to consider, in the words of one anonymous pamphleteer, "[H]ow far they encourage the oppressors, by purchasing their commodities, thus defiled with blood?"[63] In these interpretations *of* commodity-exchange, we can begin to see the vision of the sympathetic consumer.

The Vision of the Sympathetic Consumer in the Abolitionist Movement

Published in 1792, *Considerations Addressed to Professors of Christianity of Every Denomination* was hardly the first or even the most noteworthy appeal for the abstention from slave-made sugar and rum. A bevy of pamphlets, speeches, artwork, and even poetry were published between 1791 and 1793, all inciting people to abstain from purchasing West Indian sugar. These ideas worked their way into abolitionist reports distributed to members of Parliament, letters to the royal family, and in public conversations in periodicals. In the later iterations of the abolitionist movement, these ideas grew in scope, if not necessarily in popularity. The understanding of the consumer on display in this sugar campaign includes an important feature: Abolitionists envisioned the consumer as central to mercantile capitalist circuits of commerce.[64] Through this central position, the consumer was expected to "feel *with*" invisible workers throughout these networks. This vision entails a distinct reflection on, or interpretation *of*, commodity-exchange that aims to unsettle interpretations *in* exchange. Before we see this vision, however, it is important to consider what commodity-exchange was like for many Britons.

Common shopping

While not quite flush with all manner of mass-produced goods, Britons—especially those in London—had many opportunities to shop. It is important to appreciate that the enclosed brick and mortar shop, while more and more common, was still in the process of becoming typical. These enclosed shops jostled with open markets, street selling, and hastily assembled street stands. A grocer would have stowed the bulk of his salable goods behind a counter,

sometimes made of glass, in drawers and on shelves, perhaps with several bar-
rels of goods placed around the store interior.[65] Of particular interest is sugar.
By 1800, the British were importing 23 pounds per head.[66] It was typically sold
as solid loaves or viscous treacle.[67] The loaves were finished in Great Britain,
not in the sugar colonies. This meant that sugar could well be identified by the
location where it was finished, not necessarily its precise colonial origins. By
the end of the eighteenth century, some sugar loaves were recognizable by their
packaging—often tin canisters.[68] But the sugar itself, of course, did not readily
announce its origins.

Many grocery purchases involved direct cash transactions, but, at their discretion, shopkeepers could also extend credit to customers. Moreover, while pay-
ments in cash and small credit predominated, shopkeepers sometimes accepted
payment in kind. These tendencies toward cash and credit transactions of fixed
prices also made their way into advertising for groceries and other goods.[69] This
suggests that shopkeepers could try to gin up business through appeals to price
alone. At the same time, shopkeepers distributed "trade cards" with attractive
and often exotic imagery that associated goods with imperial commerce. But it
was tea especially, not sugar, that stood in for the exotic reaches of the British
empire.[70] Regardless, many ordinary Britons would have been able to shop by
price. In addition, they would have had at least some sense that many grocer's
goods would have arrived from the outer reaches of the British empire.

In this context the shopkeeper, not just the goods, helped to define the ordinary experience of shopping. Stores were commonly organized around the
shopkeeper, who literally and figuratively stood between the consumer and an
increasing array of goods—sugar, spices, tobacco, nuts, dried and fresh fruits,
and more. Given this appearance, it would have been easy to arrive at the conclusion that the shopkeeper, not the consumer, deserved pride of place in a
system of imperial commerce. Such interpretations characterized campaigns
against the consumption of tea and other imperial goods in colonial America.
Although the American colonists insisted that people abstain from the purchase and use of British imports, the point was to dissuade merchants and
sellers from stocking those goods.[71] It was not the consumer but the merchant
who occupied a powerful position in networks of imperial commerce. From
the consumer's perspective, it was merchants who could bleed them dry by
marking up prices, adulterating goods, and adding false weights to the scales.[72]
Although those concerns would remain, the abolitionists asked consumers to
imagine themselves as the most powerful figures in imperial commerce. They

did so by shifting focus away from the merchants and onto the goods themselves as well as the people who purchased them. By calling attention to hidden labor, abolitionists hoped to upend the taken-for-granted desires bound up with personal needs, appetites, and prices at the point of exchange.

The sympathetic consumer in the abolitionist movement

The tract that spearheaded the campaign against the purchase and use of West Indian sugar arrived in 1791. William Fox, a radical abolitionist and bookseller, anonymously published *An Address to the People of Great Britain on the Consumption of West-India Produce*. Within a year, the publishers had cycled through twenty-six editions in London, as well as other editions in the rest of Great Britain and America. According to the best estimates, the address reached a circulation of 100,000 at the lower bound and 250,000 at the upper.[73] These figures would make it the most widely distributed tract of the eighteenth century, eclipsing even Thomas Paine's *Rights of Man*. Within two years, there were no fewer than twenty responses—some expanding on, some challenging—Fox's proposals. In subsequent pamphlets he wrote on the French Revolution, the *Address* had such cachet that Fox was identified as the author of *An Address to the People of Great Britain*.

In the *Address*, Fox located the consumer in a larger network of imperial commerce. He argued that abstention from West Indian sugar was an ethical and political duty, one that could undermine the system of colonial slavery. "The consumption of sugar in tea, wines, pastry, and punch, in this country," he wrote, "is so considerable, that by abstaining, we shall have an important effect on the Slave Trade, the colonial slavery, and on the other European markets where the consumption of sugar is but small, because the above articles, which occasion its consumption in this country, are on the continent very little used."[74] In the earliest editions, Fox calculated that a family using 10 pounds of sugar and rum per month would be responsible for 1 murder every 21 months.[75] Such calculations would become a staple of abolitionist consumer propaganda. By acknowledging the scale, scope, and significance of British sugar consumption, the consumer was in a position to affect the slave trade, slavery, *and* other European markets. Those European markets, it is important to recall, were also receiving slave-produced sugar, whether from British colonies or their own. "If we, as individuals concerned (either by procuring or holding the slaves or receiving the produce)," he reasoned, "imagine that our share is so minute that it cannot perceptibly increase the injury; let us recollect that, though numbers partaking in a crime may diminish the shame, they cannot diminish its turpitude."[76] The consumer was, here, a role that anyone could and did occupy. Europeans or any other body of consumers were, at least in principle, equally susceptible to this argument as British ones. The sympathies of the consumer, then, depended on an interpretation *of* commodity-exchange wherein the consumer occupied a privileged position in networks of exchange and commerce—a position that was easily taken for granted.

This vision of the sympathetic consumer appears in many contributions to the abolitionist campaign against sugar consumption. All consumers, aware or not, were involved. After detailing the nightmarish worlds of the slave trade and sugar production, Thomas Cooper condemned the consumer as a perpetrator of mob violence: "Shall it be said that an individual can produce no effect? When a thousand musquets are levelled at an innocent bosom, is it no crime in me to direct another bullet at the victim?"[77] The author of another pamphlet implicated thoughtless consumers: "There are some people who appear fearful of countenancing any thing that seems new; and, having been accustomed to the use of sugar, and their parents, whose memory they respect, having without compunction used it before them."[78] Still others cast the consumer as the cause of slavery. Andrew Burn wrote, anonymously, "[I]t is evident beyond a doubt, that the Consumers of Sugar and Rum, innocent or guilty, are actually the first and moving cause of all those torrents of Blood and Sweat that annually flow from the body of the poor African."[79] Even a letter to the Duchess of York observed, "It is . . . the buyer and consumer who form the first spring which sets in action the several engines of injustice and oppression, which annually destroy several hundred thousands of our fellow-creatures."[80]

In these interpretations *of* commodity-exchange, abolitionists painted a picture that begged consumers to rethink their purchasing. Even a strident critic of the sugar campaign recognized the implications of this vision of the consumer: "Is rum a luxury? Is cotton a luxury? Is ginger a luxury? Are spices luxuries? These are all very useful and highly necessary for various important purposes; and, if the system of the author is rigidly adopted, not only sugar and rum, but cotton, ginger, and various other articles, must never more be used by Europeans."[81] Perhaps better than many advocates of abstention from sugar, this critic identified where these sugar campaigns were heading. If consumers occupied such a prized structural position, then these relations and responsibilities would necessarily attend the users of many "useful and highly necessary" goods.

As the "prime mover" or "spring which sets into action," the sympathetic consumer had the ability to transform the slave trade. William Allen, a young, earnest abolitionist illustrated this ability with a typical chain of deductions:

> Nothing can be more evident . . . than that the Consumer *of West India Produce* is the principle cause, both of the continuance of the Slave Trade, and of the prevalence of Slavery. For, I would ask, *why* is the Slave Trade pursued at all? Is it not to supply the Planters with *men* to cultivate their lands? and why are the *lands* cultivated, if not to furnish the people of Europe with their produce? It must be clear then, that if that produce were not *consumed*, it would not be imported—if it were not imported, it would not be raised—and if it were not raised, there must an end of the whole system of Slavery. These deductions . . . serve to illustrate the *connection* existing between the CONSUMER of West India Produce, and the MEANS by which is it obtained.[82]

While I will explore the significance of these deductions in Chapter 5, for now it should be obvious that consumer power derived from their position in the system of imperial commerce. In testimony before Parliament, abolitionists invoked the specter of consumer power as a way around the MPs refusal to take on the slave trade.[83] This vision suffused William Fox's speculations about the consequences, were the consumption of West India sugar to decline: "The diminution of the consumption of West India produce, would also have a powerful effect by sinking the price of the commodity; . . . The effect a small variation in the supply or demand has on the price, we have recently experienced. The small interruption of the supply in the continent, by the disturbances in the French sugar islands, has suddenly raised some of the markets, which were 20 or 30 per cent lower than the British, much above it."[84] Although the insurrection in St. Domingue would threaten the efficacy of the sugar campaign, Fox took it as proof of the consumer's systemic centrality.[85]

Sympathies, too, worked their way from consumers to laborers through commodities in this system of merchant capitalist commerce. Several years before Fox's pamphlet, in 1788, poet William Cowper penned a popular sympathetic poem entitled "The Negro's Complaint." Cowper urged the reader to acknowledge the natural and ineradicable dignity of the enslaved African: "Men from England bought and sold me / Paid my price in paltry gold; / But, though slave they have enroll'd me, / Minds are never to be sold." But after decrying the tears, sweat, and toil of the slaves, Cowper joined this suffering to thoughtless consumers of sugar: "Think, ye masters, iron-hearted, / Lolling at your jovial boards; / Think how many backs have smarted / For the sweets your cane affords." Unlike Cowper, Fox and the advocates of the anti-sugar campaign made commodity-exchange into an explicit medium for sympathy. They presented enslaved Africans as victims of murder and robbery, with consumers as the perpetrators.[86] And it was through commodity-exchange that Britons could make these sympathies felt. William Allen cautioned against false sympathies: "But if, while we *pretend* to commiserate with *them* [the "poor Slaves"], we CONSUME *the fruit of their* MISERY, we falsify our Sentiments."[87] Not only could sympathies travel through these chains of commerce, but they could be perverted into their opposite. This fits the tendency, identified by Marx, for commodity-exchange to turn our reason and sentiment against us.

There were even more dramatic ways to pique the sympathies of consumers. One pamphlet entitled *"No Rum!—No Sugar!"* imagined a conversation between "a Negro [called Cushoo] and an English gentleman [called, inventively, Mr. English]." Through their conversation, Cushoo described, in an agonizing patois, the conditions of enslaved Africans, from their capture in Africa, to their passage across the Atlantic, and then to the cruelties of plantation life. The conversation, designed to reveal the truth of slavery and the slave trade, rested atop a weighty foundation of footnotes. These footnotes mentioned eyewitness accounts of slavery, government reports, testimony before Parliament, historical documents, and even biblical denunciations of human trafficking. But more than mere reportage, the dialogue was designed to encourage sympathy with enslaved people, trumpeting how the slave trade subjected Africans to unfathomable suffering—suffering that poisoned or diminished Africans' generally noble and kind natures. After tale upon tale of violence, debasement, and suffering, Mr. English protested, "Well, I wish to hear no more of this subject however—you know I can't help it." The Englishman suggested that he was both helpless to prevent and not responsible for these atrocities. But Cushoo demurred, ". . . You drink Rum and Sugar . . . den you support Slave Trade." The remainder of the conversation unspooled the familiar argument about Mr. English's responsibility for slavery via his purchase of sugar and rum. Through an imagined, face-to-face conversation between an Englishman and a formerly enslaved African, the pamphlet courted the consumer's sympathy with enslaved Africans in virtue of the former's position in imperial commerce.[88] The conversation revealed features of the system that bound these two men together—two men who would, otherwise, never set foot in the same room.

To cultivate people's sympathies, abolitionists offered an elaborate account *of* commodity-exchange, one designed to upend interpretations *in* exchange. In the eyes of some abolitionist leaders, this vision of the sympathetic consumer posed a radical, uncontainable threat to polite dissent against slavery. As such, in 1793 they reneged on a plan to escalate the anti-sugar campaign when parliamentarians like William Wilberforce expressed concerns that "turbulent elements" would push moderates away from the antislavery movement.[89]

While the campaign was initially limited to sugar, it expanded slightly in the second major wave of abolitionist mobilization. By the 1820s, abolitionists included projects to import and market East India sugar as a substitute for West India produce.[90] Purportedly cultivated from free labor, sugar from India was more palatable to abolitionists. Advertisements for "East India sugar basins" included an adaptation of Fox's calculations from 1791: "A family that uses 5lb. of Sugar per week will, by using East India, instead of West India, for 21 months, prevent the Slavery or Murder of one Fellow-creature!"[91] An appeal to British women, in particular, announced, "By the simple substitution of East for West India Sugar, the slave-owners themselves confess that slavery may be annihilated."[92] Women's antislavery societies frequently took it upon themselves to advocate the purchase of free labor sugar over that of slave labor.[93] In the middle of the 1820s, some enterprising abolitionists approached the Quakers and other abolitionists with a proposal for a "Tropical Free Labour Company." While this venture failed to find adequate support, the proposal was noteworthy for two reasons. First, it included cotton as well as sugar. Second, the author noted "the great advantage of this plan is that its influence will extend far beyond the bounds of the British Empire."[94] There is, here, a tacit recognition that the demands upon the sympathetic consumer would only increase. Within twenty years, there would be abolitionist pamphlets that identified sugar, coffee, cocoa, rice, tobacco, tea, spices, and more as the product of free or slave labor, allowing consumers to give their money to free labor over slave.[95]

Expanding the Sympathetic Consumer

It is difficult to assess these early efforts to mobilize people as sympathetic consumers. At the time, eager abolitionists estimated that at least 400,000 people participated in the campaign.[96] But several things may have thwarted any market impacts on the slave trade and slavery. First, as mentioned earlier, the anti-sugar campaign coincided with the slave revolt in St. Domingue. This disturbed French sugar production and would have enabled the owners of British sugar to offset any potential decline in British demand by selling in other markets abroad. Second, the actual provenance of sugar on the market would have been difficult to trace. Like many other commodities, sugar doesn't make its origins known. I will detail some of the tactics and strategies that abolitionists and others used to unveil these origins in Chapter 4. Either way, in a pinch, the unscrupulous merchant could offer up slave sugar in place of free labor sugar and none would be the wiser. Moreover, East India sugar did not necessarily offer a palatable solution, even if one were to accept the thinnest notion of free labor as the standard. There were well-documented reports of slave labor and deeply coercive free labor associated with East India sugar production going back to the 1770s.[97] Thus, the safest choice for concerned consumers would have been complete abstention from sugar. And given growing significance of sugar to the British diet, this kind of wholesale abstention would have been difficult to accomplish.

But as a vision, the sympathetic consumer was not merely a claim about what the consumer did; it was also a claim about what the consumer *could* do. In these early years of mobilization, British abolitionists presented the consumer as the heart and soul of imperial commerce. Abolitionists' promoted this vision to challenge the taken-for-granted nature of commodity-exchange. It was broad enough to attract all manner of supporters—men and women, white and Black, radical and conservative.[98] Over the years, they expanded beyond sugar into a range of other staple goods including cotton, cocoa, tea, and more. We will see the vision of the sympathetic consumer expanded even further by the end of the nineteenth century. Yet this expanded account merely elaborates on this abolitionist vision of the sympathetic consumer at the center of commerce; it doesn't dispense with or supersede it. We should remember, too, that the abolitionists were not a consumer movement as such. Their focus was, always, on the legal abolition of slavery and the slave trade. Thus, this account of the sympathetic consumer drew these interpretations associated with commodity fetishism into the abolitionist movement. Abolitionists did not organize their whole movement around such interpretations. It was turn-of-the-twentieth-century activists like the National Consumers' League and the consumer co-operatives that did so. I turn next to their visions of the sympathetic consumer.

3

Turn-of-the-Twentieth-Century Visions

IN 1913, when tasked with writing a history of the Co-operative Wholesale Society on their fiftieth anniversary, Percy Redfern—journalist, historian, and co-operative member based in Manchester—described this as the discovery of the consumer:

> The co-operative voyagers came across it [an organic commonwealth] accidentally rather than of intent—as Columbus sailed to the West "Indies." They landed on the shores of this unexplored continent when they discovered the consumer, and found that everybody is a consumer and that an organization of consumers is an organized whole.[1]

As a teenager, Redfern had been apprenticed as a draper and took initially to labor-centered socialism mixed later with Tolstoy's Christian anarchism.[2] But by his mid-twenties, upon taking up a job with the Co-operative Wholesale Society in 1899, he became transfixed by this co-operative discovery of the consumer.

Across the ocean in the United States, the same year Redfern began to work with the Co-operative Wholesale Society, another group—the National Consumers' League—codified this vision of organized consumers in their founding document:

> Recognizing the fact that the majority of employers are virtually helpless to maintain a high standard as to hours, wages, and working conditions under the stress of competition unless sustained by the cooperation of consumers,

the National Consumers' League propose to educate public opinion and to endeavor so to direct its force as to promote better [conditions] among the workers, while securing to the consumer exemption from the dangers attending to
unwholesome conditions.[3]

Taken together, these statements offer a vision of consumers' political and ethical role in social life. The consumer stood, unwittingly, at the center of a system
of industrial capitalist production, distribution, and exchange. Again, like the
abolitionists, in virtue of this structural position, these consumers had a special
ability and duty to feel with distant laboring strangers through their purchases.
Further, they had a responsibility to remedy exploitative practices all along the
supply chain. While the abolitionists pioneered the vision of the sympathetic
consumer in their movement against slavery, turn-of-the-twentieth-century
activists expanded on it. They did so in a way that reproduced the basic ideas
but extended their reach to more and more goods.

How did these turn-of-the-twentieth-century activists build and expand
on the vision of the sympathetic consumer after abolition? To discover the
consumer did not mean to find an isolated shopper alone with their conscience; it meant to discover that the consumer, when properly organized and
aware, would trade on their crucial position in networks of industrial commerce to bring about a more just society. More than the abolitionists, turn-of-
the-twentieth-century activists made organizing people as consumers into a
priority.

The similar visions of abolitionists and turn-of-the-twentieth-century
activists across the Atlantic allows us to reconsider the nation-state as a self-
evident axis of cultural variation, an idea that structures comparative and
historical social science as well as histories of consumers and consumption.
In much of this work, researchers treat culture as organized around national
borders—especially, though not exclusively, prior to the Second World War.[4]
Similarly, by default, many classic works in comparative and historical sociology have hitched cultural variation to the nation-state.[5] Yet, when we consider
how these consumer activists—from the abolitionists to the National Consumers' League—arrived at a common vision of the sympathetic consumer, another
option presents itself: Work on culture must remain open to identifying and
accounting for more general tendencies that manifest in and through particu-
larities. My point is simply that the comparative foundations for many accounts
of culture privilege the nation-state, or even more local or regional forms of belonging, as sources of variation. If we are to understand the cultural dynamics

of capitalist societies, then we must be prepared to recognize more general cultural tendencies and patterns even amidst genuine differences.[6]

From the Late Eighteenth to the Early Twentieth Centuries

When the abolitionists took their first steps toward consumer activism, western Europe and those in the path of their imperial expansion had begun to experience great transformations in industry, technology, and trade. Machines that enabled more efficient production and energy consumption developed rapidly in the period after 1820, and the volume of trade increased markedly.[7] The train and the telegraph promoted the spread and distribution of people, goods, and information at unprecedented rates of speed.[8] Technological and organizational advances facilitated more efficient production of goods through the disaggregated collective of efforts of enslaved Africans in the Americas, industrial workers in England, as well as the other laborers up and down the supply chain.[9] The extraction and processing of fossil fuels began in earnest, particularly in the coal mines of northern England.[10] Others in northern England were drawn into textile factories and factory towns like Manchester that were blackened with soot. These experiences in northern England anticipated developments elsewhere in the British Isles, the United States, and other rapidly industrializing regions. In England and the United States, immigration from southern and eastern Europe became more pronounced in the late nineteenth century and contributed to urbanization.[11] By the last third of the nineteenth century, these industrial dynamics, begun decades and centuries earlier,[12] yielded more goods in circulation and denser networks of commercial and cultural connections across the globe.

These technical developments in industry were aided and abetted by strenuous, unhealthy, and exploitative working conditions. While chattel slavery was officially discredited in the wake of slave revolts, legal abolition, and the American Civil War, workers continued to find themselves in harrowing conditions. Those working in and around industrializing regions often lived in cramped, filthy areas with minimal privacy and ghastly health.[13] As migrant workers were crowded into growing cities, they found work in industrial production and in small tenement homes. In tenements, especially, women and children placed the finishing touches on otherwise mass-produced clothing, food, and other goods. Late nineteenth century investigators like Charles Booth in England and the women of the Hull House in Chicago (including Florence Kelley, who became the leader of the National Consumers' League) or Jacob Riis in New York documented the living conditions of working people at the heart of this industrial growth.[14] Moreover, the formal abolition of slavery did not, of course, eradicate slave labor, impressment, and other explicitly violent labor regimes. The rubber trade in King Leopold's Congo infamously relied on grotesquely violent labor repression to meet stringent quotas.[15] Similarly, the cacao industry experienced shocks in the early 1900s when activists exposed that enslaved children were harvesting cacao in the African islands of São Tomé and Príncipe.[16] Thus, labor—undertaken by men, women, and children under explicit and implicit coercion—played an essential role in this industrial expansion.

In the last half of the nineteenth century, there was a well-documented trend toward large-scale industrial and machine production in Great Britain and the United States.[17] The modern, hierarchical corporation, funded through the stock market, rose to prominence in the United States and subsequently made its presence known around the world.[18] These industrial and corporate transformations had the very important consequence of expanding access to mass-produced consumer goods. In England, for instance, prices for many goods fell by about 40 percent from the mid-1870s to the mid-1890s.[19] The United States experienced an analogous period of declining prices and increases in real wages, particularly in urban areas.[20] Because laborers were especially vulnerable to the late nineteenth century boom-and-bust cycle, they experienced these benefits in fits and starts. But they too began to leverage their role as consumers through demands for a "living wage."[21] Moreover, the trend toward machine production increased the capital required to initiate it. This placed workers who wanted to control their workplaces at a disadvantage— they would have struggled to raise the capital necessary to control fully mechanized production. Thus, for the working classes, amalgamation in the sphere of consumption would have been a reasonable alternative for those seeking to avoid direct confrontation with anti-labor forces.[22]

Of course, these transformations did not turn people into consumer activists on their own—otherwise, millions upon millions more would have participated. Like the abolitionists before them, then, the turn to consumer activism occurred when other ways of getting involved in public political life were blocked. The lack of access to politics can necessitate a search for other opportunities to bring about social change or participate in public life.[23] As women's groups, the National Consumers' League and the Women's Co-operative Guild encountered distinct obstacles to public participation. Most notably, women in England and the United States did not win the unrestricted right to vote until the 1920s (1920 in the United States and 1928 in England). But in late Victorian England, politics would have been predominantly a spectator sport for working-class men, too, even if they were periodically enamored of William Gladstone or other Liberal politicians.[24] Moreover, historian Gareth Stedman Jones argued that a working-class culture defined in part by political apathy emerged in the late Victorian era.[25] Thus for prospective participants in co-operative societies, various trade unions would have been a more plausible course for participating in public life and politics than the Liberals or Tories of electoral politics. In the midst of these social and industrial transformations, with the levers of power jammed or turned against them, many people cast about for other ways to bend these transformations to more desirable ends. Some turned to the world of consumers and consumption.

Shopping at the turn of the twentieth century

Along with these industrial transformations, there were also shifts in selling, shopping, and consumer culture.[26] While historians have shown that consumer culture has a long and storied history,[27] nineteenth century industrialization and urbanization brought with it arcades, department stores, exhibitions[28]—all essential to the development of consumer culture as we now know it.

As people were drawn into cities and mass production escalated, workers were also more likely to rely on the market for basic provisions. While elites helped themselves to luxury consumer goods, more working people purchased bread, margarine, jam, tobacco, and other staple goods through the market.[29] Poorer workers were not entirely aloof from luxury consumption either. The practice of "shop window ranting" came up for heated debate in co-operative publications. One member of a co-op described the practice in industrial York-shire: "Those who by force of circumstances, are compelled to earn their livings in factories and workshops are quite fond of feasting their eyes on dainty and beautiful things as are girls who move higher in the social scale."[30] These young working women engaged in playful, imaginative shopping, even without easy money to buy fashionable clothes and other goods. Shop window ranters held forth on "the merits or demerits of 'hobble-skirts' or 'pennier-skirts' . . . the lat-est creations in the hat line, the 'merry widow,' 'the beehive,' the inverted 'pud-ding basin,' the most remarkable colors of fruits, flowers, feathers, the ribbons, the lace . . ."[31] By the turn of the twentieth century, public displays in depart-ment store windows, early cinema, mass market journals and newspapers, and other forms of mass entertainment had begun to gain popular traction.[32] Even those without great fortunes had opportunities to participate in the spectacles of a budding mass consumer culture.

Across the nineteenth century, the rise and growth of the department store changed the shopping experience in many ways. Department stores turned dramatic displays of mass-produced abundance and standardized, competitive pricing into selling opportunities. The increased circulation of mass-produced goods accelerated a shift toward fixed or standardized prices.[33] Outside, the ornate displays of goods behind plated glass offered a feast for the eyes. Inside, the consumer in the department store could wander, section by section, through an unprecedented range of goods, from home furnishings and clothing to jewelry and china. Clothing was displayed on mannequins, which became more lifelike by the 1920s. In the department store, consumers could walk right up to the goods and, at the very least, appraise them without requiring the assistance of the store proprietor. But this apparent immediacy did not diminish the significance of the counter and the salespeople. The shop proprietor—or in the larger retail and department stores, the shop assistants—were often responsible for attending to the customer. Moreover, the counter remained crucial to any and all transactions in brick and mortar shops, whether a local grocer or large department store. This was the site of sale. Service, too, became an explicit selling point.[34] One could visit a department store and expect to encounter courteous and knowledgeable assistants, not just an unparalleled display of industrial consumer culture. At the same time, the visitor of such a "cathedral of consumption" could feel more anonymous, especially when compared to the small shop.[35] They were not, at every moment, susceptible to the pressures of the proprietor, who could guilt or talk them into purchases.

We must be careful, though, about taking the spectacular cornucopias in department stores—like Bon Marché in Paris or Selfridge's in London or Macy's in New York City—as the rule, for two reasons. First, department stores would have spread inconsistently throughout the areas around the metropoles. Smaller towns would sometimes have retail shops that employed similar presentations of goods, methods of selling, and breadth of options—but not always.[36] At the same time, other forms of retail like the mail order catalog extended the sales reach into towns and villages where department store-style presentations were slow to arrive. But either way, it is certain that more and more people were aware of the department store as well as the methods of display and retailing associated with them. Second, then, as now, stores were stratified by wealth and status. The working-class "shop window ranters" in Yorkshire may not have been comfortable walking into the store, but they were happy to speak their piece outside. Department stores, too, gained reputations associated with higher- and lower-status shoppers.[37] The degree to which these stores mirrored the metropolitan department store may have varied with the status of the clientele. Of course, many of the women—and shop assistants were predominantly women, while men occupied managerial, stock, and de-livery positions—who staffed these stores were drawn disproportionately from the lower rungs of class and status.[38] To the obvious class distinctions that or-ganized these stores, it is important to add also race and gender. Women were often the principal targets of department store advertising and design; such marketing unleashed, what seemed to many contemporaries, salacious and unruly desires.[39] Unlike other stores that were officially segregated under Jim Crow laws in the United States, the open style of department stores yielded more subtle forms of racial discrimination like poor service for Black consum-ers and less desirable jobs for Black workers.[40] In this context, other types of markets often persisted, not merely as vestiges of a bygone era, but as an alter-native to class- and status-based trappings of department stores.[41]

The spectacle of consumer culture extended beyond the stores through novel forms of advertising and mass media. While historians trace imagina-tive and spectacular advertising strategies back to the eighteenth century, there is no question that the advertising landscape had changed by the turn of the twentieth century. For one, advertising agencies emerged as legitimate, even global, professions—though these agencies often sold space to prospective ad-vertisers, they did not necessarily take on campaigns themselves.[42] With the de-velopment of photography and advances in printmaking, advertisers had easier access to spectacular visual tools for enticing consumers. The last half of the century also witnessed the spread of commercialized mass media, especially nationally circulated newspapers and digests.[43] Turn-of-the-twentieth-century consumer activists, we will see, often debated the question of whether to use "modern" advertising techniques. And they lamented the concessions made to a public in the thrall of such consumer spectacles.

Finally, by the end of the nineteenth century the consumer would have had even more opportunities to buy goods for standardized prices on credit. Al-though formalized systems of credit would arrive later in the twentieth century, retailers played a role in elaborate, often informal networks of credit and debt. By the 1890s, the United States was on the vanguard of consumer credit with the founding of the Provident Loan Society, which ostensibly sought to protect consumers from loan sharks and other unsavory figures. But buying mass-produced goods on installment and credit through retailers themselves would have been familiar in Great Britain, Europe, and beyond.[44] These nascent developments in consumer credit were accompanied by vigorous denunciations of desire, often specifically feminine desire, and paeans to thrift.[45] Conflicts over women's spending, for instance, revealed anxieties about the gendered consequences of access to credit and feminine desire. In late nineteenth century England, husbands were responsible for the debts that their wives accrued. Many such families ended up in court, the targets of lawsuits by proprietors and owners who sought to collect on unpaid debts.[46] Moralists and activists would often share stories about the ruin that met those tempted by credit, glamour, and cheap prices. These and other cautionary tales play into a larger series of debates about the gendered moral consequences of consumer culture and industrial capitalism.

A consumer culture around mass-produced goods began to emerge by the end of the nineteenth century. When looking out on a world that encouraged people to buy more things in new ways, there were many opportunities for people to partake of this consumer culture, both as purchasers and spectators. In contrast with the world that confronted abolitionists, the turn of the twentieth century offered a more spectacular world of consumption to more consumers.

The consumer in the zeitgeist

In the midst of such developments, more people began to think about the consumer. If we return to the language of commodity fetishism, there were abundant opportunities for people to offer interpretations *of* commodity-exchange. This is evident in the ways that these consumer-oriented interpretations of commodity-exchange proliferated across the nineteenth century. After the abolition of the slave trade in 1807, the abolitionist movement lost some of its vigor, though it regained much by the 1820s in Great Britain as well as the United States. There antislavery societies of both women and men set up markets dedicated to the sale of "Free Labor Produce." These projects, still associated with abolitionists and Quakers, in particular, continued well into the century, up to the American Civil War.[47] But other reformers picked up the mantle of the consumer, too. In the United States, the followers of temperance and dietary reformer Sylvester Graham—Grahamites, as they became known—were concerned with meat, store-bought bread, and pollution in industrial food production. In the 1830s and 40s, they worried, among other things, about commercial bakers who produced adulterated loaves for private profit rather than public benefit.[48] Graham aimed to purify the diets and souls of an overstimulated public with more abstemious patterns of consumption.

Over in England in the 1830s and 40s, insurgent liberal reformers raged against the Corn Laws, which placed tariffs on imported food and grain. But they did so in the name of the respectable masses as consumers, not the bourgeois merchants who stood to profit on unrestricted free trade.[49] These tariffs, the reformers argued, burdened consumers with higher food costs. It was, therefore, consumers who stood to benefit the most from free trade. In the decades after the Corn Laws were repealed, the British social critic John Ruskin imagined the consumer's role in production and vice versa in naturalistic terms. He worried about the corruption of virtue as people succumbed to the temptations and artlessness of industrial productions. Ruskin insisted a "general law" of just exchange required "advantage on both sides," that is, both the producer and consumer should benefit.[50] Given that law, the effects of shoddy craft traveled from the producer to the consumer and from the consumer to the producer. "If our consumption," he wrote, "is to be in anywise unselfish, not only our mode of consuming the articles we require interests him [the laborer], but also the *kind* of article we require with a view to consumption."[51]

At this same time, in the last third of the nineteenth century, government statisticians in Germany, the United Kingdom, and the United States had begun to take an interest in measuring national living standards with greater precision. Knowing, more accurately, how their populations lived would enable more effective state policies to remedy the social ills that accompanied industrialization.[52] In the last half of the nineteenth century, laborers, too, developed notions of a living wage that reframed workers' interest in terms of consumption, evident in the union product label.[53] These strategies were subsequently adopted by some trade unions in the UK, who consciously built upon the perceived successes of their American brethren.[54]

Toward the end of the nineteenth century, economists began to treat the consumer as a distinct, even privileged figure.[55] William Jevons—a crucial contributor to the so-called marginal revolution in economic thought—insisted in 1871 that political economy "need[s] a theory of the consumption of wealth."[56] Jevons viewed consumers, not producers, as the source of a good's value. Further, these values were variable (e.g., the more you have of something, the more likely you will reach a point where additional consumption of that same good will yield diminishing returns or value). And, finally, these variable consumer preferences or values, evident in greater pleasure or pain, could be measured with mathematical precision. Although Jevons died before articulating a comprehensive theory, his successors placed the consumer at the heart of demand and economic thought. Among them, Alfred Marshall—the founder of economics as a discipline at Cambridge—published a major work on the principles of economics in 1890. In that work, he foregrounded the consumer and wrote, in words redolent of John Ruskin: "The world would go much better, if everyone would buy fewer and simpler things, and would take trouble in selecting them for their real beauty; . . . preferring to buy a few things made well by highly paid labour rather than many made badly by low paid labour."[57] Such an ethical injunction spoke directly to the anxieties of an age where, perhaps unlike any other before, the consumer was on the verge of becoming a mass phenomenon. But Jevons and Marshall were not alone. Other economists like Charles Gide in France, Simon Patten and Thorstein Veblen in the United States, and J. A. Hobson in Great Britain carved out a place for the consumer— for good or for ill—in economic thought at the turn of the twentieth century.[58]

These interpretations *of* commodity-exchange flourished in the midst of the industrial, technological, political, and cultural transformations of the nineteenth century. They reveal the backdrop against which activist groups like the National Consumers' League, the Co-operative Wholesale Society, and the Women's Co-operative Guild began to build entire movements and organizations around a vision of the consumer.

Turn-of-the-Twentieth-Century Consumer Activists

It is clear that the National Consumers' League, the Co-operative Wholesale Society, and the Women's Co-operative Guild were not alone in offering interpretations *of* commodity-exchange at the turn of the twentieth century. Nor were they alone in placing the consumer at the heart of industrial capitalist production, distribution, and exchange. But, as movements of consumers who employed a common repertoire of tactics across regions and nations, they offer an instructive comparison to the abolitionists. Before I address their visions of the sympathetic consumer, there are some important questions to answer: Just who were these turn-of-the-twentieth-century consumer activists? How were they organized? From whom did they recruit and whom did they target? What kinds of campaigns did they pursue? These brief histories underscore the sociological significance of their consumer campaigns. And they begin to illustrate how developments in the nineteenth century informed their ideal of the sympathetic consumer.

Backgrounds
The National Consumers' League
As department stores gained a foothold in late nineteenth century America, some women began to worry about the conditions under which saleswomen and messenger boys worked—long hours, no breaks, constant standing, low pay. In 1890, several high-society women—including prominent philanthropist Josephine Shaw Lowell and budding social reformer Maud Nathan—founded the Consumers' League of New York City. Inspired by the investigations of the store clerk Alice Woodbridge and the Working Women's Society, the Consumers' League attempted to raise consumer awareness of exploitative working conditions. The league appealed, primarily, to wealthy women who shopped in department stores like Lord & Taylor and Macy's and who found their conscience pricked by the strenuous working conditions for the young women and boys employed there. The group developed a "white list" for identifying shops that treated their employees well and advocated state regulation of working conditions in these shops.[59] Founding members Maud Nathan and Josephine Goldmark preached their gospel of consumer responsibility to women throughout the northeast and midwest. This led to the formation of consumers' leagues in Massachusetts, Pennsylvania, Brooklyn, and Syracuse. But the members' interest in the working conditions of department store employees began to touch on the workers behind the cornucopia of goods on display. Consequently, the members of these leagues began to meet in earnest in 1898 to discuss the possibility of forming a National Consumers' League. In 1899, the local leagues agreed to form a National Consumers' League out of these concerns for the working conditions of salesgirls, messenger boys, and others in a range of industries.

Florence Kelley—a fiery, hard-nosed socialist with Quaker roots—led the league from its inception until the early 1930s. An unusually educated person, Kelley received her undergraduate degree from Cornell, studied at the University of Zurich (one of the few universities to grant advanced degrees to women at the time), and completed a law degree at Northwestern in 1894. Her English translation of Engels's *Condition of the Working-Class in England* is still in use to this day.[60] Kelley's blunt, no-nonsense insistence on justice mingled with a social scientist's desire to seek out the causes of injustice. In the 1890s, she resided at the Hull House in Chicago with friend and fellow reformer Jane Addams. Kelley led the research and publication of their seminal *Hull House Maps and Papers*, which presented a comprehensive sociological portrait of the neighborhoods and tenements around the Hull House. Speaking at her memorial service, W. E. B. Du Bois remarked on Kelley's ability to galvanize a "dead board."[61] Du Bois knew Kelley as a founding member of the NAACP from 1911 until her death in 1932, among her many other social reform efforts.

Kelley directed many of her monumental talents toward the National Consumers' League, which incorporated a host of regional and local groups of mainly middle- and upper-class white women who sought to reform workplace conditions by encouraging ethical purchasing and state regulation of labor conditions. The group contributed in numerous ways to the efflorescence of voluntary reform work associated with the progressive era.[62] The National Consumers' League set itself to these tasks: "investigate, agitate, and educate." They investigated working conditions, publicized the frequently disturbing results, and organized campaigns for ethical purchasing as well as legal changes. In its constitution, the league emphasized "the duty of consumers to find out under what conditions the articles they purchase are produced and distributed."[63] As we will see, members pursued a range of tactics to educate consumers about their complicity in the exploitation and oppression of invisible workers.

The league did not participate in electoral politics—after all, most members were women who had at best limited franchise during the period—but it did concern itself with advancing legislation that protected workers. The NCL's contribution to the political and cultural legacy of the progressive era punched far beyond its weight class. There were roughly 7,000 members in 1906 and upwards of 15,000 dues-paying members at the dawn of the First World War.[64] The majority of these consumers' leagues were located in the northeast and midwest. However, there were consumers' leagues from Kentucky and Georgia to Colorado, Oregon, and California up through the First World War. The NCL often tapped into larger networks of clergy and women's clubs to disseminate league campaigns beyond their membership.[65] Furthermore, members' participation in public life ensured that the league could shape the enforcement of existing legislation. Members often served on committees designed to investigate the efficacy of factory and workplace regulations. Their relations with legal and political figures such as the lawyer and Supreme Court Justice Louis Brandeis enabled the league to contribute to the development and defense of legislation that protected vulnerable workers, especially women and children. Most fa-mously, league members contributed to Louis Brandeis's famous court brief in *Muller v. Oregon* (1908). In defense of a maximum hours law for women, Jose-phine Goldmark and Florence Kelley documented the ill effects of overwork on women with an exhaustive array of empirical data. Much of the data had been compiled by members of the NCL, too. Such prodigious work ensured that the league had an outsized influence on life and politics in the progressive era and beyond. In addition to its national influence, the NCL worked indirectly with consumers' leagues in France, Belgium, Germany, Switzerland, Spain, and else-where in Europe.[66]

The Co-operative Wholesale Society

Inspired by earlier co-operative projects, in 1863 a group of working men opened a store in Manchester. With the goal of building working people's wealth and power, they pooled their money in order to cut out middlemen and secure better prices for participants on staple goods. To replace the middle-men, early co-operators founded local stores where members could purchase food, clothing, and household items. The stores were collectively owned by the members, who received any profits via quarterly dividends that varied with the volume of purchases made in the store.[67] From 1863 to 1890, the member-ship grew by a factor of 39 from 18,337 to 721,316 as the stores proliferated, especially throughout the industrial north of England. Over that same period, profits grew more than 414 times from £306 to £126,979.[68] Through 1920, most Co-operative Wholesale Society members were men. Local societies often re-stricted membership to men alone, with women granted membership in the event of a spouse's death. These local stores were incorporated into the CWS and members were encouraged to participate in annual meetings, local co-operative projects, and their communities.

Like the National Consumers' League, the Co-operative Wholesale So-ciety devoted an immense amount of energy to popular education. To this end, the CWS published a bevy of newspapers and journals. *The Co-operative News*—a weekly publication dedicated to co-operation as a global movement—offers a valuable window into co-operative visions, practices, and assump-tions. It had a liberal editorial philosophy that resulted in the publication of serious debates about the value and practice of co-operation. But, of course, the co-operative movement contained many distinct opinions and tenden-cies. Local co-operative societies also published their own newspapers and reports. Historian Peter Gurney reports that, by 1900, 32 co-operative societies published monthly or quarterly records with a total circulation of 384,000 per month. These newspapers and records encouraged participation in the co-operative movement, from purchasing goods at the stores to attending co-operative exhibitions and social events. Officially, the Co-operative Wholesale Society remained aloof from politics until 1917, when the tumult of the First World War spurred the formation of the Co-operative Party. Until that time, the CWS would periodically comment on budgets, the law, and other political issues, but it was officially unaffiliated with the Liberal or Conservative parties. In 1927, the Co-operative Party made an agreement with the recently formed Labour Party, which remains in place to this day.

While it was always a working-class organization and movement, by the 1880s and 90s the CWS began to tout itself as an organization of consumers. Upon the outbreak of the First World War, the CWS could claim over 3 million members, and its total capital placed it as one of the twenty largest companies in England.[69] The majority of these co-operative societies were located in northwestern England, the locus of England's industrial working class. In 1914, for instance, there were over twice as many co-operative societies in the northwestern region of England (485) than in the southern region (205) or the Midlands (218).[70] In addition to the extensive retailing, the Co-operative Wholesale Society owned ancillary organizations including a number of co-operative "productions" or industries. These industries produced a wide range of goods including biscuits, boots and shoes, tea, soaps, tobacco, bacon, furniture, flour, and clothing.[71] As we will see, the Co-operative Wholesale Society approach to managing workers sometimes conflicted with their commitment to consumers—especially when trade unions sought to organize co-operative productions or even store employees. Coupled with its contributions to working-class culture in England, the size and scope of the CWS made it an important public, organized voice for consumer politics in the era. Given their comprehensive emphasis on sales, consumption, and production, co-operators aimed at nothing less than a wholesale transformation of social life on co-operative, not competitive, terms.

The Women's Co-operative Guild
The group that would become the Women's Co-operative Guild formed in 1883. Founded by the middle-class Oxford don and active co-operator Alice Acland, the guild became a formidable organization of working-class

housewives.[72] Acland hoped to support the education of women and girls in co-operative principles, as women were commonly barred from direct membership in many co-operative societies. Women were permitted to be members only through their spouses, although a membership was not necessary to shop at co-operative stores. By 1884, the group became known as the Women's Co-operative Guild. Like their brethren in the Co-operative Wholesale Society, the guild members were committed to the co-operative movement. The Women's Co-operative Guild flourished under the leadership of Margaret Llewelyn Davies. Davies energized the membership and steered the organization from 1899 until her retirement in 1921. From an established, liberal Victorian family, she became a member of the women's guild in the late 1880s. She directed her unusually extensive educational background and talents to building the guild as a political force, dedicated to the rights of women and working people. A remarkably independent and self-effacing presence, she convinced many workingmen's wives to join the guild. In celebration of her work, one guildswoman recalled, "I remember you saying that our husbands would be willing to stay in one night a week to let us go out to the Guild and if there happened to be one who could not be persuaded to give up an evening to his wife, you quoted a verse which I cannot now remember except that it ended with, 'well then give him the rolling pin.'"[73] Davies's stalwart independence, guidance, and, indeed, humor shaped the guild's development.

In many ways, the women's guild amplified the work of the Co-operative Wholesale Society. Members of the guild sought to educate others about the co-operative movement. They published pamphlets, held public meetings, helped found co-operative stores in poor communities, and discovered a range of ways for women to participate in the movement without becoming members of the Co-operative Wholesale Society. They arranged conferences and engaged in dialogues with the CWS. Like many central members of the National Consumers' League, guild members participated in settlement houses and public educational projects, a testament to their wide-ranging activism on behalf of co-operative principles.

But the guild did not always march in lockstep with its co-operative brethren. It often challenged the CWS on issues ranging from the labor conditions of co-operative employees to divorce laws. In 1914, the guild refused to quiet its outspoken advocacy for divorce law reform, which made it difficult for working-class women, especially, to leave abusive spouses. This resulted in a direct confrontation with the Co-operative Wholesale Society and the

Co-operative Union, where the guild renounced some funding from the other organizations to preserve its independence.[74] In more mundane ways, too, the women's guild remained distinct from the Co-operative Wholesale Society. Once formed, the Women's Co-Operative Guild had its own weekly section in the main intellectual organ of the co-operative movement, the *Co-operative News*. It retained its own records and pursued explicitly political campaigns such as advocating for women's suffrage and rights. Throughout the period, the guild developed a robust program of social activism from investigations of workplace issues to the promotion of ethical purchasing. Its membership, while smaller than the CWS, grew to more than 30,000 by the First World War.[75]

The sympathetic consumer at the turn of the twentieth century

Each of these groups addressed consumers and identified themselves as consumer organizations. Yet, in important ways, they drew from different constituencies (by class, gender, nation) and had distinct organizational characteristics (operating stores versus advocacy; political versus nonpartisan). Thus, one might expect these groups to offer fundamentally different interpretations *of* the consumer in commodity-exchange. But while there are indeed differences, there are also important points of overlap. Like the abolitionists before them, they envisioned the consumer as the hub of a system of production, distribution, and exchange—this time, industrial capitalism. Moreover, in virtue of this centrality, it was incumbent upon the consumer to sympathize with the laborers through the purchase of commodities. These interpretations *of* commodity-exchange aimed to remake interpretations of goods as anonymous *in* commodity-exchange.

The National Consumers' League (US)

When, in 1898, the regional consumers' leagues met to discuss the prospect of a national league, Maud Nathan told them, "[The City of New York league] has succeeded in great measure in arousing public sentiment against long hours for clerks and paved the way for a Consumers' Label if sufficient demand for it is created."[76] But the league members believed that they needed to create demand through patient and prudent organization. Future secretary Florence Kelley summed up the prospects for a national league and label: "It was made clear that a Consumers' Label should deal first with a higher class of goods—which would be in demand by the constituent of the various leagues."[77] Thus, members were aware of their elite constituency. This approach, however, did not reflect a narrow understanding of the consumer—one limited to elites. From the founding, the consumer was very much a systemic figure, central to industrial capitalist commerce.

The league's first official constitution included the following statement:

> That the interests of the community demand that all workers shall receive fair living wages, and that goods shall be produced under sanitary conditions:
>
> SEC. 2. That the responsibility for some of the worst evils from which producers suffer rests with the consumers who seek the cheapest markets regardless how cheapness is brought about:
>
> SEC. 3. That it is, therefore, the duty of consumers to find out under what conditions the articles they purchase are produced and distributed, and insist that these conditions shall be wholesome and consistent with a respectable existence on the part of the workers.[78]

As a statement of purpose, these principles mark out a field of broad public interest and assign a specific role to consumers, that is, to uplift the conditions of laborers. But while this would be significant in itself, the NCL grounded this moral claim in a specific interpretation of the consumers' role—in their slavish pursuit of bargains, consumers brought about evils in the realms of production.

Despite its prudential judgment to begin their work by focusing on a "better class" of goods, the league assumed that everyone was a consumer. In 1915, Florence Kelley characterized her work with the NCL as relating to the "public as consumers."[79] An early piece of NCL propaganda asked prospective members: "Will you help to form an intelligent public opinion as to the responsibilities of consumers?"[80] This rhetorical gesture identifies the public as consumers—it was a role that everyone played, at least in a capitalist social order where basic provisioning occurred more and more through the market. The general failings of consumers—thoughtlessness, pursuit of cheapness, lack of organization—were not limited to the small numbers of wealthy consumers whom they targeted in their early campaigns. Kelley observed that many Italian immigrants relied on adulterated and contaminated staple products such as olive oil in their "disorganized" quest for cheaper goods: "[T]he demand of the Italians in America for Italian products, although large, persistent, and maintained at a heavy sacrifice on the part of the purchasers, is not an effective demand, because the immigrants have neither the knowledge nor the organization wherewith to enforce it."[81] This is, in other words, a systemic vision of the consumer's role in these circuits of commerce.

Consumers, furthermore, had a political and ethical duty to act through this structural position to transform the working conditions for many different unseen laborers—in other words, to remake the conditions upon which depersonalized goods and their interpretation as anonymous depended. In its constitution, the NCL made this clear: "Recognizing the fact that the majority of employers are virtually helpless to maintain a high standard as to hours, wages, and working conditions under the stress of competition unless sustained by the co-operation of consumers."[82] The consuming public stood as the sole guarantor of co-operation between employers and workers. One NCL ad listed off a collection of "Do's and Don'ts for Shoppers":

> Do ask for garments bearing the label of the Consumers' League. Do your shopping before 5 o'clock and don't shop on Saturday afternoons. Do give your address plainly when goods are to be sent. Do your Christmas shopping as early as possible. Don't waste Salesman's time looking over goods you do not intend to buy. Don't receive goods sent on Sundays, holidays, or after working hours.[83]

These "Do's and Don'ts" appealed to a consumer who sought convenience for him- or herself, above all, and one who sought cheapness regardless of how it was brought about. But these moral imperatives hinted that consumers should "feel with" those workers responsible for producing and delivering their goods. One advertisement addressed consumer sympathies directly:

> And you! Oh power possessing shopper, do you realize that by the simple act of asking for (and insisting upon having it) the Consumers' League Label when you buy, you will help obtain benefits for many of your sister women? Use your power, therefore, to change conditions and to make the demand for labelled goods so effective that sweated work, child labor and unsanitary conditions will be abolished.[84]

These workers weren't just strangers; they were "sister women" who labored under oppressive conditions.

The NCL's vision of the sympathetic consumer comes into relief when compared with the work of John Atkinson (J. A.) Hobson, the radical English economist who also took an interest in the consumer. Maud Nathan, a founding member of the Consumers' League of New York City, cited Hobson to justify the league's own work. Hobson was a self-professed "economic heretic" who is perhaps best known for his work on imperialism, which influenced Lenin's well-known critique.[85] But Hobson wrote widely on matters of political economy and became an improbable inspiration for the consumers' leagues—improbable because the inspiration seems to rest on a misreading of his work. Nathan, along with other early figures, claimed Hobson as both an inspiration and justification for the National Consumers' League.

Nathan described Hobson's vindication of the consumers' leagues as follows: "Hobson . . . had proclaimed that the wealth of a nation could be increased far more rapidly by educating consumers than by increasing the work of producers."[86] In *The Evolution of Modern Capitalism*, Hobson did assert that social progress depended on the "improved quality and character of consumption."[87] But he did not understand "educating consumers" as Nathan did. Whereas Nathan insisted that consumers required education to sympathize with unseen laborers, Hobson thought that consumers required education in a "just economy of individuality."[88] By this, Hobson meant that industrial capitalist society would be improved insofar as it balanced machine and artisanal (or artful) production appropriately. The former would satisfy needs that were common to all, while the latter would satisfy individualized needs. In the best case, Hobson suggests that the "cultivation of individual taste . . . shall graft a fine-art upon each machine-industry." Moreover, such cultivated tastes would apportion "to machinery that work which is hard, dull, dangerous, monotonous, and uneducative, while that which is pleasant, worthy, interesting, and educative [will be] reserved for the human agent."[89] In fact, Hobson distanced himself from consumer movements. When writing about the Victorian critic John Ruskin, whose influence upon this "just economy of individuality" is clear, Hobson dismissed consumers' leagues: "Something, doubtless, may be done by 'white lists' and Consumers' Leagues. . . . But this 'something' is infinitesimally little."[90] Nathan's misreading of Hobson actually speaks to her distinct assessment of the consumer's systemic significance.

Ultimately, the National Consumers' League envisioned the consumer as the systemic source of the demand for goods—a shoddy buyer was a shoddy maker.[91] The consumer benefited and depended upon others to supply the goods he or she bought; the interdependence of consumers and laborers, all along the supply chain, secured this obligation. "To buy a sweated garment," wrote NCL president John Graham Brooks, "is to have someone work for you as definitely as if she were in your own house."[92] In the NCL's vision, sympathies with unseen laborers could travel from consumers to laborers, through the commodities that circulated through networks between them.

The Co-operative Wholesale Society (UK)

The Co-operative Wholesale Society made this vision central to its project as well. Percy Redfern (1913) claimed that the mid-nineteenth century founders of consumer co-operation accidentally "discovered the consumer" as a means of organizing entire societies. While these pioneers created the template for the CWS, they did not describe themselves as a consumers' movement.[93] The CWS began to describe itself as a consumers' movement in the 1880s and 1890s.

Redfern's claim that "everyone is a consumer" may seem banal. But it reveals a crucial feature of co-operative thought: In a system of industrial capitalist commerce, the consumer would lead the way to a genuinely democratic future. This vision was most evident when the Co-operative Wholesale Society contrasted consumer co-operation and worker co-operation. In response to an address advocating workers co-operation, co-operative members argued, "In acquiring fields, farms, and factories, [consumer co-operatives] produce for their own consumption. They have no need of capitalistic channels in order to sell their goods. But it is quite otherwise with societies of producers [i.e. worker co-operatives]."[94] Worker co-operatives were at a disadvantage because they needed to work through "capitalist channels" like private sellers and businesses. For this reason, the path beyond capitalist modes of commerce went through the consumer, not the worker. To some in the Co-operative Wholesale Society, worker co-ops remained dependent on owners, management, and "middlemen,"[95] and therefore "capitalistic channels," to secure their demands as workers.

In this co-operative imagination, contemporary industrial conflicts could also reveal the privileged systemic position of the consumer as arbiter between capital and labor.[96] Redfern put this succinctly: "[In co-operation], labor and capital become the consumers' agents."[97] The systemic weakness of labor could render any gains won through workplace struggles temporary. Take, for instance, a report in a 1911 edition of the *Co-operative News* concerned with the exploitation of consumers at the hands of private producers. The commissioner (otherwise unidentified) wrote, "No doubt, as a result of labour upheavals, the profits of these men [private producers] will be increased, whilst the workmen's gains will be snatched from him in increased prices of food, clothing, coal, and shelter. . . . The consumer pays the piper."[98] Though the striking workers might win some small gains in wages or benefits, the author cautioned against corresponding cost of living increases. Furthermore, the piece concluded with an affirmation of the consumer's position of strength: "But is it right that small groups of men should be permitted to enrich themselves by taking advantage of social and industrial changes? Of course, that is the *consumers' own lookout*. He has the remedy in his own hands by means of co-operation."[99]

In discovering the consumer, co-operators also discovered the consumer's responsibilities and duties—among them was the responsibility to sympathize with those who produced their goods.[100] In an 1890 letter titled "Worker, Consumer, and Capitalist," co-operator Joseph Tyldesley addressed tensions between consumers' desire for cheap prices and workers' desire for high wages—a repeated concern for the National Consumers' League as well. He argued that such "skirmishes between the 'worker' and 'consumer' could be overcome by the co-operative model." Tyldesley continued:

> Speaking as a consumer—I am also a worker—I would say that the only solution . . . lies with the consumer. Let him make his own capital or covering the risk and hire of it, pay fair price to all workers, and take the breeches [cutting out the capitalist]. Carry this plan not only into boots, as at Leicester [co-operative boot manufacturer], but into hats at Denton, clothes at Batley, providing all our wants on this plan.[101]

He drew an explicit connection between consumers and laborers. After all, co-operators were also workers. This provided a basis through which consumers could sympathize with many different, unseen laborers' (boots, hats, clothes) desires for higher pay. But he also insists on the systemic privilege of the consumer. Both CWS leadership and members insisted on this duty to sympathize. In an article on the employment of women in shops, the editors wrote, "[F]or the sake of the customers who are profoundly anxious not to assist either knowingly or otherwise at oppressions of workers, we wish somebody would undertake to make known the shops in all big towns where buyers can go with a clear conscience."[102] Many co-operators wanted "an assurance that the clothes we wear and the foods we eat are made under proper conditions."[103]

There were times, as I will discuss later, where tensions bubbled up between the co-operators and laborers over the former's vision of the consumer and management of workers. But co-operators often insisted that co-operation "provides a ready means of enabling workmen to translate their professions into deeds."[104] By this measure, co-operation made sympathy with other workers into more than a dream. In the same piece, the author suggested that the co-operative store bound the trade unionist, consumer, and proprietor into a "whole being dominated by the democratic principle."[105] An article condemning "the sweating system" concluded with the words of Beatrice Pot-ter: "[C]o-operators are more or less responsible for the life and labour of every man, woman, and child employed in the production of the commodities they consume."[106] When food prices spiked in 1912, co-operators insisted, "in the amalgamation of consumers for their own help and protection, lies the only power that can break the spell of high prices and exorcise those spirits of greed and selfishness that give capitalist the mastery and confer misery upon the workers."[107] This was a systemic vision of the consumer's role in an industrial capitalist society, where the masses, properly educated, would be able to make their demands known through co-operation.

Though its emphasis on consumer democracy offered a distinct gloss, the Co-operative Wholesale Society, too, envisioned a society of sympathetic consumers. By making consumers privy to their commercial centrality, co-operators hoped to eradicate unsavory business practices and the undemocratic accumulation of wealth. Through the co-operative movement, consumers had the ability to trade on this commercial centrality and sympathize with those who labored to make all manner of everyday and luxury products. When mak-ing sense of commodity-exchange, the Co-operative Wholesale Society arrived at a now familiar interpretation of the consumer.

The Women's Co-operative Guild (UK)

An ad in the 1908 *Bolton Co-operative Record* read: "All Women should Vote . . . for, and try: 'Wheatsheaf' Boots and Shoes, 'Symergon' Hosiery, Bury Dress Linings, Littleboro' Flannels." These brands were "Made for Co-operators, in their own Factories, under their control, in which Women share . . . Standard Hours and Wages for Women workers."[108] While the Co-operative Wholesale Society, especially through the First World War, used the generic masculine pronoun to identify consumers, many within the movement were aware that most of the actual shopping at co-operative stores was done by women.[109] The Women's Co-operative Guild emerged in response to this situation. As an af-filiated yet independent co-operative organization, the Women's Co-operative Guild's image of the consumer shared the same ethical thrust as the CWS. It stressed the duties of consumers and decried the thoughtless search for cheap-ness as a "false economy," one that reproduced profit-seeking, sweatshop labor, and other social problems. Yet, the guild re-imagined the consumer as a woman, thereby making the claim that social progress depended upon the "woman with the basket." Although the Women's Co-operative Guild insisted

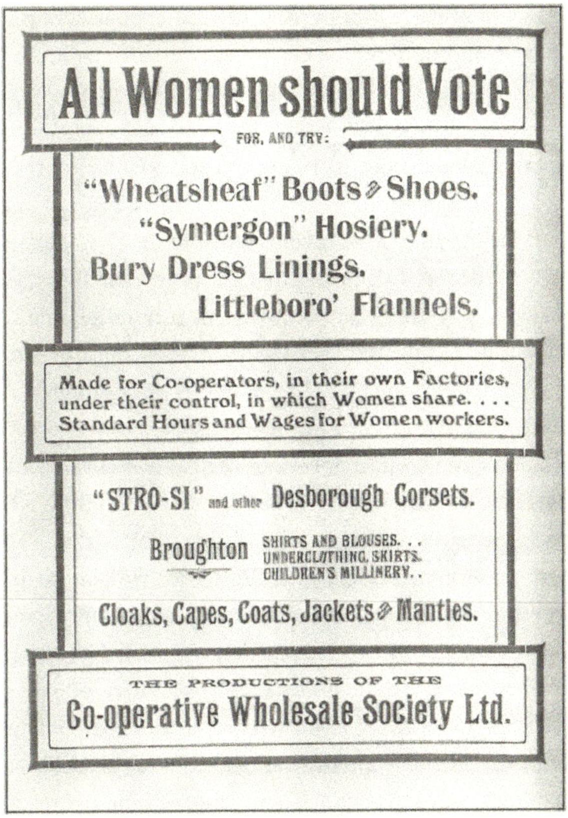

Figure 1 Advertisement from the *Bolton Co-operative Record*, March 1908.

Source: National Co-operative Archive, Manchester, UK. Reproduced with the permission of the Co-operative Heritage Trust (May 2020).

on the gendered nature of the consumer in practice, its vision of the sympathetic consumer accords with that of the Co-operative Wholesale Society and the National Consumers' League.

From its formation in 1883, the Women's Co-operative Guild sought to reform the co-operative societies as well as the competitive capitalist social order. The founders of the women's guild voiced concerns about the limitations of consumption that have plagued consumer activists of many stripes: "We can be independent members of our store, but we are only asked to come and 'buy.'"[110] The hostility to women's roles as mere purchasers reflected the gendered nature of co-operative politics. At the same time, it anticipated concerns that arose with each of these groups: how to use the politics of purchasing as a means of encouraging more robust community involvement. As the Women's Co-operative Guild grew, it promoted co-operation and encouraged women to take an interest in co-operative principles. This included campaigns to educate younger generations about co-operation and to improve the condition of women in the United Kingdom.[111] The Women's Co-operative Guild embedded its concerns about the role of women as consumers, as well as consumers in general, within this framework of improving women's condition. Consequently, the guild took a complicated attitude toward consumption and consumers: It wanted women to be recognized as more than mere consumers or purchasers, yet it also built on many women's practical role as a consumer.[112]

Through the First World War, the Women's Corner was one outlet for the Women's Co-operative Guild members in the *Co-operative News*. In practice, many of these articles dealt with issues that women would face as consumers. From the vagaries of fashion to the virtues of thrift, the Women's Corner provided open discussion, advice, and counsel for women for navigating the world of shopping. The themes ranged from grocery shopping and appropriate dress to supporting co-operative stores and sweated goods.[113] All of them provided guidelines as to the consumer's responsibilities, often responsibilities that implicitly and explicitly fell upon women. They inveighed against a "false economy" that would have women chasing fashion or bargains at the expense of "store discipline"[114] and thoughtful shopping. On the matter of store discipline, or the failure to shop consistently at co-operative stores, one member noted that the typical co-operator

> lives among women who think that shopping is a kind of diplomatic game, in which, if you are only sharp enough, you manage to outwit the shopkeeper, and get things for less than they are worth; or who conveniently pin their faith to some grocer, whom they praise among their acquaintance as "such a very fair-dealing man," forgetting that the public has very little means of judging whether he is a fair-dealing man or not.[115]

In general, the advice squared with that suggested by the co-operatives: As a consumer one had a duty to make wise and thrifty decisions that promoted co-operation between people as opposed to self-interested individualism and competition. But unlike the Co-operative Wholesale Society, the explicit focus on women's roles appears, at first glance, to narrow the guild's vision of the sympathetic consumer to women alone.

A closer look, however, reveals a now familiar interpretation *of* commodity-exchange. In a paper intended for "Junior co-operators," guild member Geraldine Hodgson made the structural position of the consumer explicit: "The fact is, from the street arab to the Queen, every one of us is a *consumer*."[116] Similarly, guild members committed themselves to the notion that co-operation was ultimately a consumer movement. In a guild pamphlet introducing co-operation, M. C. Spooner cited social reformer Beatrice Webb's description of co-operation approvingly: "The unit of the co-operative movement is the customer—almost invariably a woman."[117] Like their co-operative brethren, guild members knew *who* played the role of consumer, but also insisted on the importance of the consumer's role in an industrial capitalist social order.

When members of the Women's Co-operative Guild discussed the consumer's sympathies, it was clear that these obtained for any purchaser—even if women were in fact the primary purchasers. In one explicit account of consumer sympathy, Margaret Llewelyn Davies wrote, "Now the first duty of consumers is that they take care to consume nothing which is not in some way beneficial to the producers and sellers thereof as to the consumers themselves."[118] This description—where consumers seek benefit not merely for themselves but for "producers and sellers"—illustrates that the role of the consumer entailed the capacity for sympathy with producers. In principle anyone could occupy this role. Davies drove this sympathetic role home with a familiar Ruskin-esque turn of phrase: "When we women buy anything, let the question in the back of our minds be, is making this worthy to be the bread-winning work of a human being? Would I care to have it for my own employment?"[119] Again, this practical acknowledgment of women as consumers worked in concert with the broader vision of the consumer's systemic role. Her conclusion made this clear: "Let us [women] start then and set the fashion, for it directs the greatest consumers' organization in the whole world, and thus controls the industry of the world."[120]

This vision of the sympathetic consumer appeared in the guild's iconic image of the "woman with the basket." Introduced in the first decade of the twentieth century, this image—a woman with woven basket resting upon her knee, looking out into the dawn over an urban, industrial landscape—accompanied a manifesto that identified the woman's power of purchase as "the greatest earthly power." The introductory paragraph is an ode to consumer power in a system of capitalist commerce:

The "Woman with the Basket" is one of the great Types of Humanity. She has a place beside the Sower, the Master Builder. She is the ingatherer of the produce of the Earth; the inbringer of the provisions of the Household; the distributor of all succour and help. She is mistress of the markets of the world, for what she will not buy, men need not make nor procure.[121]

With this great power, came the responsibility to sympathize:

> If we women would cease to buy what is not bread, and begin to search out all that is honest and of good report—if we would but cease to admire and imitate some whom we should rather regard as awful warnings, and learn to honour instead the home-maker and the fellow-worker—if we would cease sinking into apathetic indifference, and bend our energies to make the world better worth living in, we should speedily have a new, happier, and fast-developing social state.[122]

Through her consumption, the woman with the basket honored the "home-maker" and "fellow-worker." The woman with the basket appeared on guild membership cards and became a way for active members to rally women to the cause. It also incarnated the guild's vision of the sympathetic consumer.

Whereas the Co-operative Wholesale Society offered an image of the universal male consumer, the Women's Co-operative Guild proceeded from many women's practical roles to a universal female consumer—both needed to use their structurally derived power to usher in a better, more just world. There were obvious gender differences within the co-operative movement.[123] And the Women's Co-operative Guild raised the question of who did the actual purchasing rather pointedly. But it also articulated a vision of consumers' transformative social role that shared basic features with the Co-operative Wholesale Society and the consumers' leagues. The consumer occupied a decisive role in a system of industrial capitalist commerce—everyone was at some point, or had the capacity to be, a consumer, even if—in practice—women were more commonly consumers. Moreover, through this decisive role, consumers were expected to sympathize with the producers of their goods.

National Consumers? Comparison, Culture, and Commodity Fetishism

Like their predecessors in the abolitionist movement, turn-of-the-twentieth-century consumer activists promoted a vision of the sympathetic consumer. Even as they molded the vision to their distinct ends and social contexts, these groups shared an interpretation. This vision entails a specific interpretation *of* commodity-exchange, wherein the consumer has the responsibility to feel with unseen laborers. These interpretations *of* commodity-exchange both question and take for granted the nature of such exchanges. Thus, this vision speaks to the fetishism of commodities. Moreover, this illustrates something important about the search for a capitalist culture, whether via commodity fetishism or other phenomena. Rather than insist that observed differences are inconsequential, we can discover a similar pattern in these distinct interpretations of commodity-exchange. Where investigations into market cultures or cultures of capitalism might discover only a plurality of interpretations, I find a common pattern bound up with a recurring phenomenon crucial to a capitalist social order. To illustrate, consider how a de facto emphasis on national cultures informs some historical accounts of consumption.

Historians of consumer politics commonly stress the national differences between England and the United States.[124] The curious history of consumers' leagues in the United States and England exemplifies this narrative of national difference. In 1887, the first consumers' league was established in London by a member of the Women's Trade Union Association named Clementina Black. This league sought to secure fair wages and safe workplaces by mobilizing consumers to patronize approved shops. The league held meetings over several years before they disbanded in or around 1892. Consumers' leagues in England never recovered, and Black continued to support the trade union movement in other ways. Across the sea, in 1889, women in New York formed a group called the Working Women's Society. They desired to "investigat[e] and redress the hardships and abuses endured by women and children in shops and factories."[125] In one of their meetings, the Working Women's Society resolved to draw up a list of approved shops where workers received adequate wages and labored under fair conditions. Upon learning of the London-based consumers' leagues, the members took on their name and eventually organized the Consumers' League of New York City. Within seven years, the consumers' leagues became a nationally federated organization and inspired similar projects throughout Europe. Thus, while consumers' leagues originated in England, they failed to take root there. In the United States, the consumers' leagues found their footing and, eventually, influenced the work of European reformers. This series of events reinforces the narrative of cross-national difference.

Consequently, some historians reject any suggestion that co-operatives and consumers' leagues share similar visions or commitments. Matthew Hilton draws a bright line between the co-operative movement and the work of consumers' leagues. He writes of a "much more divergent body of consumerist thought" in turn-of-the-twentieth-century England in contrast with the sharper focus on consumer citizenship in the United States.[126] In so doing, Hilton distinguishes between co-operatives, free trade liberalism, and consumers' leagues. The latter were seen as a "support to existing labour concerns" and therefore less radical as a consumer movement.[127] Similarly, Julien Vincent insists that consumers' leagues "should not be confused with workers' consumer co-operatives."[128] Hilton and Vincent are correct; it would be a mistake to conflate the National Consumers' League, the Co-operative Wholesale Society, and the Women's Co-operative Guild. At the same time, to stress British and American peculiarities alone makes it easy to overlook intriguing similarities in their visions of the consumer.[129]

That American and British consumer activists shared a vision of the sympathetic consumer should encourage us to rethink conventional practice in histories of consumption.[130] Many compelling works of historical social science have used cross-national comparisons to discover common tendencies without writing around national differences.[131] The point is not that it is wrong to identify national differences or that these turn-of-the-twentieth-century groups were really all the same. Rather I want to suggest that the framings of these arguments can blind us to the kinds of similarities that the search for a capitalist culture reveals. By leaning on analytical and explanatory frameworks defined by nation-states and regions, regardless of the kinds of practices and patterns we seek to explain, we risk finding nothing but national differences that produce national difference. One could make a similar argument for historical time periods. That the abolitionists and turn-of-the-twentieth-century activists promoted visions of the sympathetic consumer offers an opportunity to inspect this curious alignment. By discovering this elementary point of overlap, we find a reason to look more closely at other obvious contrasts. While such investigations need not yield surprising parallels and connections, it is surely better to investigate than to assume.

Commodity fetishism—which includes these interpretations *of* and *in* commodity-exchange—lends itself well to such investigations. Thus far, we have seen how these interpretations *of* commodity-exchange manifest in a variety of ways—even in identifying basic similarities like the vision of the sympathetic consumer. It should be clear already that, in many ways, abolitionists and these later activists thought very differently about the consumer and the world. For instance, the unapologetic gospel fervor of the abolitionists seems foreign to the National Consumers' League or the Women's Co-operative Guild. The reformist rhetoric of the NCL, moreover, does differ from the frequently anti-capitalist rhetoric of the co-operative movement. At the same time, as we explore different features of the sympathetic consumer, it will become clear that interpretations *in* commodity-exchange were associated with some important limits on what all of these activists do. This sensitivity to variety and uniformity befits a mode of investigation, such as the search for a capitalist culture, that must render both.

*　*　*

When Percy Redfern, the co-operative historian, compared the founders of consumer co-operation to Columbus in the West Indies, the metaphor was perhaps truer than he intended. After all, like Columbus, the shores these co-operative voyagers "discovered" were already inhabited. These co-operative forebears had a vision that abolitionists, aghast at the world Columbus helped to create, would have recognized. Over the course of the nineteenth century, more and more people discovered this vision of the sympathetic consumer. Because it evolved in relation to a common phenomenon like commodity-exchange, the sympathetic consumer was not the sole possession of some special class of consumers. But this did not mean that the vision was common. Thus, these advocates—from the abolitionists to the Women's Co-operative Guild—did their best to bring their vision to others. This tells us that there is more to the sympathetic consumer than a mere dream or vision. If we want to understand the sympathetic consumer as more than a mere dream, we need to look into these efforts to share it with the world. We need, in short, to look at the practices bound up with such a vision.

4   Practicing Sympathetic Consumption

IN 1791, abolitionist William Fox declared, "[E]very person who habitually consumes one article of West Indian produce is guilty of the crime of murder."[1] As you may recall, Fox's *Address to the People of Great Britain* called for consumers to abstain from the purchase and use of sugar and rum from the British West Indies, where enslaved Africans were purchased to work on elaborate sugar plantations. But Fox's rhetoric went further than indicting consumers for murder. He also asserted that, unbeknownst to consumers, the blood of enslaved people polluted the sugar that British colonists purchased. Fox explained the need for organized consumer action to avoid figuratively ingesting the blood of the enslaved: "The laws of our country may indeed prohibit us from sugar cane, unless we will receive it through the medium of slavery. They may hold it to our lips, steeped in the blood of our fellow creatures; but they cannot compel us to accept the loathsome potion."[2] In continuing to purchase and use slave-grown sugar and rum, consumers were "virtually" agents of "the slave-dealer, slave-holder, and the slave-driver."[3] Fox's rhetoric drew attention to the depersonalized labor that went into the cane sugar, which had become a staple of the British diet.

One century later, in 1892, the Women's Co-operative Guild staged its essay competition on the theme of shopping. We can return to the words of Katy, who mused: "It does seem strange, when we think of it, how lightly and thoughtlessly we go out shopping, how easily we let the money slip through our fingers, money that has cost thought and toil and weariness." Poignantly, Katy condemned the thoughtlessness evident in the search for cheap bargains:

I don't think any of the readers . . . would say—"Well, what does it matter if someone did have to pay more, so long as we get a bargain?" or "It is no affair of ours if work is not properly paid for—if we don't buy them, someone else will." Though we would scorn to hold such sentiments, we may *act* as if we held them, just for want of thought and looking into things.[4]

She then lamented, "If we could only have a 'magic mirror' that would show us the beginning and end of the 'bargains' and cheap goods which look so attractive . . . we should need no more arguments."[5] Her sympathetic prose invited readers to peer into the dingy, desolate rooms where depersonalized goods were produced so that they could see the "pale women and girls" who produced them. Moreover, her use of "we" asked readers to identify as consumers, whose duty it was to remedy inhumanely sweated labor and other unjust conditions through conscientious purchasing.

These attempts to mobilize sympathetic consumers appealed to the senses. They offered *ways of seeing*, to lift a phrase from the art critic John Berger[6]— ways of seeing the links between producers and consumers in goods that didn't otherwise reveal them. In these ways of seeing, activists responded to the curious anonymity of consumer goods—what I have called interpretations *in* commodity-exchange. To make such ways of seeing possible, activists deployed a whole range of tactics. Katy and William Fox depicted the worlds behind these commodities: the suffering, toil, and blood, all hidden from the consumer. Their interpretations *of* commodity-exchange presented the labor behind the goods as both imperceptible and as an intrinsic source of value, just as we would expect given Marx's description of commodity fetishism.

But we will also see that interpretations *in* commodity-exchange had tactical consequences for abolitionists and turn-of-the-twentieth-century consumer activists. Katy's desire for a "magic mirror" that would expose the suffering hidden behind goods captures the essence of these tactics well. Such a magic mirror would elicit sympathy with those suffering. That sympathy, in turn, would lead consumers to a different interpretation *of* commodity-exchange, as a way to transform the world, not just to sate some desire or another. In short, the anonymity of commodities—interpretations *in* commodity-exchange—informed the practices meant to promote the vision of the sympathetic consumer— interpretations *of* commodity-exchange. While this anonymity can lead to thoughtlessness, as both Marx and Katy noted, it can just as well lead people to wonder what lies behind the commodity.

Thus, this chapter highlights the techniques and practices, ways of seeing, bound up with the sympathetic consumer. It traces two ways of seeing common to abolitionists and turn-of-the-twentieth-century activists: imaginative and sensuous. The former involves techniques that would induce people to imagine the toil and suffering and dignity of invisible laborers. The latter involves techniques that literally placed images and objects before people's eyes and in their hands. These techniques appear both in early abolitionism and turn-of-the-twentieth-century consumer activism. This brief comparison also reveals some differences between the abolitionists and their successors, especially with respect to the role of Christianity in their advocacy. But more important, the comparison illustrates how the fetish of commodities can inform the practical development of the sympathetic consumer in similar ways: Interpretations *in* commodity-exchange shape the strategies and techniques through which activists may seek to spread the vision of the sympathetic consumer. For these consumer activists, commodity fetishism yielded a paradoxical result. The anonymity of goods led not to pacification and isolation but to social engagement. Ironically, this very engagement reproduced the depersonalized conditions of commodified labor that created the fetish in the first place, conditions that could encourage pacification and isolation.

Abolitionists' Ways of Seeing

Many in the abolitionist movement devoted imaginative and practical resources to making slave labor visible. Moreover, they asked consumers to imagine the plight of enslaved Africans behind otherwise depersonalized goods. As Fox noted, "A family that uses 5lb. of sugar *per week* . . . will, by abstaining from the consumption 21 months, prevent the slavery or murder of one fellow creature."[7] But abolitionists also devised ways to have consumers directly perceive the tools and products of the slave-grown goods as well as those goods produced by free labor. These ways of seeing point to the taken for granted interpretations of goods as anonymous *in* exchange.

Imaginative ways of seeing

William Fox's 1791 pamphlet occasioned several responses, each of which stressed the ways that British consumers were responsible for the horrors of slavery. One of them, *Considerations of the Slave Trade and the Consumption of West Indian Sugar* by Thomas Cooper, repeated and extended Fox's calculation about the murders that would be avoided if British consumers were to abstain from the consumption of sugar and rum: "A family that uses five pounds of sugar *per week* . . . will, by abstaining from the consumption 21 months, prevent the slavery or murder of one fellow creature." He continued, "[E]ight such families in nineteen years and a half, would prevent the slavery or murder of 100, and 38,0000 would totally prevent the slave trade, by removing the occasion to supply our islands."[8] Even over sixty years later, in the early 1850s, Elihu Burritt—an American diplomat and activist—published a pamphlet entitled "Twenty Reasons for Total Abstinence from Slave-Labour Produce." His first reason recapitulated Fox's legal metaphor for imagining consumer responsibility and seeing through anonymous goods, though Burritt opted for a lesser charge: "[A]ll the products of the labour of the slave are the fruits of an aggravated robbery perpetuated on him daily, and are therefore stained with all of the crime and guilt that can attach to stolen goods."[9] Abolitionists found many ways to draw the consumer's thoughts to the nature of the work that went into their produce.

The most obvious of these imaginative tactics involved gut-wrenching descriptions of slavery—from capture on the African continent, through the Atlantic middle passage, to life in the British colonies. Years before the anti-sugar campaign, abolitionist pamphlets described Africans

> being sold to the highest bidder, and branded with a hot iron . . . unpitied . . . and under the merciless control of unprincipled and unfeeling men, without proper food or clothing, or any encouragement to sweeten their toil; whilst every fault, real, or imaginary, is punished with a rigour which is but weakly restrained by the colony laws.[10]

Although these were general tactics for abolitionists, they put them to use consistently when advocating abstention from West Indian sugar. Abolitionist Andrew Burn commenced an essay on the evils of purchasing West Indian sugar by detailing the chain gangs into which enslaved Africans were organized. He included personal testimony:

> I have myself seen the poor offending Slave, flogged in such a horrid, cruel manner, as really baffles all descriptions, and immediately after the dreadful operation, fastened with both Legs in the Stocks, for days and nights together; while his raw back has been constantly washed with the strongest brine; putting him to the most excruciating torments.[11]

He then appealed to the special sympathies of British women:

> The tender Mother with her sucking Infant tied to her shoulder, is obliged to work
> equally hard, as if she carried no such burden. And when the hardened Wretch
> of a Driver cuts his dreadful whip across her back, of which he is not sparing, we
> cannot suppose him always so dexterous, as to avoid touching at times, the harm-
> less Innocent at the breast. Think on this, ye Mothers who use Sugar![12]

Thus, the consumer was encouraged to turn her thoughts of sugar toward the
ruthless treatment of enslaved Africans.

Into the nineteenth century, antislavery societies—especially those run by
women—used the imagination to personalize slave-produced commodities.
Literary scholar Charlotte Sussman has shown how abolitionists used poems
and literature to convey images of suffering workers and attach them to specific
commodities like rum and sugar—from the poetry of William Cowper to work
penned by members of local antislavery groups.[13] One such poem, printed in
William Lloyd Garrison's antislavery publication *The Abolitionist*, appeared
under the name "The Sugar-Plums":

> No, no pretty sugar-plums! Stay where you are!
> Though my grandmother sent you to me from so far;
> You look very nice, you would taste very sweet,
> And I love you right well, yet not one will I eat.
>
> For the poor slaves have labored, far down in the south,
> To make you so sweet, and so nice for my mouth;
> But I want no slaves toiling for me in the sun,
> Driven on with the whip, till the long day is done.
>
> Perhaps some poor slave-child that hoed up the ground,
> Round the cane in whose rich juice your sweetness was found,
> Was flogged till his mother cried sadly to see,
> And I'm sure I want nobody beaten for me.
>
> So grandma, I thank you for being so kind,
> But your present to-day is not much to my mind;
> Tho' I love you so dearly, I choose not to eat
> Ev'n what you have sent me, by slavery made sweet.
>
> Thus said little Fanny, and skipped off to play,
> Leaving all her nice sugar-plums just where they lay;

As merry as if they had gone in her mouth
And she had not cared for the slaves of the south.[14]

The poem joins the brutal portrait of slavery to the sugar plums, offered as a gift. Though some abolitionists like Garrison personally disdained consumer activism, these sentimental appeals worked their way into abolitionism on both sides of the Atlantic. People—and women in particular—were asked to imagine the violence inflicted upon slave laborers and to see themselves as responsible for this violence in their role as consumers. Many abolitionists made use of these images to encourage abstention from the purchase and use of the goods by enslaved Africans.

In the 1820s, British women's antislavery societies reported projects to circulate information about slavery and slave-grown goods:

> The mode pursued for awakening attention, circulating information, and introducing to the notice of the affluent and influential classes of the community a knowledge of the real state of suffering and humiliation under which British slaves groan, experience has proved to be one of the most eligible that could be devised, viz. the dissemination of current information through the medium of the societies workbags and albums, of the former of which about 2,000 have been disposed in England, Wales, and Ireland.[15]

Such societies enjoined members to "use . . . the produce of *free labour*, in preference to that of *slave labour*."[16] Thus, the spread of information included, among other things, emotional appeals that redounded to the purchase of free labor sugar. These appeals elicited sympathy with enslaved people, often by targeting women as the "softer sex."[17]

The most dramatic, and certainly the least common, of these rhetorical, imaginative efforts warned that slave-produced commodities were morally and physically polluted. In William Fox's wildly popular pamphlet on abstention from British imperial sugar, he adapted this passage from Benjamin Franklin's memoirs:

> An eminent French moralist says, that when he considers the wars we excite in Africa to obtain slaves, the numbers necessarily slain in those wars, the many prisoners who perish at sea by sickness, bad provisions, foul air, &c., &c. in the transportation and how many afterwards die from the hardships of slavery, he cannot look on a piece of sugar without conceiving it stained with spots of human blood! Had he added the consideration of the wars we make to take and

retake the sugar islands from one another . . . he might have seen his sugar not merely spotted, but thoroughly dyed scarlet in grain.[18]

Andrew Burn, most hysterical of all, cast sugar consumers as literal cannibals, as the bodily excretions and effluvia of maltreated African slaves suffused West India sugar:

> [M]y business . . . is, by plain manners of fact, of which I have frequently had ocular demonstration, to convince the inhabitants of Great Britain, who use Soft Sugar, either in Puddings, Pies, Tarts, Tea, or otherwise, that they literally, and most certainly in so doing, eat large quantities of that last mentioned Fluid [blood], as it flows copiously from the Body of the laborious Slave, toiling under the scorching rays of a vertical sun, mixed with many other savory ingredients . . .[19]

These dramatic accounts of polluted sugar worked their way into broader denunciations of slave-grown produce including cotton. A speech on slave-grown produce published in the year after Fox's pamphlet noted, "Here's the smell of blood on the hand still, and all the purfumes [sic] of Arabia cannot sweeten it."[20] Almost sixty years later, an 1848 pamphlet advocating abstention from slave-grown produce bore the title "There Is Death in the Pot!"[21] The biblical title suggested that slave labor poisoned these goods both spiritually and physically. In each of these, the consumer was implicated in a rotten system of slave labor and exploitation; as a result, the consumer upheld such exploitation.

When dealing with depersonalized goods and seeking to drum up support for a broader campaign to abstain from the purchase and use of sugar, abolitionists relied, in part, on these rhetorical tactics that depicted slave labor as well as consumers' relations to enslaved Africans. Such images aimed to prick the consciences of unthinking British consumers into participation in nonconsumption campaigns and abolition in general.

Ordinary, sensuous ways of seeing

But abolitionists didn't rely on imaginative and vivid rhetoric alone. They also relied on creative and documentary attempts to show people the conditions under which enslaved Africans lived and worked. They circulated paintings and images as a means of identifying with the abolitionist cause.[22] Perhaps the most famous of these was Josiah Wedgwood's antislavery medallion: "Am I Not a Man and a Brother?" Wedgwood manufactured these medallions in London, and they became readily identified with the abolitionist movement.[23] The medallion featured a stylized image of a supplicating African slave, chained arms clasped in front of him, with the phrase like a halo encircling his body. Other artists and campaigners produced pictures of slavery's cruelties as well as its systematic, exploitative character. These paintings were useful to abolitionist campaigns in the early nineteenth century.[24] One of the most powerful images of the slave trade's brutality came in the diagram of Africans stacked head to toe in the hold of the *Brookes* slave ship. On its own, the image testified to the dehumanization of the slave trade. But when joined with the campaign against sugar consumption, the ordinary British consumer would have had cause to see sugar and rum as bound up with a monstrous traffic in humans.

There were also efforts to brand sugar in ways that would allow consumers to distinguish slave-grown and free labor produce. In the 1820s, many abolitionists pushed free labor sugar manufactured in India and elsewhere. The Liverpool women's antislavery society announced the substitution of free labor produce as one of three major planks in their platform, alongside disseminating information about slavery in the British colonies and illustrating the ill effects on British imperial rule. One member wrote: "[W]e may hope that more than one-tenth of the population would be willing to make some small temporary sacrifice for the accomplishment of so great an object as that of the *Abolition of West Indian Slavery*. If only this proportion would give up the use of sugar grown by slaves, and substitute that which is the produce of free labour . . ."[25] Abolitionists could place their free labor sugar in East India sugar basins with "East India Sugar not made by slaves" in gold lettering.[26]

But to encourage the purchase of free labor sugar, abolitionists could go to free labor depots like those that cropped up in London in the 1830s and 40s. In these depots, one could find sugar and cotton sourced from India as well as American produce with a certificate from the Free-Labour Produce Association of Philadelphia.[27] One pamphlet, published in 1848, listed sugar, coffee, cocoa, rice, tobacco, and spices by region of origin, divided into three categories: "produce of free labour," "produce of slave labour," and "partly free, partly slave, or uncertain."[28] The consumer could observe, for instance, that slaves produced tobacco from Virginia, Kentucky, Maryland, and Cuba while free laborers produced tobacco in British India, British West India, Ohio, and Santo Domingo (now, the Dominican Republic).

Although they relied heavily on imagined and stylized images, the abolitionists sought to connect those images of enslaved labor to otherwise depersonalized goods. This work was required because consumers were easily able to ignore their implication in the system of slave production. "Reader! We solicit

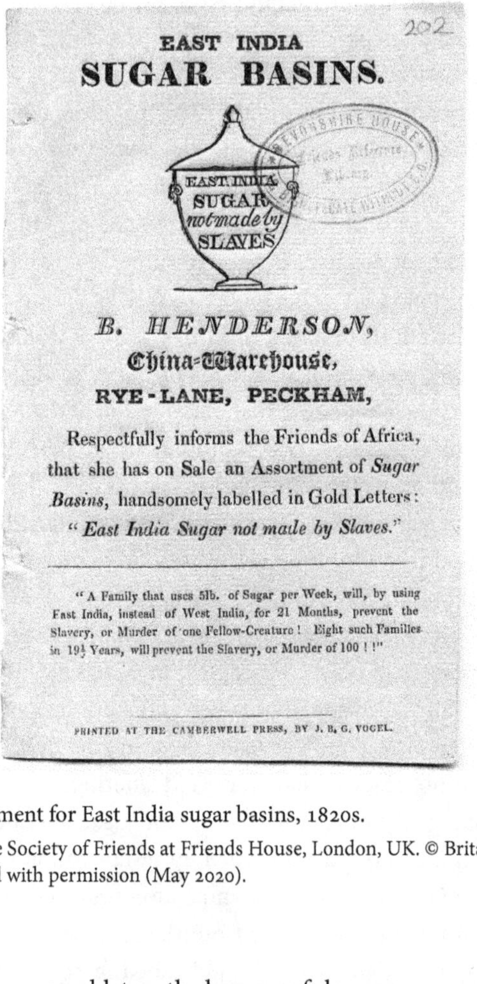

Figure 2 Advertisement for East India sugar basins, 1820s.
Source: Library of the Society of Friends at Friends House, London, UK. © Britain Yearly Meeting. Reproduced with permission (May 2020).

your attention," one pamphlet on the horrors of slave-grown sugar began, "[W] hile we bring under your notice a case of cruelty, in which, as a nation, we are deeply implicated; not *intentional* cruelty . . . it is true, but equally oppressive in its results, and evincing, to say the least, a remarkable want of consideration for the feelings of others."[29] The pamphlet went on to make the nature of this consumer cruelty explicit:

> [The lady] little thinks that to enable her to sweeten her daily meal, the African village may have been fired—the horrors of the middle-passage inflicted— human beings brought to the auction-block and sold into interminable slavery, the wife from husband, and the child from parent—the gang, male and female,

driven to the cane-field with a cart-whip—herded together at night like cattle—systematically kept in heathen darkness and degradation![30]

The pamphlet's author then paired these rhetorical images with goods, identified according to their place of origin and character of labor. All of this information ostensibly empowered consumers to choose goods with those images of slave and free labor in mind. When consumers saw the goods, they would be able to imagine the kind of work that made them possible. This pattern reappears when we look into early twentieth century consumer activism.

Early Twentieth Century Consumer Activists' Ways of Seeing

Like the abolitionists before them, the National Consumers' League, the Co-operative Wholesale Society, and the Women's Co-operative Guild engaged in similar projects to connect producers to depersonalized goods with imaginative ways of seeing. In an address to the National Consumers' League, social reformer Homer Folks noted,

> What we all need, as Consumers, is a little more information and imagination. If we could only look behind the price and appearance of products to the processes and conditions by which they are produced, we would be better consumers and better citizens. If, in some manner, the personality of the workers could be impressed upon the product, not merely their skill, and their industry, but their fatigue, their strain, their suffering, how our work would be simplified.[31]

In the *Manchester & Salford Equitable Society Monthly Herald*, the editors attributed exploitative labor to the workings of the market: "Sweating is, say *The Morning Post*, far less the result of any deliberate grinding of the faces of the poor than of ignorance and inadvertence, and the blind ruthlessness of economic laws."[32] Both writers grappled with the anonymity of goods in commodity-exchange. They expected, like Marx, that the commodity was, at first sight, a trivial or obvious thing. But unlike Marx, they hoped that ways of seeing might dispel this interpretation.

Imaginative ways of seeing

The imaginative techniques of the National Consumers' League, the Co-operative Wholesale Society, and the Women's Co-operative Guild took two distinct, but interrelated forms. First, activists used sensory metaphors to describe changes in consciousness. By awakening the consciousness of the consumer, he or she would be brought to moral action. Such metaphors are common and do not necessarily, in and of themselves, tell us anything about activists' interpretations *in* and *of* commodity-exchange. Second, like the abolitionists, activists used rhetoric to unveil the social conditions behind depersonalized goods and attach such images to commodities. This rhetoric attempts to challenge the interpretation of goods as anonymous *in* exchange. With this awakened imagination, the consumer could "perceive" the social relations of production in otherwise depersonalized goods. Because activists relied on these ways of seeing to connect producers and consumers via commodities, they refer to conditions specific to capitalist societies. In the work of these activists, then, even generic sensory metaphors for awakened consciousness often called on the consumer to imagine the conditions of production. Therefore, as we will see, both imaginative forms engaged with depersonalized goods.

These sensory metaphors for awakened consciousness appeared repeatedly in propaganda. Florence Kelley asked whether purchasers could be induced to give preference to justly made goods, by which league members meant goods made in clean environments by workers treated fairly. If such an awakening were possible, it required the dedicated work of league members: "In view of our investigation, the bargain counter is seen in a new light. . . . The point is henceforth to *know how the cheapness of our bargains is attained.*"[33] The task of the consumer activist was to attach sentiments such as pity to the knowledge of existing conditions. How could one induce such an attachment? The National Consumers' League sought to cultivate a spirit that "changes passive approval, appropriation, and sympathy into that dynamic conscience which constrains its owner to *look* into a subject and act upon the convictions gained in *looking.*"[34] Kelley captured the league's work to transform consumer consciousness with a visual metaphor. By looking into the origins of the commodities they bought, consumers would learn to purchase justly.

Co-operators followed a similar pattern. Percy Redfern of the Co-operative Wholesale Society used sensory terms to identify producing and consuming powers:

> The powers of producing and consuming are to the normal human being as left hands and right. Or, better, still, the hands are the producers, and the mouth that eats and the eyes that see the beauty of the world are consuming powers and those that feed the desires of the heart by which the hands are governed.[35]

Vision and taste, the consuming powers, nourished the heart and, by extension, *guided* the hands that produced. The guild's iconic image of the "woman with the basket" traded in similar visual metaphors. With a woven basket resting on her knee, gazing out over an urban, industrial landscape into a sunlit sky, this woman possessed the earthly power to shape and reshape not only what was produced, but the lives of those that produced it. Further, the image emphasizes her ability to see far beyond her immediate surroundings—an unsubtle metaphor for the consumer's profound effects on the world beyond.

Figure 3 "Woman with the Basket," an image published in the *Co-operative News*, 2 January 1909.

Source: National Co-operative Archive, Manchester, UK. Reproduced with the permission of the Co-operative Heritage Trust (May 2020).

Of course, at least since Plato's *Republic*, sensory metaphors for knowledge and consciousness have been common in Western culture. To illustrate a direct connection to commodity-exchange, then, these sensory metaphors must connect consumers to producers explicitly. In describing the work of the Consumers' League of New York City, the tireless Maud Nathan used sensory metaphors to render the "dark places" where "unseen and unheard" workers toiled in dismal conditions. Like Katy with her magic mirrors, Nathan reported, "[T]hose who go down into the depths, never return with the same light hearts."[36] Perceiving the cloistered processes of production became the source of conviction, a means of transfiguring passive sympathy into an active ethical practice. These ways of seeing promoted a change in consumer consciousness as they revealed the social relations of production behind commodities.

Members of co-operatives and the consumers' league made such connections explicit when they lamented consumers' failure to perceive as well—a failure that was tied to capitalist commodity-exchange. An editorial on "The Poor Consumer" in the *Co-operative News* bemoaned the noxious influence of advertising and asked, "Will the consumer also awaken from his long Rip van Winkle sleep and rub his eyes till the truth dawns upon him?"[37] In the National Consumers' League, Florence Kelley suggested that a failure to see undermined the power of the purchaser:

> The power of the purchaser, which is potentially unlimited, becomes great, in practice, just in proportion as purchasers become organized and enlightened, place themselves in direct communication with the producers, inform themselves exactly concerning the conditions of production and distribution, and are able thus to enforce their own will instead of submitting to the enticement and stimulus of the unscrupulous advertising seller.[38]

The separation of producers and consumers allowed consumers to be manipulated by unscrupulous merchants and advertisers. In an article from 1908, Kelley described the responsibilities of the consumer to the "unseen young servants" who both manufacture and deliver goods.[39] These visual metaphors were also tools for consumers to "perceive" the social organization of labor behind depersonalized goods. Furthermore, they steeled the consumer against the appeals of advertisers, who made it more difficult to overcome the banal mystifications of commodity-exchange.

Sometimes, however, these activists fretted over their dependence on imaginative ways of seeing. In justifying the NCL's exhibits (see next section), Florence Kelley voiced frustration with these ways of seeing:

> We are an eye-minded nation. We love shows and pictures of all kinds. We buy our food and clothes according to the shop window displays, or to pictures and legends painted on barns and hoardings, or printed on the covers of magazines ... the multitude of thoughtless spenders are guided by their eyes.[40]

But Kelley's lament did not precede a call for different techniques. Rather, she treated this sensory dependence as a fact: "The exhibit is prepared and kept in circulation in recognition of these facts."[41]

Co-operators expressed similar concerns. One co-operator explained that a longstanding suspicion of advertising "died hard," despite the ill effects on co-operative trade: "Paint, paste, and polish would not be necessary, and glare and glitter could very well be done without."[42] Many co-operators and guild members viewed advertising as manipulation, which clashed with the co-operative educational mission. The simultaneous embrace and wariness of visual techniques suggest anxiety over the interpretation *in* commodity-exchange of goods as anonymous. But despite their reservations, both co-operators and league members did their best to appeal to "eye-minded" nations.

While it would be a mistake to claim that all of activists' techniques addressed depersonalized goods directly, those imaginative attempts to illuminate obscure chains of working conditions *and* connect them to such goods clearly did so. Furthermore, we have seen that activists often combined these imaginative ways of seeing in practice. Rather than merely replicating a common Western intellectual idiom, these sense metaphors acquired a more precise meaning in activist propaganda and advocacy. When the NCL's Florence Kelley wrote of "convictions gained in looking," the metaphor resonated with the project to reinterpret anonymous commodities. In fact, Kelley used that phrase to respond to the question, "Could purchasers be induced to give the preference to goods made under the right conditions?"[43] To look into one's purchasing decisions, she implied, one must imagine the labor behind the commodity.

Such imaginative ways of seeing advanced the vision of the sympathetic consumer. But turn-of-the-twentieth-century activists took advantage of more than imagination. There were many new opportunities to actually show consumers the people and places behind their goods.

Ordinary, sensuous ways of seeing

Upon opening a copy of the *Annual Report of the National Consumers' League* 1900–1901, one finds an image of the league label. Underneath the label is the following explanation: "Goods bearing the above label are made in factories in which—The State factory law is obeyed; All the Goods are made on the premises; Overtime is not worked; Children under sixteen years of age are not employed."[44] The label announced to consumers that they were not spending their money on a business that employed sweatshop labor.

The NCL label illustrates one common way that turn-of-the-twentieth-century consumer activists combined imaginative and sensuous techniques to personalize anonymous goods. When a shopper saw the label, activists hoped they would imagine a clean, fair workplace—as well as the dirty, unfair ones to which they were compared. But here sight was not just a metaphor. The label appeared on or with particular products and, as such, began to make the associations for the consumer. These sensuous ways of seeing went beyond the label, too; activists often relied on the circulation of workplace photographs via "lantern lectures" (lectures accompanied by photographs projected as slides), pamphlets, and newspapers as well as public and private exhibitions of goods.

For the National Consumers' League, the label was a tool to remind consumers to engage in thoughtful shopping by keeping labor in mind. The league supplied approved factories with the label, which the manufacturers affixed to the goods—mostly clothing—in the factory. When the goods arrived at the shops, the label was already attached. Because the NCL did not operate its own stores, members thought it vital that the label remained attached to the goods. After all, the label brought the labor behind goods in view. If the label was stripped from the clothes, this undermined its entire purpose. Members of the Consumers' League of New York City raised the issue that some stores, concerned that there was insufficient demand for it, were removing the league label *prior* to putting the goods out for sale. But these same stores assured worried purchasers that the goods were league-approved. In response, a member wrote, "New York merchants frequently 'hide their light under a bushel' and though selling garments properly bearing our label frequently cut it off, or stow the clothes away in such quiet corners that customers are not aware of their presence."[45] Like a string tied around a finger, the label served to remind consumers where to direct their attention. It was meant to induce sympathetic consumption.

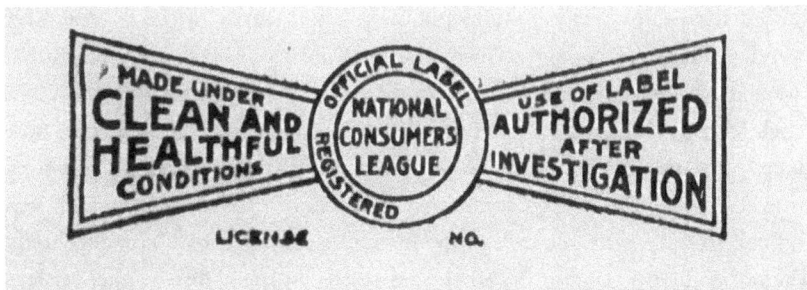

Figure 4 National Consumers' League label. Source: Library of Congress, Washington, DC. Reproduced with the permission of the National Consumers' League (June 2020).

Like the NCL members, co-operators used their brand to induce sympathetic consumption. In Great Britain, the Co-operative Whole Society also labeled goods. Staple goods bore "the Wheatsheaf" logo—a bit of heartland imagery that often included the phrase "Labor and Wait," which came from the Scottish theologian and novelist George MacDonald—a friend of John Ruskin. The CWS wanted the logo to stand for pure goods in the broadest sense.[46] Because the CWS operated stores and store owners could stock co-operative products directly from the wholesale society, co-operative shoppers could be relatively certain that co-operative goods would bear the label.[47] One who saw the CWS brand would be able to envision a clean, wholesome workplace where the employees were well treated and fairly compensated. As one co-operator observed, "[T]he stores can be made the medium for the sale of pure products, using the term in the widest sense."[48] This wide sense included the notion that co-operative goods would be "produced for sale under . . . equitable conditions."[49] As such, many co-operative advertisements announced that the products were made under "the best conditions of labor."[50] The superiority of co-operative working conditions was a matter of pride for members, which they touted in public exhibitions and ad campaigns. The Women's Co-operative Guild trumpeted the "superior" co-op conditions when supporting bills to regulate working hours and conditions for shop assistants in co-operative stores.[51] In co-operative publications, one can find in-depth descriptions of co-operative goods at various moments in the supply chain. A story about co-operative tea, for instance, began in the tea plantations and ended in the London factory where the tea was cured and packaged.[52] Such accounts included pictures of the workers and their environment. Both in practice and principle, the co-operative brand mattered.

But it was not always easy to maintain the integrity of the co-operative brand and label. In 1906, the Co-operative Wholesale Society discovered that sweated laborers in London were producing matchboxes bearing the CWS label. Disgruntled co-operators opined that the co-operatives claimed to produce "pure" goods, even if they were unable to "scent" out traces of sweating in every case.[53] The editors contrasted the "scent of the sweater," which was difficult to trace, with the case of the matchboxes, which had "come to light." The possibility of keeping the label pure rested on the ability to uncover and see sweatshop conditions in an imaginative sense. Provided that co-operators could preserve the integrity of the brand, actually seeing a co-operative label would allow consumers to imagine co-operative goods in relation to fair working conditions. As with the abolitionists before them, the label was a tool for associating the commodity with images of the labor process—imaginative or sensuous. But labels did not supply their own images; rather they relied on others. As such, the label encompassed both imaginative and sensuous techniques.

There were more straightforward ways of seeing, of course. The National Consumers' League, the Co-operative Wholesale Society, and the Women's Co-operative Guild took advantage of developments in photographic technology to document and expose the labor behind goods. With the emergence of mass-produced film materials, decreased exposure time, hand-held cameras, and social documentary photography, photographs of workplaces and workers were more readily available. In the United States, the NCL circulated photographs of working conditions extensively. Between 1905 and 1914, the NCL annual reports included photographs of tenement working conditions that identified the goods produced there, from cigars and artificial flowers to clothing and bread.[54] The annual report for 1905–06 displayed photographs of flower makers; workers finishing garments in their homes in a New York City tenement; workers in a garment sweatshop; pasta drying in a tenement hallway; a cake and cruller bakeshop in a tenement; a candy factory with an adjoining bedroom; an overcrowded tenement house; a shack to house berry pickers during the picking season; and cranberry pickers. Some NCL pamphlets consisted almost exclusively of photographs of workers and their working conditions.[55] In contrast with the NCL members, British co-operators often used photographs to document virtuous co-operative events rather than to illuminate the obscure conditions of production.[56] But co-operatives did circulate images of co-operative productions in movement periodicals such as *The Wheatsheaf*. These photographs and accompanying stories were reprinted in local co-operative publications. From bacon and cake flour to biscuits and tea, co-operators presented virtuous working conditions in co-operative productions.[57] In general, these tactics allowed consumers to see photo-realistic images of workplaces—often in the context of specific commodities.

Another common tactic, one that incorporated photography as well as other ways of seeing, was the exhibition. By the turn of the twentieth century, the exhibition was well established as an opportunity to display the prowess and progress of the Western world, while also to display the curiosities and eccentricities of the rest.[58] At world exhibitions, people could take in scale models of street scenes, new technologies and inventions, and accoutrements of life, both "modern" and "premodern." Consumer activists made use of these major exhibitions and also staged their own local exhibits. In the former, they displayed sweated and non-sweated goods, as well as workplaces. In the latter, attendees were able to see, touch, and sometimes taste goods, while learning about their origins.

Exhibitions were a regular feature of co-operative life.[59] A member of the Oldham co-operative society described an 1894 exhibition as "an object lesson in co-operation."[60] This meant that co-operative exhibitions celebrated the ability of the working classes to produce high-quality, non-sweated goods that reflected principles of democratic, mutual uplift. The CWS referred to exhibitions as "avenues through which the members of society may be familiarised with Co-operative productions, so that they may become purchasers of these goods rather than those of private manufacturers."[61] Attendees could take these goods in, appreciate their working-class origins, and be encouraged to buy them. It is important to appreciate that co-operative store managers were not required to stock co-operative-made goods in their stores. Thus, exhibitions were designed to make co-operative goods attractive both to store managers and ordinary co-operative members. At a co-operative demonstration in Bolton, one attendee noted the "fragrant whiffs" of co-operative tobacco, as well as pickles, gums, sauces, clothing, and boots.[62] When taken together with the emphasis on the virtues of co-operative working conditions and working-class roots, these exhibitions provided an opportunity for British consumers to develop a taste for wholesome commodities.

Members of the Women's Co-operative Guild developed similar exhibitions of co-operative products for use at conferences throughout England: "Our idea is that the guild shall possess a box of goods which shall be sent round to the various towns where the conferences are held."[63] It was also common for local guild conferences to provide samples of co-operative goods, while also offering lectures on the virtues of co-operation or pressing social issues. Sometimes these events involved lantern lectures on co-operative principles.[64] While the slides were not preserved in co-operative records, it is clear that guild members used them to encourage sympathetic consumption. Several reports of women's guild events identify lantern lectures on "Cocoa," "Soap," "Flour," and a range of other goods.[65] These events paired photographic images and accounts of working conditions with demonstrations of co-operative goods; there the consumers could perceive the producer and commodity together.

The National Consumers' League engaged in similar exhibitions of goods, justly and unjustly made. Exhibitions of labeled garments were so common that one member wrote, "[C]hronicling them would be a hopeless undertaking."[66] These events displayed goods bearing the NCL label alongside photographs of the factories from which these goods originated.[67] For major expositions such as the 1915 Panama–Pacific in San Francisco, the league used large screens or slides that depicted "unfavorable industrial conditions" and the NCL's work to remedy those issues, including samples of goods made in tenements.[68]

In the years from 1914 to 1917, this major exhibit visited twenty-eight states. Smaller exhibits were available by request for smaller local groups. These comprised photographic replicas of the large screens, samples of tenement-made goods, and slides of ideal working conditions.[69] In at least one instance, a Massachusetts garment factory hosted a lecture, an exhibition of labeled goods, and a tour of the premises.[70] The league also constructed exhibitions for other groups that addressed themes such as industrial conditions, urban congestion, public health, and more. Florence Kelley described the league's contributions as "bringing out in every way the relation of the consumer to the conditions under which work is done."[71] Designed to "attract the attention of the passer-by," these exhibitions relied on photorealistic images of production to elicit consumers' sympathies.[72] In addition, league members could also host private exhibitions in their homes, where members encouraged the purchase of ethically made goods.[73]

By placing sample goods alongside images of their origins, activists joined sensuous ways of seeing to imaginative ones. As one co-operator wrote, "[T]o me distributive co-operation is chiefly valuable because it provides a ready means of enabling workmen to translate their professions into deeds—in plain words, to give them the opportunity of purchasing for their daily use goods

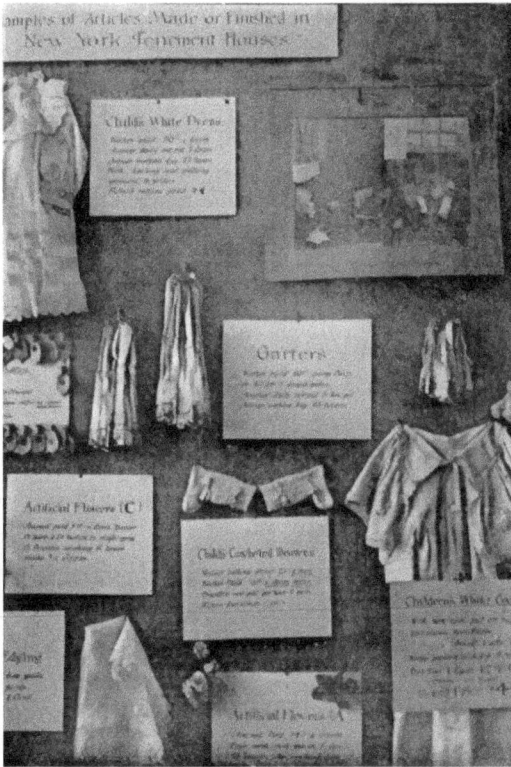

Figure 5 An image from an exhibition. Printed in the pamphlet, "Children Who Work in the Tenements: Little Laborers Unprotected by Child Labor Law," Consumers' League of the City of New York, March 1908.

Source: Kheel Center for Labor-Management Documentation and Archives, Cornell University Library. Reproduced with the permission of the National Consumers' League (June 2020).

produced under the same equitable conditions they seek for themselves."[74] These ways of seeing followed, directly, from depersonalized goods in exchange and their associated anonymity *in* commodity-exchange. At the founding of the National Consumers' League in 1898, Maud Nathan wrote of precisely this:

> The mysterious power that expands and contracts our sleeves that arrays us one year in shining mohair and another in clinging cashmere, sets in motion hundreds of looms and changes the labor of thousands of men and women . . . our ignorance and fears justify us no longer in remaining indifferent. Whether we will or not we are parts of a social system and are bringing to bear upon it our individual touch for good or evil.[75]

Nathan captures the encounter with depersonalized goods, the effort to shed light on their origins, and the ethical imperative that such exposure sets in motion. As with consumer co-operation, the NCL worked to rationalize this mysterious power that courses through capitalist channels of production, distribution, and exchange.

These ways of seeing—both ordinary and imaginative—were not the only techniques employed to advance their vision. The National Consumers' League and the Women's Co-operative Guild worked fervently to pass legislation that would regulate wages, hours, overtime, working age, and other concerns. The Co-operative Wholesale Society and the Women's Co-operative Guild sought to make consumer co-operatives a social and cultural hub, one that would uplift the working classes. Many NCL and women's guild members participated in efforts to secure women the vote and in the settlement house movement. Members also engaged in straightforward labor organizing, though only the guild did so as an organization. These groups were not, in other words, monomaniacally committed to these ways of seeing and consumer activism alone. But such ways of seeing tell us something important about their appeals to sympathetic consumers. They tell us that these appeals, as with the abolitionists' pleas before them, rested on their efforts to dispel the anonymity of goods in commodity-exchange.

Thinking with Differences

In practice, activists' visions of the sympathetic consumer—interpretations *of* commodity-exchange—depended on anonymous goods—an interpretation *in* commodity-exchange. Imaginative and sensuous ways of seeing—the prose, pictures, photographs, labels, exhibits, and more—were tactics designed to promote a vision of sympathetic consumption. There is, here, a close connection between these two aspects of commodity fetishism. But these basic commonalities also index some noteworthy differences between abolitionists and turn-of-the-twentieth-century activists. Abolitionists appealed to people in the context of a broader movement against slavery, and often as good Christians—not just or primarily as consumers. By contrast, turn-of-the-twentieth-century activists insisted on a more comprehensive role for consumers to root out sweatshop labor. Even as their work was informed by religious organizations and sentiment, they mobilized people as consumers. In addition, abolitionists relied on a more limited set of tactics associated with ordinary ways of seeing. They lacked the ready access to photorealistic images of labor conditions that later activists used in exhibitions and propaganda. Together, these changes also manifest in distinct ways of talking about contamination and purity.

Eighteenth and early nineteenth century abolitionists encouraged tactical ways of seeing with the tools available to them. With the exception of the artistic images of slavery and enslaved Africans, abolitionist ways of seeing remained largely imaginative—that is, they relied on the ability to conjure images of slavery in the heads of consumers with stomach-churning rhetoric.[76] At the same time, there was a robust discourse attesting to the horrific facts of slavery. Abolitionists drew on reports from sailors, slavers, agents of the British empire, and dedicated advocates like Anthony Benezet. But they had more limited means of bringing these images of brutality into view, literally, than turn-of-the-twentieth-century activists. As such, they relied more exclusively on artistic renderings—paintings, literature, poetry—as well as evocative, mind-searing prose.

In the middle of the nineteenth century, free produce supporters in Great Britain and the United States continued in the manner of earlier abolitionists.[77] Some identified American slavery as a way to supply consumers with commodities—an explicit description of the consumer in a system of production, distribution, and exchange.[78] Free produce advocates, many of them Quakers, opened stores dedicated to the sale of non–slave-made goods. One supporter wrote of stores that sold goods from the southern states: "Go to yonder store, and the products of oppression will stare you in the face. Look! And you will see the pro-slavery pictures there exhibited."[79] While these stores were not filled with "pro-slavery pictures" in a literal sense, these free produce advocates sought to brand slave-made products by using imaginative ways of seeing. In 1851, abolitionist Henry Highland Garnet stated, "The sugar with which we sweetened our tea, and the rice which we ate, were actually spread with the sweat of slaves, sprinkled with their tears, and fanned by their sighs."[80] These familiar visions and practices were designed to encourage both ethical purchasing and broader participation in the antislavery movement. Also, like earlier abolitionists, free produce supporters saw themselves not as consumer activists, but as abolitionists.[81] Lawrence Glickman notes that free produce advocates, Sabbatarians, and southern advocates of nonintercourse with northern states "neither defined themselves as consumer activists, nor understood themselves to be fighting on behalf of consumers."[82] They saw themselves as antislavery advocates (or pro-Confederate, in the case of southerners who avoided the purchase of northern goods). Nevertheless, as consumers, their vision and practices bear a striking resemblance to those of later activists.

There are other differences between abolitionists of all stripes and later consumer activists that bear mentioning. For one, abolitionists insisted on purity and contamination of the soul, above all else. The abolitionist William Fox warned, "[I]f we purchase the commodity, we participate in the crime."[83] Although framed in legal terms, the guilt was existential and spiritual—not legal. Only the paranoid fears of abolitionist Andrew Burn—who insisted that all consumers of West India sugar and rum ingested the blood, pus, diseases, and insects associated with sugar production—anticipated later concerns about physical contamination. And even Burn's pornographic descriptions reveled in an acute, racialized moral disgust seemingly motivated by enslaved Africans themselves more than sickness or ill-health.[84]

Consider, by contrast, the NCL's concerns about the damp, dark, disease-ridden tenement. Or Katy of the Women's Co-operative Guild, who worried about the dark "unwholesome rooms" where Jewish children and women worked.[85] In this later activism, the worries over spiritual and existential pollution did not disappear—one can still hear overtones of racism and xenophobia in these fears of uncleanliness; but such concerns were sublimated into worries about bad air and lack of sunshine and debilitating chronic conditions and infectious diseases. For another, abolitionist groups focused exclusively on physically remote enslaved Africans, while much of the later activism emphasized mainly invisible domestic workers. While this shift may appear surprising, especially in light of the nineteenth century industrial and technological developments that rendered the world functionally smaller, it is explicable in terms of global geopolitics. After all, the rise of an international system of nation-states could quite plausibly induce a temporary contraction in horizons—a situation where the nation-state came to define the spheres where activists felt they could be effective. It is telling, after all, that cooperators—still living in the heart of the world's greatest colonial empire—were more likely to respond to labor issues outside of the United Kingdom than the National Consumers' League, which was based in the United States.

But for all of these differences, even here, we should not lose sight of their overlapping concerns with matters of purity, invisible labor, and the consumer. Though the substance may have varied, the form of the sympathetic consumer remained. In these ways of seeing, an interpretation *in* commodity-exchange—anonymous goods—informs the interpretations *of* commodity-exchange—the idea that personalizing the origins of these goods would induce sympathetic consumption. The character of capitalist commodity-exchange, in other words, shaped the practices and ideas associated with the sympathetic consumer.

From What to Why

Ultimately, these discussions suggest a basic proposition: To avoid errantly attributing visions or practices to commodity fetishism, one must demonstrate that these visions or practices depend on specific interpretations *in* and *of* commodity-exchange. In these last three chapters, I have shown precisely that. The vision of the sympathetic consumer involves a specific interpretation *of* commodity-exchange, one that simultaneously takes commodity-exchange for granted and calls it into question. At the same time, the encounter with anonymous goods, an interpretation *in* commodity-exchange, conditions the interpretation *of* commodity-exchange—these ways of seeing so crucial to the activism on behalf of the sympathetic consumer. The vision of the sympathetic consumer, therefore, appears as a condition of these ways of seeing; but this vision and the practices essential to the sympathetic consumer are also conditioned by commodity-exchange.

This proposition has other implications. With respect to ways of seeing, it reveals how the character of the problem can inform activist tactics and strategies when seeking to remedy it. To mobilize around the problems hidden by depersonalized goods, abolitionists and turn-of-the-twentieth-century activists employed various ways of seeing. In this way, the interpretive frameworks that they used to build sympathetic consumption—what social movement scholars call "frames"—were structured around problems associated with depersonalized goods. While social scientists have long recognized the relevance of framing to social movements, they have treated social problems as things that are framed above all else. But if we look at abolitionists and turn-of-the-twentieth-century activists, there are good reasons to understand their parallel tactics as built around problems associated with commodity-exchange in a capitalist society. As such, we ignore the converse relationship—how the experience of social problems informs framing—at our peril.[86]

As ways of seeing evolve through interpretations *in* commodity-exchange, the work of these consumer activists exposes a paradox. The anonymity of commodities has invited political engagement, not just disengagement. These activists did not simply ask consumers to buy the right goods and then leave them to their own devices as individuals; they campaigned to address workplace conditions and provided ways for people to engage in activism. To bring their vision of the sympathetic consumer into being, activists showed people the origins of their goods. In doing so, activists focused on the nature of the goods themselves—the circumstances and consequences of their production. Their activism was, in this way, provoked and shaped by the depersonalized goods in exchange. To William Fox and Katy and Florence Kelley and many others, commodities were a riddle that begged for a solution. Thus, early efforts to promote the sympathetic consumer illustrate that commodity fetishism does not inexorably lead to political pacification, individualism, and total quiescence—though it certainly can.

Ironically, however, this engagement reproduces the fetishism that activists sought to penetrate. Contra the intuition that such campaigns dispel the fetish by revealing the labor behind the goods, the work of these consumer activists would be more accurately described as uniquely fetishistic. By connecting consumers to producers by means of the commodity, activists channeled capitalist relations of labor and exchange. Their interpretations assumed depersonalized labor in commodity-exchange as a measure of worth. In the marketplace, sugar made in the East Indies or a bathing suit with the National Consumers' League label confronted the private laborer as anonymously as West India sugar or a sweatshop-made bathing suit. At the point of purchase, the sympathetic consumer, for his or her part, replicated an interpretation *in* exchange—even as activists attempted to reinterpret the meaning *of* exchange as including the "pale women and girls" or "oppressed Africans" tasked with making those goods. Marx considered this very situation—where people relate to other people through commodities—to be implicit to all purchases occurring under capitalist conditions. Thus, activists' reliance on ways of seeing may help explain, more precisely, the limits of consumer activism.[87] Typically, critics point out that ethical purchasing reinforces the expansion of the capitalist market—the very condition that underlies commodity fetishism. But in addition, although activists unveiled some of the labor behind the goods, this very act depends on a taken-for-granted interpretation *in* commodity-exchange—the anonymity that accompanies depersonalized goods and labor in a capitalist social order. This, then, is the paradox: The vision of the sympathetic consumer appears simultaneously as a condition of these ways of seeing and as a consequence of the depersonalized and anonymous goods that call for ways of seeing.

*   *   *

When the Consumers' League of New York City discovered that some retail outlets were selling league-approved garments without a label, Louise

Lockwood Thurber, the chairwoman of the Committee on Label, had some advice: Consumers should pressure those retailers to include the labels and stock labeled goods. She wrote:

> [W]e hope the pressure will result in the [shop] window's being dedicated to a fine assortment of white goods and children's clothes bearing our label; that the general public may thereby have an object lesson of the quantity and quality of clothes that are made in healthful, happy, properly fire-protected and properly paid factories![88]

Thurber's description recalls several features of the sympathetic consumer.

We find the vision of a consumer, the source of desire, as the sympathetic figure at the heart of a wide-ranging system of production, distribution, and exchange. Her description of the laborers performed a doubly sympathetic maneuver. The labeled goods hail from healthful, happy, and safe places of work. The workers, one might assume, must also be healthy, happy, and safe. One could surely imagine a worker happy with her job, one who feels a sense of security owing to a regular paycheck in a safe workplace. But in 1915, just four years after the devastating fire at the Triangle Shirtwaist Factory in Greenwich Village, the phrase "fire-protected" would have evoked the suffering and death of 146 garment workers—mainly women and young girls—as well as dozens more injured. The consumer stood to make these sympathies felt by demanding goods from the happy, healthy, safe, and properly compensated worker.

We also find certain practices, ways of seeing, to promote the sympathetic consumer. Imagine a shop window with an attractive array of clothes, all bearing the league label. As shoppers pass, their eyes are drawn to the neatly folded clothes and smartly dressed mannequins. These are, Thurber knew, an "object lesson"—not only of the quality and quantity of goods, but of the principles behind the label: that the goods should be made under healthy, safe, and happy conditions. This array of label-bearing goods in a large-paned shop window is a sensuous way of seeing, indeed! It is a way of seeing that, at the same time, calls upon the consumer to imagine those pleasurable and painful feelings of the workers who make, deliver, and sell the goods bearing the label as well as those without it.

But there is a third feature of the sympathetic consumer, one that I have, thus far, taken for granted: an account of why one should be a sympathetic consumer in the first place. Thurber also implies such an account. After all, she called on league members to make their desire for the label known. This assumes that these desires would resonate through the shop and goods in question to the workers involved all along the supply chain. They would not only increase happiness and diminish unhappiness in the world, but they would give others permission to see and do the right thing. The power of organized consumer demand as well as the imaginative reveries of the shop window testified to this moral rightness and efficacy. However, like the commodity in exchange, these moral accounts or justifications may seem obvious and trivial, but when we look into them, they reveal some mysteries and surprises, too. This is the next stop on our journey to track the sympathetic consumer.

5

Moral Arguments

WHEN, IN 1792, the abolitionists made their case against the slave trade in the English House of Commons, William Crafton presented the evidence of its horrors along with a declaration: "Should the Legislature of this country contrive to withhold its protection from that part of its West-Indian subjects, distinguished by a different colour of the skin, or find itself unequal to secure them from oppression, still it will be in the power of the PEOPLE here to afford that redress to their sufferings, which has been solicited from the guardians of our liberties."[1] But what power could the people exercise over and against a recalcitrant legislature? After quoting liberally from William Fox's address, Crafton stated, "The Legislature being unwilling or perhaps unable to grant redress, it is peculiarly incumbent upon us . . . to abstain from the use of sugar and rum, until our West-Indian planters themselves have prohibited the importation of additional slaves."[2] Over one hundred years later, the National Consumers' League described employers as "virtually helpless" against market forces that would drive down working standards and conditions; the public, as consumers, assumed the power to elevate standards and protect workers.[3] Faced with recalcitrant forces, activists turned to a higher power: the consuming public.

By focusing on consumers, the abolitionists, co-operators, and consumers' leagues set themselves a monumentally difficult task: convince the purchasing public to transform their habits and ethics of buying in the name of a humanitarian cause; in so doing, they would transform the world. But how could they justify this project and the vision of the sympathetic consumer? After all, these were unabashedly moral projects that hitched large-scale social reforms and transformations to people's roles as consumers. Historians have dated the novel emergence of collective action based on consumer identity to the late eighteenth century, from the refusal to consume British tea in colonial America to the abolitionist rejection of slave-grown sugar. The abolitionist movement, as many have noted, was also a watershed in the history of global humanitarianism—it was a popular social movement on behalf of distant strangers. Not only was the task itself immense, but given its novelty, others were likely to notice and question the approach.

In this chapter, I look into the ways that activists justified the sympathetic consumer as a moral project. It focuses on two deeply related aspects of these justifications: First, activists explicated the role of the consumer in capitalist circuits of production, circulation, and exchange, and second, they grounded these justifications in both deontological and consequentialist ethics. Gabriel Abend has shown that moral arguments—including public moral arguments—depend on a "moral background," that is, assumptions about the nature of morality.[4] These assumptions, he argues, can condition moral arguments and actions. By examining the moral arguments in favor of the sympathetic consumer, I disclose how activists' "moral background" depends, in specific ways, on commodity fetishism and related capitalist phenomena. At the same time, their reflections on commodity-exchange bring a distinctive set of moral concerns into focus. Scrutiny of these moral arguments allows us to appreciate the role that religion—especially Christianity—played in emergent consumer activism. This approach brings a fresh perspective to longstanding debates about the role of capitalism in the development of humanitarian concern for distant, suffering strangers.

What Is a Moral Background?

Five years after the formation of the National Consumers' League, it had managed to run afoul of local labor leaders. A representative of a group advocating union labels, Mary Kenney O'Sullivan, asked whether the NCL's activities were "standing in the way of the Unions for needle trades, or [were] simply accomplishing in a more indirect way a work which [the unions] are unable to do because of the unstable nature of their constituency."[5] Several years later, in 1908, the Massachusetts branch received a letter from a petticoat manufacturer, "protesting against our becoming identified with trades unions."[6] Faced with such challenges, league members often felt compelled to explain why they organized around the consumer. After all, a consumer could also be a laborer or a citizen or a merchant and so on. In many instances, league members as well as abolitionists and co-operators anticipated resistance and folded such arguments into their propaganda. But what do these arguments and justifications reveal? How can we interpret them? Gabriel Abend's notion of the moral background provides some guidance.

The moral background describes the collection of assumptions that are necessary to make moral judgments and act morally. In other words, these are cultural conditions that must obtain in order for one's actions to be moral and to render moral judgments of actions. To illustrate, activists' visions and practices indicate that they understood the consumer to be a relevant moral actor in the first place. They reveal a sense that the consumer had the power to affect the character of production. These visions and practices can disclose, further, a method or methods for determining and explaining the consumer's special moral role. Abend characterizes these assumed cultural conditions as "second-order understanding[s] about the nature of morality"—interpretive tools that people use, often implicitly, to act and think morally.[7] These tools can include (a) the grounds or reasons for moral judgments and actions, (b) the concepts used in moral judgments and actions, (c) the objects judged or acted toward, (d) the allowable methods of argumentation that undergird moral judgments and actions, (e) the degree of objectivity accorded to moral reasoning, and (f) the metaphysical assumptions that attend moral thought and activity.[8] I will be especially concerned with (a) moral grounds (why be a sympathetic consumer), (c) the objects judged or acted toward (the consumer as a relevant moral actor), and (d) methods of argumentation (specifically, the chains of reasoning that characterized these arguments about the sympathetic consumer). From these arguments, then, we can glean insights into some assumptions that undergird sympathetic consumption as a moral project.

In his history of American business ethics, Abend uses the moral background to reveal points of difference where others might find only "monotonous and predictable" condemnations of greed and the feckless pursuit of profit.[9] He unearths two distinct paths to these condemnations of greed: standards of practice and Christian merchant.[10] Those following the standards of practice model take a scientific and pragmatic path, while those following the Christian merchant model take a theological and universalist one. According to the standards of practice model, one denounces greed because it harms the businessperson, business in general, and society. This is broadly consequentialist reasoning; that is, it focuses on whether an action promotes the greater good. Greed isn't bad because the associated actions are intrinsically immoral, but because greedy actions create more pain than pleasure in the end. By contrast, according to the Christian merchant model, one denounces greed because greedy actions are themselves immoral. This is broadly deontological reasoning; that is, it focuses on whether the action, in itself, is right or wrong. Greed isn't bad because it creates more pain than pleasure, but because the associated actions violate the golden rule. Thus, the moral background reveals a dynamic world of ethical assumptions and models beneath a placid surface of moral agreement.

There is, perhaps, a monotonous predictability in consumer activists' accounts of morality and economic life. But when considered in relation to commodity fetishism and the conditions of a capitalist social order, this predictability may reveal the workings of a capitalist culture with greater precision. We will see how the capitalist tendencies and phenomena toward which we direct our moral judgments and through which we carry out moral projects can affect moral background assumptions. This reveals how social conditions and phenomena invite activists to understand consumers as crucial moral agents.[11] When the NCL members were called to justify themselves before unions or business owners or the consuming public, how did they respond? What modes of reasoning did they employ? What justifications did they offer? I demonstrate that the coherence of their reasoning depended, in a nontrivial sense, on commodity fetishism and the capitalist conditions that made it possible. In short, how abolitionists, co-operators, and consumers' league members justify the sympathetic consumer can highlight the manner in which social phenomena and conditions inform moral presuppositions.

Abolitionists Justify the Sympathetic Consumer

The moral imagination of the abolitionists was profoundly systemic. By this I mean that abolitionists reasoned on the basis of the consumer's position in imperial capitalist circuits of commerce—from production and distribution to exchange and consumption. They argued for the sympathetic consumer by tracing the depersonalized links in the supply chain that joined producers to consumers—a mode of reasoning that I will call capitalist. But, of course, identifying the consumer as a relevant moral object and building an argument that mirrored capitalist supply chains did not yet explain *why* one should be a sympathetic consumer. For this, abolitionists leaned especially on deontological ethics. At the same time, they were happy to rely on consequentialist ethics, too, if it gave someone a reason to be a sympathetic consumer.

The corrupt system of imperial commerce

After William Fox denounced consumers of British rum and sugar as co-conspirators in the violence and brutality visited upon enslaved Africans, the floodgates opened. Abolitionists made the British consumer's structural role in the slave trade and slavery explicit. But even in the years leading up to this explicit turn to consumer activism, the abolitionists used systemic images of imperial slave trade to vindicate moral denunciations. They were especially keen to denounce those who were "interested in" or profited from imperial commerce, including British people in the colonial metropole. In the main, these moral denunciations reflected a broadly Christian sensibility. But the moral critique also unfolded through systemic exposés of imperial commerce that presented the links between enslaved producers and British consumers.

What aspects of this system did these abolitionists find relevant? A 1784 pamphlet, *Thoughts on the Slavery of the Negroes*, gives a sense. The work, published anonymously by Quaker Joseph Woods, began by appealing to the reader's sympathy:

> [T]he sick, the lame, the blind, the insane, those whom disease or accident, united with poverty, have rendered helpless, become the objects of compassion and assistance to their more fortunate neighbours. But as it is an observable characteristic of the human mind, to be more affected by objects which are near, than by those which are remote, their vicinity is an important circumstance in the incitement and application of this benevolence.[12]

Woods then distinguished suffering that produces only "temporary sympathy" and "[is] beyond the reach of our succour" from one particular kind of suffering in which Britons were "interested":

> [M]ultitudes of unhappy and unoffending creatures are exposed to sufferings that humanity shudders at, and in which relief is withheld though within our power, because the scene of oppression is distant and the hearts of those who are immediately engaged in it, are hardened by the powerful influence of avarice

and habit, and because these very sufferings are the source of public revenue and private wealth. The subject alluded to, is the System adopted for employing the negroes in West-Indian Islands and the ignominious traffic called the Slave Trade.[13]

In virtue of their standing within a system of transatlantic commerce and slavery, Britons benefited from slavery, *and* they sloughed off their moral responsibility owing to the obscured, distant scenes of oppression.

Woods alluded, later, to the benefits that may have accrued to British consumers. At one point, he took commercial arguments for and against this slavery and the slave trade on their own terms. This required him to hold claims of religion and morality in abeyance. Having considered the claim that the climate for sugar cane required "involuntary servitude" to work the plantations, Woods concluded:

> The objection, from motives of commercial policy, amounts to this, that the claims of religion and morality ought to be subservient to those of avarice and luxury, and that it is better that thousands of poor unoffending people should be degraded and destroyed in the most abject slavery, than that the inhabitants of Europe should pay a higher price for their rum, rice, and sugar.[14]

By acknowledging the prospect that the renunciation of slavery could increase the cost of consumer goods, Woods revealed how the moral critique engaged slavery as a matter of British imperial commerce. In effect, he admitted that morality could cost, literally. Although it may have made the argument more difficult, Woods engaged on the terms of merchant capitalism.[15] This was not a simple, abstracted moral calculus.

This kind of systemic imagination was commonplace in the moral arguments against slavery and the slave trade. Seven years prior to the beginning of the anti-sugar campaign, abolitionists published, *The Case of Our Fellow-Creatures, the Oppressed Africans*, a pamphlet written by William Dillwyn and John Lloyd. After insisting that the "species of oppression" in which the British empire trafficked was "not equaled, even in the most barbarous of ages," they quoted an "eyewitness account" that asked readers to, quoting the Book of Job, "put our soul in their souls stead."[16] Dillwyn and Lloyd described enslaved Africans, trapped in the tyrannical system of slave-driven commerce: "When a trade is carried on, productive of much misery, and they who suffer by it are some thousand miles off, the danger is the greater of not laying their sufferings to heart."[17] While this language hinted at the complicity of metropolitan Britons, others were much more direct. An imperial bureaucrat denounced the slave trade as "that corrupted system of commerce, which pervades every civilized nation at this day."[18] Such barbarous trade perverts the noble end of commerce, "an institution which promoted the free circulation of commodities, the increase of knowledge, and the wealth and prosperity of nations."[19] To many abolitionists, the tyrannical institution of slavery contributed to a system of commerce that was, by its nature, obscure to those in the colonial metropole.

This system of commerce persisted, they argued, through its opacity as well as the spoils claimed by various participants. Abolitionists described these participants as "interested," that is, invested in the perpetuation of slavery and the slave trade. The most obvious interested parties were the slave-traders and slave-holders themselves. In *The Case Against Our Fellow-Creatures,* they asked the reader to put themselves in the enslaved person's stead: "Did we, in such case, behold an increase of luxury and superfluity among our oppressors, and therewith feel an increase of the weight of our burdens and expect our posterity to groan under oppression after us?"[20] Those trading and holding slaves were enriched at the expense of the enslaved, and, in that sense, they were interested. More broadly, Swedish abolitionist Carl Bernhard Wadström asked,

> Are not the governments of the two most flourishing nations, England and France, who give laws to the rest of Europe, influenced by powerful possessors of the ancient colonies and opulent merchants of their productions? It is impossible that information of so delicate a nature should be obtained pure and unadulterated through the medium of surly, sordid planters and sugar factors who are acting only from a vile self-interest.[21]

Broader still, Reverend James Ramsay asserted,

> I am seriously of the opinion that the sugar trade, with which that for slaves is connected at present, is of the utmost importance to the state; and that any sudden shock, that affects it, will be widely and deeply felt: and it must be confessed, that several of the sugar colonies shewed, in the beginning of the late disputes, strong signs of an unaccountable bias to the ideal empire of America.[22]

This dependence on slave sugar extended to the British public: "[S]uch indeed is the growing demand for sugar in Britain and Ireland, as to call for all that will ever be produced on our remaining Islands."[23] In Ramsay's estimation, the slave trade contravened efforts to improve the conditions for existing enslaved

Africans in British colonies, given the significance of sugar throughout the British empire. They all agreed, whatever else, that an "interest" in slavery could radiate throughout the British empire via networks of commerce—from the slavers and slave-holders in the colonies to the legislators and public in the British Isles.

When abolitionists began the anti-sugar campaign in 1791, this systemic imagination, born of encounters with slavery and imperial commerce, became even more crucial. A letter from Thomas Cooper, published in the same year as Fox's address, prefaced an indictment of the British public with accounts of the transatlantic slave trade and the lives of the slaves. He made a grisly calculation:

> The average import of slaves into the European colonies may be 100,000; but these are only two-thirds of the import previous to seasoning, for one-third dies in the seasoning; therefore the actual import into the European colonies is at this rate 150,000. But this latter number is only four-fifths of the cargo when first laden; for one-fifth at least dies in the passage, therefore the cargo when first laden was 180,000 men. Moreover, it has been observed before . . . that for *one* man actually sent down to the coast, at the very least *ten* were slaughtered. Hence, *one million, eight hundred thousand* people are annually murdered at the instigation of Europeans.[24]

Cooper insisted,

> [T]he most callous heart cannot reflect upon [this circumstance] without emotion, and every one who possesses a common degree of humanity is ready to imprecate the vengeance of heaven upon the authors and abettors of such unparalleled barbarity. What then must be his anguish on finding that he himself has, thoughtlessly indeed, but really, been accessary to the crime, and is partaker in the guilt?[25]

To demonstrate his reasoning, Cooper posed a series of questions and answers:

> For why is the Slave Trade carried on? To supply the West India planters with hands to cultivate the islands. And why are the islands cultivated? To furnish the inhabitants of Europe with sugar!! If sugar were not consumed it would not be imported—if it were not imported, it would not be cultivated, if it were not cultivated there would be an end of the Slave Trade, so that the consumer of sugar is really the prime mover—the grand cause of all the shocking cruelty which accompanies the treatment of the wretched African Slaves.[26]

Whether one agrees with such reasoning is immaterial: This particular chain of deductions seems to follow interpretations of imperial commerce, as a train follows the tracks.[27] And one can find it repeated in pamphlet after pamphlet advocating that the British public abstain from the purchase of sugar. "Take away the cause," one affirmed, "and we all know the effect will cease. Abstain from Sugar, and Slavery falls."[28] "If the cultivation of Sugar be the sole cause of our Negro Trade," proposed another, "let us no longer partake in the fruits of that cultivation."[29]

Yet Cooper did not seek only passive reasons for the British public's consuming guilt; he sought to compel with blunt force. After establishing the moral complicity of conspirators to an assassination, he turned to the situation of the British consumer:

> A number of persons offer a large sum of money for a certain natural production. The merchant is by this induced to import it and the planter to cultivate it. But as the merchant will of course prefer the cheapest market, the planter must adopt the cheapest mode of cultivation, i.e. in the present case, must purchase slaves. He, therefore, in his turn, offers a reward for *this commodity*, by which others are tempted to procure *it*, and, since it is not otherwise to be obtained, to procure it *by the annual murder* of *many hundred thousand of their fellow creatures*. The load of guilt bears equally upon every brink [sic] of this infernal chain, upon every one who is either directly or indirectly engaged in the cultivation or consumption of West India produce; but as in the case above, the first mover seemed more criminal than the rest, so in this case a larger portion of guilt may perhaps, not unjustly, be attributed to the consumer. The conclusion appears inevitable.[30]

To be a consumer was to be not just another link in an infernal chain of commerce, but the first cause of injustice and suffering in this infernal chain. Cooper indicted the British public as consumers. Abolitionists asked consumers to see the suffering that, according to their reasoning, consumers called into being. Thus, their moral object (the consumer) and argument (chain of reasoning) revealed a specific debt to the world of merchant capitalism.

Deontological and consequentialist ethics in abolition

While abolitionists' reasoning and objects reflected this substantive engagement with merchant capitalism, such reasoning and objects just as evidently reflected their moral groundings. As one abolitionist wrote, "Most of us, though not all, laid aside the use of sugar, because we thought it was what a regard to right required of us; because we were persuaded that the contrary practice was wrong, morally wrong, in persons who judged of the matter as we did."[31] We have already seen these grounds in abolitionists' denunciations of imperial commerce. Their deductive chains of reasoning, which followed circuits of imperial commerce, also entailed reasons why one should be moral in the first place. If there were no reasons to be moral, then the causal connections between producers and consumers would not motivate sympathetic consumption. While these reasons were, in general, deontological, we can also see a kind of consequentialist ethic at work—often in the same argument. These arguments tied claims about the causal structure of the world to ethical ones about its moral structure.

Many of the abolitionists, it is well known, were informed by deep Christian commitments. Yet in their public arguments, these Christian commitments often appeared only after the advocate had clinched the guilt of the consumer. In a speech, William Allen bore out the consumer's guilt in a familiar fashion: "[British commerce in sugar] is a *chain of Wretchedness* every link of which is stained with blood! and it involves in *equal criminality* the African Trader—the West India Slave-Holder—and the British Consumer!"[32] Only after establishing this guilt did Allen explain why such complicity was criminal: "You know, Sir, we argue against the practice of Moral Evil, from its apparent *consequences*, supposing it to become *universal* throughout the Creation—the desolation and ruin it would every where occasion. Every act of vice is a tendency to *this*: it is that *begun*, which *carried on*, would end in defacing the beauty of all the Creator's works."[33] The evil of slavery, therefore, issued from the offense to God's creations. While the causal chain implicated the consumer, one's Christian duty would motivate the consumer to abstain from sugar.

After Thomas Cooper indicted consumers for the murder of millions of Africans, he called them to a higher judgment:

> Remember, friends, there is another tribunal, before which sooner or later we must all appear; the best of us will with reason tremble when that awful day approaches; but let it not be said, in addition to our other crimes, that we encouraged a traffic fatal to the happiness of so many of our brethren—of the children of that great Being, before whom we then shall stand.[34]

To refrain from the purchase and use of West India sugar, and to join the abolitionist cause, would lighten one's spiritual burden come the final judgment. William Fox concluded his address with a reminder of God's ultimate judgment: "In proportion as we are under their influence, we shall exert ourselves to remedy these evils, knowing that our example, our admonitions, our influence, may produce remote effects, of which we can form no estimates; and which, after having done our duty, must be left to *Him who governs all things after the counsel of his own will.*"[35] The abolitionists were willing to call people to account as Christians to justify their duties as consumers.

More noteworthy, perhaps, were the lengths to which abolitionists sometimes went to hold deontological grounds—especially Christian moral arguments—in abeyance. A letter addressed to the Duchess of York appealed to her feminine sympathies with brutal facts about slavery and the slave trade, all in the name of the "friends of humanity."[36] While this nebulous phrase could suggest a God-given natural right, these "friends of humanity" made a different case to the princess. The surprising popularity of the campaign against sugar, they noted,

> has incited us redouble our zeal in endeavouring to bring over every friend of humanity, to a practice which his unbiassed judgment must approve, which must well accord with his best feelings, and be productive of pleasing reflections. It is at the head of this body of persons, whose motives all must respect, whose resolution all must applaud, and whose object all must approve, that you are requested to place yourself;—a body not distinguished as the friends and advocates of humanity, who cherish sympathy for, and who would fly to the assistance of suffering man, whatever the colour of his skin, the form of his features, the mode of his religion, or the state of his manners; who believe that individuals enjoy most happiness when the general pulse beats highest; who conceive it to be a law of nature, that individual felicity keeps a fixed pace with the well-being of the aggregate of the species.[37]

The argument appealed to a "law of nature," wherein individual happiness depended on the aggregate well-being of the whole. If the oppressive institution of slavery placed the well-being of Africans at the expense of Europeans, then this would diminish individual happiness in the aggregate. This is a consequentialist ground or justification, where the greatest good for the greatest number ultimately clinches the argument.

But this letter did not only make a consequentialist case to the princess; abolitionists called flattery and fashion to their aid. "Her Majesty, so famed for the private and domestic virtues, and her piety" it implored, "—[and] the King . . . by rejecting the produce of [a villainous trade] will display their humility, as well as their humanity, and their other good qualities."[38] Most important, however, "the influence of your example will then spread itself through the different ranks of the nobility and gentry. Fashion will take the side of humanity. The middling orders of the community, who could stand out against the arguments and the examples of their equals, will yield to those of their superiors, and depressed, afflicted, bleeding humanity will lift up her head in triumph."[39] Rather than a deontological argument, the letter made a sociological one about the dissemination of moral ideas and practices. Fashion could serve the cause of greater justice. In this letter, then, the sociological argument mingled with a moral grounding that favored consequences rather than Christian duty.

Similar consequentialist grounds appeared in the second resurgence of the abolitionist movement in the 1820s. As some abolitionists searched for alternative sugar sources, these economic arguments against the slave trade took a number of forms. A pamphlet on West India sugar urged British consumers to purchase sugar from India or the East Indies. The text all but shouted,

> [S]o discouraging is the prospect of any thing effectual being done [to abolish slavery and ameliorate the conditions of the enslaved Africans], that the friends of humanity must chiefly depend on the consoling conviction of the undisputable truth, THAT THE LABOUR OF SLAVES IS MORE EXPENSIVE THAN THAT OF FREE MEN, AND THAT CONSEQUENTLY SLAVERY COULD NOT EXIST IN UNRESTRICTED COMPETITION WITH FREE LABOUR.[40]

Slavery should be abolished, it argued, because it was bad business practice. In her pamphlet aimed at the "hearts and consciences" of British women, penned in 1828, Elizabeth Heyrick proclaimed, "[O]bjectors to the disuse of West India produce on the ground of its ruinous consequences to the planter, forget that the ruin of the planter under present system is inevitable."[41] An 1825 meeting of abolitionists condemned imperial regulations that imposed duties on sugar cultivated outside of the West Indies. They resolved, "That in this giving a large bonus to the holders of slaves in their competition with free labour, this Country is pursuing a cause which while it is at variance with all just maxims of commercial policy powerfully and fatally tends to aggravate the miseries of the Slave & to perpetuate the evils of Colonial bondage."[42] They could justify sympathetic consumption on consequentialist grounds, even as Christian moral grounds quietly stalked in the background.

To encounter such starkly consequentialist justifications, however, was rare in the early years of the abolitionist movement. More common were justifications that traded in an admixture of consequentialist and deontological cases against slavery and the slave trade. Many of these cases landed, ultimately, on Christian grounds. Thus, Fox dedicated the bulk of his argument to excavating and tracing the links between the British consumer and the enslaved African. Having done so to his satisfaction, he declaimed:

> [I]f our execration of the slave trade be any more than mere declamation against crimes we are not in a situation to commit, we shall, instead of being solicitous to find despicable distinctions to justify our conduct, abhor the idea of contributing, in the least degree, to such scenes of misery. If these be the deductions from the most obvious principles of reason, justice, and humanity; what must be the result if we extend our view to religious considerations?[43]

He sought an argument that would work even without an appeal to Christian theology.

The status and complicity of the consumer was, in many of these arguments, presented as fact. Having laid out the case for the consumer's complicity, Thomas Cooper reasoned, "If the facts above stated are true . . . every person who habitually consumes one article of West Indian produce, raised by Slaves, is *guilty of the crime of murder*—every one who does it, when convinced that what has been said is true, is *deliberately guilty*."[44] While the moral grounds may have, ultimately, been theological, the method of argumentation was unquestionably capitalist—it depended on logical chains of causation that followed the circuits of imperial commerce. The object, too—the sympathetic consumer—entailed an interpretation *of* commodity-exchange as natural. This interpretation framed commodity-exchange in terms of the merchant capitalist system that made it possible. Thus, as revealed in these aspects of the moral background, the interpretation *of* commodity-exchange took on elements of the commercial system upon which depersonalized goods depended.

Turn-of-the-Twentieth-Century Activists Justify the Sympathetic Consumer

Like the abolitionists, turn-of-the-twentieth-century activists exhibited a profoundly systemic moral imagination. Their arguments for sympathetic consumption located the consumer in a system of industrial capitalist commerce. Moreover, they traced the causal links in the supply chain to establish the consumer's moral responsibility, though they were also especially concerned with the ways that advertising and competition obscured the consumer's systemic position and moral role. The moral object and the method of argument, in Abend's terms, followed the structure of the capitalist commerce. Unlike the abolitionists, turn-of-the-twentieth-century activists were decidedly more pluralistic in their moral grounds. While deontological Christian ethics remained relevant, the abolitionists' thunderous warnings of the last judgment gave way to more subtle allusions to Christian principles. Moreover, these allusions often mingled with a more mundane grounding in consequentialist business ethics. Either way, the moral object and method of argument depended on capitalist phenomena and institutions.

The public of consumers

In 1908, writing on behalf of the National Consumers' League, Florence Kelley declared, "[T]he prime responsibility of the consuming public is its own ignorance."[45] She meant that the public must be educated about how to purchase goods ethically. The question was not *if* the consuming public had a duty to unseen producers of goods, but whether they could become aware of this duty—whether they could become sympathetic consumers. Co-operators and NCL members alike did not believe that the public would come to understand their responsibilities spontaneously. In anticipation of a projected 1895 budget surplus, the editors of the *Co-operative News* wrote: "If co-operators do not exercise some pressure in this matter, if they give no sign that they are alive to the interests of the consumers generally, the other side—the side of the interests—will have it all their own way."[46] Speaking at the twenty-fifth anniversary of the Consumers' League of New York City, Lillian Wald trumpeted the systemic centrality of consumers:

> It [the Consumers' League] started . . . right . . . giving a respectful ear to the grievances and complaints from the people. . . . And, hearing the message, the founders of the League used their intelligence and their inspiration to interpret these grievances to the consumers, that they might be roused to a sense of their responsibility for the young girls who served them from behind the counters.[47]

In what kind of system were these consumers enmeshed? What reasons did people have to become sympathetic consumers? Turn-of-the-twentieth-century activists argued along the links in the chains of commerce. But they were also attuned to the distracting circumstances in which consumers found themselves. Consumers, they suggested, did not easily recognize their complicity in degradation and exploitation. "The principal task of the League," wrote Kelley, "is to enlighten men and women who are eager to do right if they can but know what is right."[48] A co-operative editorial took a similarly circumspect view of living, breathing consumers: "Whatever the personal merits of the consumer may be—and these are subject to wide diversity—none can doubt the social importance of his functions."[49] While the consumer occupied a vital public role, activists could not rely on consumers to discover this public role all by themselves.

"In a very real sense," alleged John Graham Brooks, the first president of the National Consumers' League, "to buy a harmful thing is to help make that thing."[50] Kelley insisted that "the consumer is the indirect employer and can by no means escape a share in the moral responsibility for the employment."[51] But how were consumers to ascertain the harm and depravity that they created? After all, the depersonalization of consumer goods aided and abetted the ignorance of the consuming public. Early on, Florence Kelley underscored this with a simple tale of two white cotton underwear manufacturers: a "well-ordered factory" in Richmond, Vermont and tenement production in New York, New York.[52] They produced competitively priced underwear under wildly different conditions. Kelley wrote, "The economy which in Richmond, Vt., is made by the application of high intelligence, using the most advanced methods of production, is made in New York City wholly at the expense of the footpower worker, her wages, her home, her health, and all the joy and comfort that depend upon these."[53] The comparison implied that producers and consumers were anonymous to one another. Without the NCL, consumers' would be unable to discern the origins of the goods they bought: "The League," Kelley noted, "now renders it easy for purchasers to select with knowledge of circumstances [of production]."[54] Thus, the depersonalization of goods and labor conditions upon which they depended supplied a clue as to the source of the consumer's duty.

Florence Kelley's crusade against the ignorance of the consuming public began with depersonalized goods in commodity-exchange and followed them back into the workplace. The consumer had some resources to remedy this ignorance "ready to hand." Consumers needed only to look around at those who sold them daily newspapers or worked in shops: "Everyone can see how small is the newsboy in the street. If, in buying papers, we give the preference to big boys, we use the obvious means to encourage big boys and discourage little ones in the newspaper business in the street."[55] But owing to the complexity of industrial capitalist commerce, consumers needed the assistance of organizations like the National Consumers' League:

> The National Consumers' League goes beyond the store to the factory, and in one narrow field of manufacture, that of women's and children's white stitched underwear, awards the use of its label to manufacturers who employ no children below the age of sixteen years, give out no work to be done away from their own premises, employ no one longer than ten hours in one day, and obey the state factory law.[56]

Teachers and state officials, further, could supply consumers with information about the conditions of labor into which vulnerable men, women, and children were thrust in the manufacture of all manner of goods. Ultimately, Kelley claimed, "The most urgent responsibility of the consumer is thus clearly to deal with her own ignorance by every possible means—to observe the visible working children, and to insist upon obtaining from the city, state and federal officials fresh and valid information about the unseen ones."[57] As "indirect employers," consumers could discover the responsibility to sympathize through knowledge of the commercial circuits of industrial capitalism.

Co-operators were also attuned to the links between consumers and producers in capitalist circuits of commerce. Under conditions of industrial capitalist commerce, Women's Co-operative Guild members saw ignorance as a sticky problem: "It will take time and friendliness and association, and a gradual acquaintance with certain economic facts, to make the ordinary purchaser into a convinced and useful co-operator."[58] Absent some familiarity with the logic and circuits of capitalist commerce, ignorance of the duty to sympathize would persist. They sometimes insisted that loyalty to co-operation would ultimately stamp out exploitative practices like sweatshops: "[L]egislation can only act as a palliative. It cannot prove to be a radical remedy for sweating, which is the inevitable outcome of unrestricted competition."[59] Competition created incentives to exploit—consumers seeking the cheapest prices, producers seeking higher wages, owners and merchants seeking low wages—that the law did not address. Only the mutual effort of consumer co-operation could radically restrict competitive capitalism. Moreover, the organization of capitalist commerce rendered the trail of the sweatshop difficult to trace: "[P]urchased through the ordinary channels of commerce, it is difficult, however strong the desire, to avoid the use of commodities in which some form of sweating or corruption has not entered."[60]

Fortunately, co-operation supplied a more salutary channel. In their roles as consumers, people could overcome the competitive, capitalist logic that governed such networks: "What we must strive for is a system of service where there will be no inducement either to exploit the worker or adulterate the goods manufactured. This can be found in a complete form of co-operative effort."[61] These co-operative efforts built on an expanded understanding of democracy, where "every one of us is a consumer."[62] In other words, co-operation made it possible that everyone could be a sympathetic consumer. To recognize that truth, co-operators reasoned, would enlarge notions of democracy: "There is a fundamental misapprehension if democracy is permitted . . . to be a mere method of government, not identified with the true life of the nation."[63] This true life of the nation included the commercial networks that joined producers and consumers. As co-operator Joseph Tyldesley wrote,

> [T]he only solution to the problem lies with the consumer. Let him make his own capital or covering the risk and hire of it, pay fair price to all workers, and take the breeches. Carry this plan not only into boots, as at Leicester, but into hats, at Denton, clothes at Batley, providing all our wants on this plan. It is the only plan on which we can hope to purge ourselves from the old leaven of, "Every man for hissel' and the de'il tak' the back most.[64]

Consumer co-operation supplied a means through which people could both understand and surmount the seductive, exploitative, individualistic, and undemocratic world of capitalist competition.

According to co-operators and the NCL, one could discern the consumer's unique public role by observing features of industrial capitalism. Co-operator Percy Redfern observed, "There is a division between a numerical minority of owners, with their friends and dependents, and a majority of workers; and there is also another division co-existing between the antagonistic interests of capital and labor and the interest of the public as the universal consumer."[65] At the founding of the National Consumers' League, Maud Nathan noted, "It [the White List] has succeeded in great measure in arousing public sentiment against long hours for clerks and paved the way for a Consumers' label if sufficient demand for it is created."[66] A Women's Co-operative Guild editorial concluded that purchasers were at the mercy of shop proprietors in particular, asserting "that the public has very little means of judging whether he is a fair dealing man or not."[67] Similarly, co-operators often contrasted the "private" appropriation of profit, which one found in a shop (non–co-operative business), with the public profit-sharing of the consumer co-operative.[68] In an essay hailing the superiority of co-operative stores, George Holyoake used "people," "public," "customers," and "purchasers" interchangeably.[69] As the true emissary of the public, the consumer was discoverable everywhere. Co-operation and consumers' leagues made it possible to hold consumers accountable to public values of mutuality, not the private values of competition.

But the publicness of the consumer's role in a capitalist social order—which was essential to the consumer's power and sympathies—also made him easy to overlook. "How long," the editors of the *Co-operative News* asked, "[I]s the consumer going to allow himself to remain the shuttlecock to be knocked about in this manner at the will of grasping capitalists?"[70] Moreover, because the consumer's power derived from the structure and organization of a system, it was difficult to see. In Percy Redfern's assessment, "What superiority there is in the consumer is simply economic. He it is who creates and determines demand, and he alone, justly may exorcise competition. Working from demand to supply—that is to say from human need to human satisfaction—co-operation has to recognize this economic priority."[71] Margaret Llewelyn Davies, the leader of the Women's Co-operative Guild, underscored the gap between consumer ignorance and control: "The power of the revolutionary weapon—the market basket—has been made clear. Women have been transformed from buyers, ignorant of the economic results of their acts, into intelligent Co-operators, conscious that they can undermine Capitalism, and making good their right to share in the control of the Movement [co-operation]."[72]

Yet it was not just the consumer's position in a system that obscured her power and responsibility; competitive pressures, prices, and advertising enticed and threatened to overwhelm the consumer. With dramatic flair, the *Co-operative News* made a point common among turn-of-the-twentieth-century activists: "In the amalgamation of consumers for their own help and protection lies the only power that can break the spell of high prices and exorcise those spirits of greed and selfishness that give capitalists the mastery and confer misery upon the workers."[73] In this competitive atmosphere, co-operators fretted that consumers would be led astray by advertising. "The ordinary purchaser," one guild member wrote,

> requires a great deal of strengthening against the urgency of advertisements. Suppose you are told that a certain soap takes all of the effort from the process

of scrubbing, or that it gives the complexion of a child of six to a woman of fifty. You do not literally believe what you are told— . . . But unless you are a very cynical or experienced character indeed, it is almost impossible not to believe that the soap of which such things could be said must be a good soap, and that you may safely put it on your face.[74]

Co-operators were leery of contemporary advertising techniques themselves and debates about its merits surfaced periodically in the *Co-operative News*.[75] In spite of their concerns, all of these activists appealed to, in Florence Kelley's words, "eye-minded" consumers.

Pressures to compete with novel forms of advertising aside, we should also recall that activists were wrestling with depersonalized goods in commodity-exchange. As such, they often needed to rely on ways of seeing themselves. Thus, British co-operators often implicitly distinguished their edifying advertising campaigns from malicious marketing ones that bred ignorance. The matter of "Bonus Tea" is a case in point. Bonus Tea described a range of marketing strategies wherein merchants sold tea at a slight markup, while offering consumers "complimentary" wares from the same store. One could purchase tea and receive credits to spend on China or silverware, for instance, or in extreme cases, an old age pension after years of loyalty to a particular brand.[76] Women's Co-operative Guild members decried Bonus Tea as "bogus." Such advertisements induced both thoughtlessness and moral turpitude on the part of consumers.[77] In these "false economies," sham and swindle masqueraded as virtues. "The delusion that in this commercial age," bemoaned one co-operator, "something may be had for nothing dies hard."[78] Many worried that opportunities to buy on credit in retail shops and department stores had similarly deleterious effects. Guild members, in particular, cautioned against credit purchases, which gnawed away at the virtues of thrift and reason.[79]

It was similar with the National Consumers' League. Once again, general secretary Florence Kelley conveyed these concerns with characteristic force: "Much of the current advertisement, of which the patent-medicine advertisement may be taken as the type, is directly aimed at the ignorance of the purchaser. Nearly all of it is aimed at the cupidity of the public; and it, therefore, offers cheapness as the one great characteristic."[80] Under the spell of cupidity, consumer demands for cheap goods pushed businesses to minimize costs and maximize profits. This understanding was codified in the NCL constitution when they asserted that the "stress of competition" rendered employers helpless against the pressure to exploit others.[81] At the 1901 World Exhibition in Buffalo, Florence Kelley described the effects of competition across the English-speaking world: "Cutthroat competition among manufacturers, merchant tailors, contractors, and workmen in turn, has forced down the cost of production until filthy workshops, starvation wages, excessive working hours and child-labor characterize the industry wherever it is found in London, New York, Chicago, or Toronto."[82] Members of consumers' leagues in Massachusetts noted the threefold competition between manufacturing firms, penal institutions, and tenement sweatshops, which created the pressure to exploit laborers all along the supply chain.[83] In their campaigns to reduce working hours around Christmas, league members depicted competition in vivid scenes of "unusual crowds" and exhausted workers: "An especial effort was made in Harlem where in December, 1913, the conditions in the stores, at night and during the few days before Christmas, were marked by unusual crowds, overwork and overfatigue of the clerks and delivery boys."[84] Both the structure of industrial capitalist commerce as well as competitive pressures, prices, and advertising kept the consumer thoughtless and distracted.

Set against such a background, arguments for sympathetic consumption revealed the systemic nature of industrial capitalism—not only consisting of commerce, but also of advertising and a consuming public insufficiently awake to its responsibilities to distant laborers. This world of industrial capitalist commerce shaped their arguments for sympathetic consumption. These arguments tracked institutions and circuits of commerce in turn-of-the-twentieth-century capitalism: depersonalized goods, lengthening supply chains, prices, competition, sweatshops, department stores, advertising. To turn-of-the-twentieth-century activists, these circuits could both manifest and conceal the consumer's status as a moral object. But activists were convinced that such knowledge of these circuits would demonstrate the empirical and moral truth of the sympathetic consumer. As one co-operator wrote, "We need not say anything more right now about the duty of seeing that luxuries are produced under fair conditions to the workers, because that duty applies to *every kind of thing produced*, as much the necessary loaf of bread as the most delicate iced pudding."[85] Thus, in their methods of argument and objects, turn-of-the-twentieth-century activists' interpretations *of* commodity-exchange—of the consumer's moral role in a capitalist world—took on features of the commercial system upon which commodity-exchange depended.

Deontological and consequentialist ethics in turn-of-the-twentieth-century consumer activism

Again, as before, we cannot understand these moral objects and argumentative methods without examining the moral grounds of their arguments for the sympathetic consumer. J. T. W. Mitchell, a preeminent member of the Co-operative Wholesale Society, identified co-operation as a beacon of moral uplift: "The three great forces for the improvement of mankind are religion, temperance, and co-operation, and as a commercial force, supported and sustained by the other two, co-operation is the grandest, noblest, and most likely to be successful in the redemption of the industrial classes."[86] The Women's Co-operative Guild, too, embraced the moral aspects of consumer co-operation. As one speaker before the guild stated, "If we have helped to train women's minds . . . developing in them a belief in the new social faith, and if we have helped to give women a field of action in which to carry out this faith, then the harvest of the seeds we are sowing will be reaped by future generations."[87] By identifying co-operation as a "social faith," the speaker amplified the moral conviction that guild members sought to cultivate. Similarly, Florence Kelley described the National Consumers' League's "underlying principles" as "partly economic and partly moral."[88] The NCL constitution, furthermore, codified the "duty of consumers to find out under what conditions the articles they purchased are produced and distributed and insist that these conditions shall be wholesome and consistent with a respectable existence on the part of the workers." It did this out of concern for the community and indicted consumers who sought "the cheapest markets regardless how cheapness is brought about."[89] There were moral reasons to be a sympathetic consumer. What were they?

At first blush, any deontological ethic appears wholly remote from their justifications for sympathetic consumption. Margaret Llewelyn Davies wrote, "Co-operators as consumers, and trade unionists as producers or workers, may be regarded as forming two halves of the same circle. And if a *man* be taken as a type of worker, a *woman* would certainly represent a body of consumers or purchasers. It has been the aim of the Guild to arouse women to a sense of the 'basket power' which they specially possessed."[90] Rosalind Nash, another guild member, explained the reasons to wield this "basket power" responsibly:

> We know, of course, that the articles that are turned out into the shops in
> such quantities do not, as they lie there, make anyone's wealth, or health, or

happiness. They are produced with the idea that they will go further and be consumed in the homes, and in order that the employer, who sets the work of production going, may make a profit. But we hardly realise that *the consumer, through being the final object, becomes the controlling power*. Too much stress cannot be laid on the part that consumption plays in controlling production and *use*, that is say in *controlling work*. And seeing that the choice of articles for consumption, or use, lies to a large extent in the hands of the women who control the homes, it is evident that the place of these women in the industrial system is a predominating one.[91]

Nash's capitalist reasoning found its moral ground in the consumer's ability to control the "wealth, or health, or happiness" of those who produce and work upon the goods; consumers were, in this sense, responsible. But whose wealth, health, or happiness should guide the consumer? The good of the many. "The consumer," reminded Percy Redfern, "is every modest one of us when we eat, drink, read, travel, go shopping, visit the theatre or rest in bed. Consumers, therefore, generally are poor, because the majority are poor, and a great number are very poor."[92] Consumers had a responsibility to purchase so as to support the health and welfare of the masses—a basically consequentialist justification. They could do so by "giving their custom to the Co-operative factories and workshops, where trade unionist conditions [were] observed, short hours [were] worked, and healthy accommodation provided."[93]

The National Consumers' League took a similar approach. Florence Kelley laid out the familiar conditions:

From the cradle (which may be of wood or of metal, with rockers or without them) to the grave (to which an urn may be preferred), throughout our lives we are choosing, or choice is made for us, as to the disposal of money. From the newsboy who fosters the cigarette and chewing-gum trades, and is himself fostered by our failure to give the preference to some one-armed father of a family in the purchase of our papers, to the self-conscious patrons of the Kelmscott sheets, we all make daily and hourly choice as to the bestowal of our means. As we do so, we help to decide, however unconsciously, how our fellow-men shall spend their time in making what we buy.[94]

Because consumers dictated the conditions of production, they had a responsibility. And, as with the co-operators, the moral imperative to shop rightly came to ground in the benefits to the majority. John Graham Brooks insisted,

"[W]e should do what we can as purchasers to raise the standard of life among the great majority."[95] Kelley stressed, in practical terms, the consequentialist ground of the consumer's duty:

> [T]he National Consumers' League acts upon the proposition that, to consti-
> tute an effective demand for goods made under right conditions, there must be
> numbers of consumers sufficiently large to assure purchases steady and consid-
> erable enough to compensate for the expense incurred by humane employers.[96]

At times, Kelley claimed that consumers had a duty to promote that "which is most wholesome for the whole community."[97] That is not a straightforwardly consequentialist claim. But these justifications allude to a basic consequential-ist idea: that people should become sympathetic consumers because it would diminish pain and increase pleasure. When tasked with justifying their activ-ism, then, co-operators and consumers' league leaders often supplied conse-quentialist justifications that followed, in familiar capitalist method, the supply chain from producer to consumer and back.

Yet neither the co-operators nor NCL members disparaged or renounced deontological justifications of duty and right. In a letter to the Women's Co-operative Guild, co-operator Edward Vansittart Neale acknowledged, "You rightly appreciate the functions of Co-operation . . . in speaking of it as a 'gospel'—the song of peace on earth and goodwill to mankind, and it must be regarded not as a substitute for the ancient Gospel, but as the *complement* of it."[98] It was quite common, for instance, to find allusions to Christian moral precepts in efforts to justify the co-operative consumer, even in these osten-sibly nonsectarian co-operative organizations. The editors of the *Co-operative News* noted a lag between scientific progress and moral progress, asserting, "One great step forward [in morals] has been made in the change from 'don'ts' to 'do's'. But that was made nearly nineteen hundred years ago when the new commandment to love was added to the old commandments of prohibition."[99]

Co-operators were happy to associate the truth of their mission with that of the Christian church; they casually integrated religious sentiments into articles that dealt with co-operative business, advertising, or news of the day.[100] While describing the duty of each co-operative store to purchase their goods from the Co-operative Wholesale Society, one co-operator recalled the Christian prin-ciple of brotherly love: "What we want today is to lift our movement out of the cold, dreary region of self-interest into the warm, bright sunlight of mutual help and brotherly love."[101] A co-operative publication out of Manchester recounted a parable by a visiting bishop that questioned the morality of consumers taking on debt and the false economies of industrial capitalism. The bishop described how he avoided a costly new cathedral that would have replaced the more austere wooden church. The co-operator followed this brief story by observing, "The contentment of this [British] Columbian bishop reminds us of St. Thomas Aquinas grim remark—that churches with wooden chalices had golden priests; but those with chalices of gold had priests of wood."[102] The co-operative leaders, it seems, certainly wanted to remind the rank and file of their Christian duties. This reflected the influence of Christian socialism on many of the co-operative leaders.[103] While many in the English urban working class were indifferent to organized religion, the co-operators' accounts of consumer morality resounded with the familiar language of reform-oriented Christianity.[104]

The NCL incorporated Christian ethics in a more strategic and oblique manner. One might attribute this attenuated Christian moral sensibility to the intellectual tendencies of Florence Kelley. Kelley was a committed socialist who agitated publicly and privately on behalf of class-based redistribution and transformations of wealth. In a letter to her son, Kelley affirmed her admiration for Marx as a political economist and puzzled over the tendency of the urban proletariat to reject socialist politics.[105] But Kelley recognized that her views would likely find little favor with the members of consumers' leagues, drawn as they were from religious, white, upper-middle-class backgrounds. In private correspondence, Kelley wrote, "[I]t *is* most encouraging to see how readily the organization [NCL] spreads. The most favorable existing organizations seem to be the churches and the women's clubs."[106] Kelley would have understood the moral and ethical appetites of group members, both active NCL officers like John Graham Brooks or sympathizers such as economist Richard T. Ely and the rank-and-file membership, recruited through churches and women's clubs.[107]

Consequently, the influence of this Christian moral sensibility on the NCL appeared "from below" rather than "from above," the reverse of co-operatives. Whether the leaders of the National Consumers' League liked it or not, they were dependent upon the Christian calendar when designing campaigns, especially their "Buy Early" campaign for Christmas.[108] And members of the leagues at the national, state, and local levels called upon friendly clergy and church communities to recruit more members and to educate the public. They circulated information about the NCL in venues such as the *Sunday School Times*.[109] In 1902, for instance, league members' distributed "one thousand Christmas circulars, with annuals, calendars, catechisms, pamphlets by John Graham

Brooks and the Menace to the Home."[110] Such arrangements between leagues and the churches were common.[111]

Furthermore, the NCL received practical support and moral ballast from clergy and church organizations. A member of a Michigan Consumers' League endorsed, for instance, the writings of Bishop Potter, a reformist Episcopal priest: "Every one who purchases goods is indirectly an employer of labor and is morally bound to give his or her trade to factories and stores which treat their employees honorably and well."[112] By giving the league's project an explicit Christian gloss, Potter revealed the ease with which NCL activities could take on the language of Christian social reform, even as the national leaders strove to avoid religious provincialism. Florence Kelley often spoke on the league's behalf at church meetings throughout the calendar year and sometimes even gave sermons from the pulpit.[113] And Kelley was always explicit about the NCL's debt to ministers: "The best help, however, which the ministers give takes the form of their sermons in the late spring on the duty of refraining from shopping on Saturday afternoons, and in the early fall on the duty of avoiding the Christmas crowds, and in general the duty of applying the Golden Rule to shopping."[114] These deontological calls to duty could appeal to members, regardless of the leader's moral convictions.

People should become sympathetic consumers, activists argued, because of the consumer's ability to do good and harm in competitive capitalist societies. While they were comfortable furnishing Christian principles of categorical right and duty, co-operators and NCL members took a pluralist approach to justifying their moral claims—both consequentialist and deontological grounds would do. But the method of argumentation and object remained profoundly capitalist. In the words of Kelley, "We are all of us spending money (however little) all the time; and every time we spend a dollar we help to determine, by our selection of goods, whether the factories and stores which are carried on righteously shall prosper, or whether the baser competitor shall thrive at the expense of the nobler."[115] By learning to see and track the links in the chains of capitalist commerce, the sympathetic consumer's duty came into view.

The Sympathetic Consumer, Justified

Abolitionists and turn-of-the-twentieth-century consumer activists reasoned in parallel. Their moral arguments for the sympathetic consumer depended on an account of the consumer as the cause of and solution to suffering in capitalist circuits of commerce. In other words, their moral objects and methods of argumentation hewed closely to their reflections on the consumer as a force in a capitalist society. Even their moral grounds were threaded together through the consumer as a moral object. To make these arguments, they ascertained the consumer's role in a system of commodity production; they elaborated the links between consumers and producers; they identified the consumer as the perpetrator of harms along these chains of commerce; and they justified their calls for sympathetic consumption, variously, on consequentialist and deontological grounds. Further, they deployed these consequentialist and deontological grounds as complements, not competitors. The object was to awaken consumers to their moral responsibilities—not to insist on only one path to these responsibilities. They often wrote as if the reasons why people should engage in sympathetic consumption were less significant than the effective, organized demand of sympathetic consumers. We can say, therefore, that interpretations *of* the consumer in commodity-exchange, as well as the capitalist institutions upon which commodity-exchange depends, informed the moral background.

Of course, the abolitionists and turn-of-the-twentieth-century activists differed in some ways. The early abolitionists gave greater weight to Christian precepts—but not, as we have seen, to the exclusion of consequentialist moral grounds. In this way, the abolitionists had much in common with turn-of-the-twentieth-century activists who dabbled in consumer activism like the Christian Social Union. Established in Oxford in the 1890s, the Christian Social Union, an organization of Christian socialists, undertook some select forms of ethical purchasing. They grounded this work, unsurprisingly, in Christian precepts. Thus, they described the "ground" of their appeals: "We are of those convinced that the ultimate solution of this social question is bound to be discovered in the Person and life of Christ."[116] These principles guided their campaigns for selective purchasing, but also non–consumer-related projects like the moral education of business owners and proper conduct within a family. By contrast, a co-operator lamented the Anglican Church's lack of explicit moral guidance on matters of political economy and morals in economic life. Anticipating Max Weber's description of the modern world as a set of value spheres characterized by distinct principles and practices, he wrote:

> The clergyman can offer less guidance in practical matters, because he must remain within his "proper sphere." This must be specially disappointing to those who feel that moral guidance is what the age needs most, and that the social

dangers looming in the future can only be warded off by practical measures founded on moral truth.[117]

Co-operation, he argued, could supply guidance where the official church stayed silent.[118]

But these differences do not gainsay a basic fact: The coherence of the sympathetic consumer depended on claims about the relations between consumers and producers in capitalist circuits of commerce and the specific role of the consumer therein. In a sense, the sympathetic consumer seemed to be in the capitalist world for these activists to discover. Their ethical arguments depended on the causal claim that consumers exercised power over producers and production.[119] This causal claim made sense in a capitalist world characterized by expanded networks of production, commodification, and depersonalized goods. Whereas Gabriel Abend demonstrates how moral phenomena depend on a moral background, I demonstrate how a moral background can, in crucial ways, depend on social phenomena. This latter approach helps us appreciate the significance of at least some of the monotonous predictability that characterizes moral pronouncements on economic life in a capitalist social order. It underscores the extent to which the sympathetic consumer is a distinctly capitalist pattern of interpretations and social conditions.

Capitalism and Global Humanitarianism

There is one task yet remaining in this chapter. I have shown that the moral arguments for the sympathetic consumer depended, in crucial ways, on capitalist phenomena and institutions. These observations allow us to reassess a vexing question for historians and social scientists: What is the precise nature of the relationship between capitalism and global humanitarianism?

Since Eric Williams published *Capitalism and Slavery* in 1944, there has been a rich and fruitful discussion about the emergence and functions of humanitarianism—that is, concern for the suffering and well-being of distant strangers and the institutions that allow people to enact such concern—for example, international NGOs and social movements, especially. Activism on behalf of the sympathetic consumer contributes to such institutionalized concern. One might also think of advocacy on behalf of culturally and/or physically distant strangers ranging from pro-indigenous petitioners in the Spanish empire to international NGOs like Doctors Without Borders or the Red Cross. These organized efforts enable people at different corners of the globe to take a direct interest in the suffering of distant strangers. This novel phenomenon—birthed over the last six centuries—tracks the development of capitalism. There appears, then, to be a connection between capitalism and humanitarianism.

Many historians have identified abolitionism as a crucial case through which to understand the precise nature of the relationship between capitalism and humanitarianism. There was, after all, a "remarkable shift in moral consciousness" toward internationally held antislavery opinions in the second half of the eighteenth century along with the rise of industrial capitalism.[120] David Brion Davis held that British abolitionists, a great many of whom were Quakers, engaged in a "highly selective response to labor exploitation." By "selective response" Davis meant that abolitionists failed to draw obvious connections between the cause of enslaved Africans in the colonies and wage workers in England.[121] Many abolitionist leaders were scions of a rising capitalist class, and, as such, they relied on wage labor—the destruction of the planter class in the colonies would not have hurt their bottom line, but restrictions on their ability to control and exploit wage laborers would have. Consequently, owners could be comfortable with disciplinary control over free laborers but not over enslaved ones. While humanitarian sentiments may have been religious and philosophical in origin, the capitalist conditions within which such sentiments took root shaped their application. "The growing power of antislavery in early industrial Britain," Davis argued, "was at least partly a function of the fit between antislavery ideology and the interests of an emergent capitalist class."[122] In this way, the spread of abolitionism was arguably compatible with the class dynamics and ideology of a capitalist social order.

In response, Thomas Haskell proposed a different relationship between abolition, humanitarianism, and capitalism—and in the process he reframed the question almost exclusively around humanitarianism's origins. He claimed that the growth of capitalist marketplaces underwrote an expansion in causal and moral perception, including a sense of how one's actions could shape the lives of distant strangers. This occurred via the spread of "promise-keeping" or contracts. These contracts extended one's obligations across space and time; they also encouraged a scrupulous attentiveness to these obligations. To invest in a sugar plantation in the British West Indies, for instance, could heighten one's sense of "causal involvement in other lives."[123] As promise-keeping and an expanded sense of causal perception became conventional, the conditions were ripe for antislavery sentiment to mature. People thousands of miles from the Caribbean could understand themselves as responsible for the conditions of enslaved Africans on sugar plantations. Haskell argued that the market, and not class interest per se, "was one of the major factors in the expansion of causal horizons," an expansion that redounded to the spread of abolition.[124]

At this stage, the debate revolved around how best to specify the relationship between capitalism and humanitarianism: Did abolition work in the service of a hegemonic class interest or did it reflect shifts in moral conventions grounded in the expansion of the capitalist marketplace? But in the wake of Haskell's emphasis on the origins of the humanitarian sensibility, subsequent responses have proposed alternative origin stories. Notably, Christopher Brown clarified how abolitionist reform efforts crystallized in the context of British imperial conflicts, especially in the North American colonies. Colonial claims of British tyranny occasioned a debate about the morality of the British empire. This mainstreamed internal criticism of the British empire and enabled abolitionists, many of whom were already marginal for religious reasons, to criticize the slave trade and slavery without appearing as fanatical eccentrics.[125]

Peter Stamatov drew on the context of empire to propose a slightly different origin story, one focused on conflicts among political, religious, and commercial emissaries of imperial expansion. In the Spanish and British empires, a pattern of humanitarian engagement emerged. Religious actors, tasked with the salvation of souls, began to take notice of the demoralizing conditions of indigenous and/or enslaved African laborers.[126] This placed them in conflict with settlers, who were tasked with the extraction of wealth, and imperial governors, who were tasked with extending the political rule of the Crown. To make their case on behalf of indigenous and enslaved African laborers, these religious advocates developed methods of documenting abuses, circulating information, allying with exploited people, and petitioning those in Europe to push for reform.[127] Thus, as the emphasis turned to origins, religion and colonial empire have taken pride of place in discussions of humanitarianism. Capitalism seems to be too bulky and imprecise to tell us much about humanitarianism.[128]

However, if we consider the consumer activists' moral background, we can describe the relationship between capitalism and humanitarianism with greater precision. Abolitionists and turn-of-the-twentieth-century activists alike made arguments for the sympathetic consumer that depended, essentially, on capitalist circuits of commerce. As consumer activists made sense of these circuits of commerce, their moral objects and methods of argument, especially, acquired a form that mirrored them. Even if their ethical frameworks and moral background assumptions preceded the development of industrial capitalism, we can see how developments in capitalism shaped their humanitarian thought and practice. Or, said differently, even if we need not claim that industrial capitalism was a necessary precondition for the development of humanitarianism, we can still recognize its importance to the form that humanitarianism has taken.

To understand why, we need only reemphasize a distinction made initially by David Brion Davis and elided by Thomas Haskell: "[I]t is important to distinguish the *origins* of antislavery sentiment . . . from the *conditions* that favored the acceptance of this ideology among various governing elites."[129] But we can return to this distinction between origins and conditions armed with a mode of reasoning from Haskell and Abend. We must scrutinize the assumptions that underlie abolitionist moral arguments for humanitarian advocacy. After all, the manner in which they condemned slavery and sweatshops and the methods they pioneered to address these wrongs depended on their attempts to make sense of capitalist institutions. To understand how capitalism relates to humanitarianism, then, it may prove helpful for others to reassess how abolitionist visions of labor, to pick just one example, relate to elements of merchant and industrial capitalism. What matters is establishing whether or not the coherence of their moral reasoning, practices, and visions depends on specific elements of a capitalist social order. The point is, we need not see accounts of culture that invoke capitalism as hopelessly imprecise. In fact, we can render such arguments with relative clarity and precision by exploring distinct patterns of interpretations and social conditions like the sympathetic consumer.

6

The Sympathetic Consumer, Challenged

THE DEVELOPMENT of the sympathetic consumer—promoted by abolitionists, the National Consumers' League, the Women's Co-operative Guild, and the Co-operative Wholesale Society—shows us that we need not shy away from or diminish difference to discover a common pattern. For all that they shared, no one would confuse the purple bombast of William Fox's *Address to the People of Great Britain* with the sober legalism of the National Consumers' League constitution—or the celebrated "woman with the basket" of the Women's Co-operative Guild with the intrepid male voyager of the Co-operative Wholesale Society. Yet thus far I have underscored the common vision, practices, and moral assumptions that appear in and across these differences. What, then, should we make of the differences between these various activists? And what can these differences tell us about the sympathetic consumer as well as a capitalist culture? After all, we must give an account of some ways that these differences matter—not just of the differences themselves. I aim to provide such an account in this chapter.

To capture some effects of these differences, I focus on the trajectories of turn-of-the-twentieth-century activists alone. The historical details of the paths taken by the Co-operative Wholesale Society, the Women's Co-operative Guild, and the National Consumers' League are intricate. These paths, we will see, are bound up with national, organizational, class, and gender differences. Let's recall some major distinctions: As an organization of working-class men who operated and belonged to co-operative stores, the Co-operative Wholesale Society understood itself as a stalwart advocate for the working-class consumer; the Women's Co-operative Guild, in contrast, was an organization of working-class women as consumers, advocating for working-class women who neither operated stores nor were allowed to be co-operative members (though this began to shift in the first few decades of the twentieth century). Both co-operative groups, however, shared a British national identity—one that sometimes surfaced in explicit commitments to free trade liberalism. In these respects, the National Consumers' League, composed largely of upper-class women with no stores to operate or national legacies of free trade, presents a helpful foil to both co-operative groups.

These differences informed how each group developed over the period from the 1880s to the 1920s. We can see this in the ways that each dealt with specific challenges from business and labor (for a summary, see Tables 1 and 2). Trumpeting its working-class legitimacy, the Co-operative Wholesale Society remained steadfast in its clashes with labor; despite its affinity with trade unions, the CWS refused to adopt trade union standards of a closed union shop. In contrast, the Women's Co-operative Guild was unwavering in its solidarity with trade unions. This difference was bound up with gender-specific efforts to secure unions and wage parity for co-operative shop assistants and other employees—many of whom were women. Yet when the CWS and the guild confronted antagonistic merchants, they jointly affirmed a uniquely British commitment to free trade. For the National Consumers' League, the major conflicts were with labor. As a result of issues with trade unions, the NCL abandoned the clothing label that formed an important part of its early activism. This conflict underscored notable class and gender differences between the NCL and segments of the American labor movement. But in virtue of its organizational character and class background, the league depended on both the labor movement *and* manufacturers to keep its activism afloat. In sum, the conflicts with labor and business elicited distinct ways of mobilizing around and on behalf of sympathetic consumers.

The sympathetic consumer unfolded amidst these differences, which, in turn, shaped how consumer activism developed in each case. Through commodity-exchange and the institutions that underwrite it, the sympathetic consumer regulated but did not necessarily dictate the choices that activists made.[1] If, then, this consumer activism depended on a capitalist social order, it is also nevertheless true that other phenomena and tendencies informed how this pattern of sympathetic consumption evolved. We will see that when

Table 1 A summary account of labor conflicts

Consumer Activists	National Consumers' League	Co-operative Wholesale Society	Women's Co-operative Guild
Main antagonists	American Federation of Labor, trade unions with labels	National Union of Boot and Shoe Operators, trade unions with labels	Co-operative Wholesale Society
Nature of the conflicts	The NCL's label sometimes antagonized the trade unions. Union leaders worried that businesses could use the league label to obscure poor labor practices.	The CWS was unwilling to implement a closed shop (open only to trade union members) in co-operative productions. It rejected a closed shop on the grounds that it would "coerce" membership.	The women's guild challenged the CWS about the wages and status of women workers in co-operative stores and productions. The guild also insisted on the complementarity of trade unionism and co-operation.
Responses	The NCL pursued a strategy that would complement trade unions. It emphasized public neutrality as a consumers' movement vis-à-vis trade unions.	The CWS appealed to its working-class bona fides. It emphasized its status as a working-class *consumers'* movement in the face of trade unions and the Women's Co-operative Guild.	The women's guild appealed to its working-class bona fides. It emphasized its status as a *working-class* consumers' movement in co-operation with trade unions vis-à-vis the Co-operative Wholesale Society.
Outcome	Eventually, union pressure, coupled with more state investigation of workplaces, led the league to abandon the label in 1918.	The CWS did not receive the trade union label from the National Union of Boot and Shoe Operators; it persisted with the co-operative label.	The women's guild achieved some wage guarantees for women workers via the Amalgamated Union of Co-operative Employees and continued to advocate for the co-operative label.

the NCL clashed with the American Federation of Labor or the CWS clashed with the boot and shoe workers, each did so in the context of advocacy for the sympathetic consumer. But in those clashes other concerns associated with class identity, gender, and organization swayed the course of their activism. These concerns manifested in a strategic divergence of the National Consumers' League and the Co-operative Wholesale Society—the former abandoned the label while the latter persisted. As we follow the baroque historical paths of these turn-of-the-twentieth-century activists, we may further appreciate how the sympathetic consumer can appear, at once, as a condition and consequence of specific capitalist phenomena and tendencies—that is, as a pattern of interpretations and features of the social order that make each other possible.

To appreciate how these conflicts with labor and business played into the idiosyncratic development of sympathetic consumer politics, we must know something of the landscape within which these conflicts arose. Tensions emerged within and around the co-operative movement, of which the Co-operative Wholesale Society and the Women's Co-operative Guild were but two contributors. The former was, however, the most powerful in a group that included co-operative productions (not worker co-ops, but productions financed by the Co-operative Wholesale Society), banks, insurance, and educational organs. These tensions played themselves out when the CWS found itself in conflicts with labor (via trade unions and the Women's Co-operative Guild) and business (non–co-operative merchants). Next, I turn to the tensions within and around the National Consumers' League. The National Consumers' League had to quell periodic labor and business discontent with the league's policies and positions; the former took issue with NCL campaigns that impinged on labor's "territory," while the latter disliked that the NCL distinguished between "moral" and "immoral" businesses and bristled at the NCL's ties to labor. A look into these conflicts reminds us never to discount the context of application, especially if we seek that which transcends these contexts.

Co-operative Conflicts over Labor and Business

Co-operators traded in the rhetoric that everyone was a consumer—from the royals to children living in tenements or on the street. As we have seen, this was essential to their understanding of co-operative democracy. Those who stood to benefit most from this realization were the masses of working poor.

Table 2 A summary account of business conflicts

Consumer Activists	National Consumers' League	Co-operative Wholesale Society	Women's Co-operative Guild
Main antagonists	Individual business owners	Non–co-operative store owners (merchants)	Non–co-operative store owners (merchants)
Nature of the conflicts	Business owners often expressed concern that the National Consumers' League was in cahoots with trade unions. The NCL also required co-operation from the business owners to place labels on goods.	Merchants organized periodic boycotts of co-operative stores. Co-operators cast merchants as the representatives of a competitive, capitalist society.	Merchants organized periodic boycotts of co-operative stores. Co-operators cast merchants as the representatives of a competitive, capitalist society.
Responses	The NCL insisted on its public neutrality vis-à-vis labor and business.	The CWS appealed to national identity and insisted on the "un-British" coercive nature of boycotts.	The guild appealed to national identity and insisted on the "un-British" coercive nature of boycotts.
Outcome	Reinforced the systemic vision of the sympathetic consumer, with minimal disruption from the business owners.	Explicitly defined the sympathetic consumer as British, with minimal disruption from the merchants.	Explicitly defined the sympathetic consumer as British, with minimal disruption from the merchants.

Thus, co-operators eagerly branded themselves as an organization of working-class consumers, first and foremost. One Mancunian co-operator spelled out the logic:

> To me distributive co-operation is chiefly valuable because it provides a ready means of enabling workmen to translate their professions into deeds— . . . In a store, the workman is not only a consumer; he is a proprietor as well. Thus, the trade unionists of the land have it in their power to produce as partners and to purchase as enlightened and conscientious consumers, the whole being dominated by the democratic principle.[2]

 Co-operation was, principally, a means of working-class uplift. Percy Redfern described the first economic principle of co-operatives as one of "mutual effort" where the "good of one" becomes consonant with the "good of all." Early co-operators (the Rochdale Pioneers, who figured prominently in co-operative mythology) "held to the older ideal of the control of industry by the working class."[3] This emphasis on the working class was common in co-operative discussions.[4]

As groups of largely working-class consumers, both the Co-operative Wholesale Society and the Women's Co-operative Guild straddled the line between the consumer's systemically privileged position and their stated working-class identity. Consequently, debates often surfaced within the movement over the appropriate balance to strike between the interests of consumers and workers. Some emphasized "bringing members to the stores" as an elemental feature of co-operation.[5] Under these descriptions, co-operation seemed like a project engaged in "the education of the consumer," in general.[6] Others emphasized the vices of the consumer. In 1911, one society president argued that the (co-operative) movement had "become too much the slave of the consumer" and, consequently, had "lost sight of the producer." He concluded, dramatically, "Dividend is the consumers' god. If the C.W.S. has to raise the price of their goods in order to pay the women's minimum scale, it will handicap all societies that have fallen to the curse of the big dividend."[7] While the co-operators wanted to support the working masses, they sometimes agonized over the question of whether to focus on them as consumers or producers.

But co-operators weren't just workers and consumers; the Co-operative Wholesale Society was a business. Co-operative life was organized around the store, where members could receive quarterly dividends on purchases made. Further, consumer co-operatives were involved in the manufacture of goods, from boots to tea, many of which were sold in co-operative stores. In this light, the project of co-operation was to dissolve the roles of worker, owner, and consumer into the solvent of democratic, mutual uplift;[8] in practice, of course, these roles still needed to be hashed out. As workers, owners, and consumers, the co-operators tried to balance their desires to turn a profit and please consumers with their desire to give labor a fair deal. Unsavory ownership decisions to seek profit could undermine the stated commitment to workers and consumers. For instance, the appearance of boots of unknown provenance in co-operative stores, neither trade union nor co-operative made, could induce an agonizing appraisal of co-operative principles. In response to one such incident, a member of the Women's Co-operative Guild sided explicitly with labor: "Trade unionism stands for industrial order against foolish and fatal competition, self help, mutual help, the constant raising of the standards of leisure and of education—all objects dear to co-operators, are the work of unions."[9] But in that same issue, one CWS member worried that unions were unnecessary and possibly counterproductive to "ideal co-operation": "Under ideal co-operation, trade unions can have no useful place, and the most effective way I can conceive of the trade unionists bringing about the conditions they desire is for trade unionists to become co-operators."[10] These conflicting statements capture the range of co-operators' attitudes toward trade unions. But they flag another important fault line between co-operative groups: that between members of the Co-operative Wholesale Society, mostly men, and the women in the Women's Co-operative Guild. The latter tended to voice unambiguous support for trade unions, while the former was more circumspect with its support.

The CWS and the guild needed to splice together distinct functional roles of labor, capital, and consumer into a harmonious whole. Thus, the co-operators had to work to ensure that the movement didn't succumb to centrifugal forces that would wrest them apart. At the same time, they often ran afoul of non–co-operative merchants, who resented the criticisms and competition of the consumer co-operative movement. We can see what this work of adhering to co-operative principles looked like in co-operative confrontations with labor and business.

When labor challenged co-operation

While they weren't especially nasty, conflicts between trade unions and the Co-operative Wholesale Society flared up in the decades around 1900. One such conflict occurred between the CWS and several British trade unions, particularly the National Union of Boot and Shoe Operators (NUBSO). In 1911, the NUBSO was planning to introduce a trade union label to adorn boots made under trade union conditions. The union had been in communication with CWS representatives about this issue as far back as 1907. At that time, a trade union representative to the Co-operative Congress—a quarterly meeting with representatives from co-operative groups such as the Co-operative Wholesale Society and Co-operative Industries/Productions, among others— sent two resolutions for consideration: (1) asking for a pledge that "only firms recognised as 'fair' by the Trade Unions affected shall be patronised by the co-operative societies in question" and (2) "the adoption by trade societies of a label to indicate to the public that the articles produced are made by Trade Unionists will tend to diminish the manufacture of sweated and non-union goods."[11] In the ensuing discussion, one co-operator, Mr. J. Argyll, raised what was to be the sticking point: "He had found the greatest difficulty had been to get the opinion of trade unionists as to what were really 'fair' shops."[12] In addition to wage and cleanliness standards, trade unions understood a "fair" shop to mean a closed union shop, open only to workers who were a part of the union; in this case, that union was NUBSO.

But co-operators, at least those involved in the CWS, blanched at this requirement for two reasons. First, they desired that the co-operative brand be a sufficient marker of both quality and fairness. Many reasoned that the co-operative brand already signaled both qualities. Caving to the demands of the boot and shoe operators would tacitly admit that the brand did not indicate quality and fairness. As one rank-and-file trade unionist and co-operator stated, "[He] was quite satisfied with the label of the C.W.S. They paid the standard rate of wages and more. It ought to be sufficient for every man or woman in the society."[13] Co-operative advertisements always stressed the quality of CWS goods, while also often highlighting the virtuous nature of co-operative production.[14] Many CWS members thought that a trade union label would dilute the CWS brand, which should have been a guarantee of quality and fairness and working-class power on its own.

Second, co-operators were not necessarily convinced of the value of a closed union shop. In this, the CWS revealed a quintessentially British commitment to voluntarism and free trade. The chairman of the CWS, J. P. Shillito, reported, "[The CWS] would have to agree to employ only trade union labour, and they could not see their way to give such an undertaking."[15] The antagonism of CWS members to a closed shop seems to have its basis in the co-operative's affirmation of consumers as the ideal remedy to the exploitation of labor by capital, as well as their unwillingness to "coerce" the workers in co-operative factories to joining labor unions. After the editors of the *Co-operative News* demanded that the CWS leadership disclose the communications between NUBSO and the CWS, Shillito argued, "The Wholesale could not be tyrants; they must allow their employees to use their discretion with regard to their joining a union."[16] His argument also stressed that the consumer, not the producer, occupied a privileged position in industrial capitalism. When, in 1911, British food prices shot up, one co-operator interpreted the increase as the result of labor unrest: "No doubt, as a result of labour upheavals, the profits of these men will be increased, whilst the workermen's gains will be snatched from him in increased prices of food, clothing, and shelter."[17] As we have seen before, co-operators would often cast their focus on consumers as a democratic defense of working-class power. Even this co-operative opposition to a closed union shop could, then, appear as consistent with their working-class identity.

Consequently, co-operators found it galling when, in 1911, NUBSO declined to offer the co-operative boot and shoe manufacturers a union label. In the midst of a healthy debate in the *Co-operative News*, E. L. Poulton, the general secretary of NUBSO, described the negotiation process between the union and co-operatives, which dated to 1909. He wrote that co-operative leadership "had every sympathy with the objects, [but] they could not adopt the stamp because it would mean they must employ only trade unionists, which would mean 'interference' with 'individual liberty.'"[18] The NUBSO monthly reports confirm that the union received a delegation from the co-operatives in September 1909.[19] Although cordial, these negotiations never resolved the basic issues of the co-operative brand and the closed shop. As a result, the co-operatives did not receive the union label (or stamp) on their boots, much to the chagrin of both co-operators and trade unionists.

This wrangling over the trade union label induced a serious discussion of co-operative goals and purposes. As representatives of the working classes, what did it mean to co-operators that trade unionists did not officially "approve" of co-operative productions? Co-operators were not shy about their ostensive support of trade unions and the working classes. And as the flurry of correspondence generated by this conflict shows, some rank-and-file co-operators were also trade unionists.[20] Co-operators' lengthy negotiations with NUBSO led to a disappointing denouement. While the CWS affirmed its class identity as a group devoted to transforming society through the organization of (working-class) consumers, it was not recognized by the boot and shoe operators as a trade union–approved employer. At the same time, the clash also affirmed the CWS as a consumers' co-operative, in so far as it pursued these principles against the wishes as the trade unionists. But in simultaneously affirming their class and consumer identities, the co-operators insisted that they were a movement of working-class consumers. Co-operation was essentially a movement for and by the working classes.

The Women's Co-operative Guild and labor against the Co-operative Wholesale Society

These clashes with labor did not just encourage co-operators to insist on their working-class bona fides. They also underscored the salience of gender to the policies and practices of the Women's Co-operative Guild and the Co-operative Wholesale Society. The guild and the CWS quarreled over the unionization of employees at co-operative stores. The Amalgamated Union of Co-operative Employees (AUCE), formed in 1895, sought to organize co-operative employees of all stripes. In doing so, the union encountered resistance from many local co-operative leaders and members. But the AUCE found a consistent ally in the Women's Co-operative Guild, which was more than willing to defy CWS leadership. In 1893, just prior to the formation of the AUCE, the guild already voiced unqualified support for trade unions: "It will be remembered that we gave an account in our last report of the two series of conferences that the guild arranged in order to promote the alliance of the co-operative and trade unionist movement."[21] In subsequent years, the guild lent public support to laborers within the co-operative movement even when it found itself lined up against the CWS leadership. In the midst of the co-operative struggle over trade union labels, the Women's Co-operative Guild defended the unionization campaign of co-operative store employees.[22]

Before delving into the guild's support of the AUCE, however, it is crucial to recall several aspects of the relationship between the Co-operative Wholesale Society and the Women's Co-operative Guild. The Women's Co-operative Guild created a space for women to take an active role in co-operative projects and in British social life. Given that women's roles in the co-operative movement were initially restricted, the guild's insistence on women's participation was bound to disrupt business as usual. Thus, from the beginning the guild adopted a critical yet supportive stance toward the CWS. As guild members described it, they had two central aims: (1) to encourage women to take administrative roles within the co-operative movement; and (2) to address both direct issues within the movement/co-operative organization (such as educating co-operators as to their duties) and indirect issues,[23] "by helping to raise the whole status of working women by means of combination, municipal activity, and legal protection."[24] This seemingly innocuous statement exposes a basic organizational difference between the guild and the CWS: Whereas the CWS was a nonpolitical entity (i.e., it refrained from engaging in electoral politics—until the First World War, which occasioned the founding of the Co-operative Party in 1917), the guild worked actively to bring about women's suffrage and took "political" stands that threatened the "independence" of the co-operatives. The unassuming word "combination" announced the guild's active support for both trade unionism and consumer's co-operation. By referring to "municipal activity" and "legal protection," the guild promised to engage in openly political activism, from advocating women's suffrage to minimum wages for workers.[25] The guild refused to compromise on these activities, even when it led to conflict with other co-operators.[26]

Many co-operative employees—that is, those who worked in the store and in the co-operative factories—were women. This was of special interest to the Women's Co-operative Guild. It published papers about the status of working women in co-operative enterprises and in employment more generally.[27] Along with investigations of working conditions, these papers clarified the goals of guild campaigns. As guild member M. C. Spooner reported,

> Twenty-four shillings per week for a man over twenty-one years is the minimum wage adopted by the Amalgamated Union of Co-operative Employees, and already many of the societies have agreed to this minimum rate; "but," as the secretary of the Union significantly remarks, "women are not included in our minimum wage."[28]

Spooner noted, further, that "it is the distinct duty of every store member to ascertain what wages are being paid by the [local] society."[29] Pamphlets like this encouraged guild members to agitate for co-operatives and the AUCE to adopt this wage scale; this was important, especially because women were offered only limited legal protections in the workplace.

In 1906, the guild approached the AUCE with a petition to extend the minimum wage to women.[30] Two years later, the guild sent a petition to the CWS publicizing members' desires to obtain "equal pay for equal work" in co-operative factories.[31] This aligned the guild with the AUCE campaigns to extend the minimum wage standard to women. By 1909, the Women's Co-Operative Guild had mounted a campaign with the AUCE in support of a minimum wage for working women in co-operatives. In fact, the guild described this minimum wage campaign with AUCE as "perhaps the most important and far-reaching agitation which the Guild has undertaken."[32] Thus, guild members sought to prod the hesitant CWS to adopt standards in advance of the going wage rate and industry practices, particularly when it came to women.

In 1914, the guild and the AUCE convinced the CWS to adopt a minimum wage for more of their women workers. Guild representatives proudly reminded the world of their unapologetic support for trade union "principles and practices."[33] In addition to this agitation with and through the union, the guild members consistently supported trade unions in other ways, from advocating trade union goods and labels to joint political and municipal agitation. Consequently, while guild members were certainly committed to consumer co-operation, they were much less concerned about an ideological commitment to the consumer above all else—especially in the event that such commitments contradicted those of labor. When the CWS finally buckled and offered a minimum wage for women, guild members declared their support of trade unionism near and far:

> The Guild has shown its . . . desire for a working alliance between the two movements [co-operation and trade unionism] in various other ways—e.g. in carrying on propaganda among trade unionists and their wives, in subscribing to the Dublin strike, and in welcoming the wives of the South African trade unionist exiles. We have endorsed the national policy of the AUCE, as regards wages, hours, *and employment of trade unionists only.*[34]

Crucially, the guild affirmed the very principle that the CWS treated as a sticking point in their negotiations with the boot and shoe operators: the closed shop.

The guild members were not just quiet organizers in the background: They made their support of trade union goods and trade union campaigns public. For instance, in the midst of the conflict with the boot and shoe operators, the women's guild voiced unapologetic support for trade unionism: "[B]ecause our movement is becoming such a huge commercial success, more than ever we are convinced that the workers should combine in their own interests."[35] In the same article, after acknowledging that nothing but the values of co-operators prevents a "society of sweaters" from taking hold, one guild member asked,

"Then how are we to know . . . that no one suffers? . . . If our minds are to be easy, we must know that the just and well-considered demands of the employed themselves are satisfied. . . . And the label . . . seems a convenient short cut to the union's opinion."[36] Guild members built on their status as consumers to support trade unions as well as co-operation.

*   *   *

The Co-operative Wholesale Society's conflicts with labor revealed several practical "deviations" from the vision of the sympathetic consumer. In general, when the co-operators sparred with labor, they emphasized a shared class identity. When they did this, however, they also acted much more like a group of working-class consumers. But the guild further distinguished itself from the CWS on this score. Guild members took it upon themselves to agitate for change as *working-class* women within the co-operative movement of consumers. If these conflicts revealed the Women's Co-operative Guild as an organization of *working-class* consumers, the CWS appeared as an organization of working-class *consumers*. We will see how these differences in emphasis—bound up with class, gender, and organization—mattered more clearly when we look at the National Consumers' League. But the co-operators also tussled with merchants.

Un-British boycotts

One of the great bugbears of the co-operative movement was the middleman—the non–co-operative merchant who, in the co-operative imagination, leeched off of labor while exploiting consumers. Co-operators saw the middleman as an avatar of a competitive, capitalist society at odds with their mutualistic vision. The Co-operative Wholesale Society traced its origins to an organized effort to cut out the middleman. In the middle of the nineteenth century, the Rochdale Pioneers sought to create an outlet for working-class men to procure goods more cheaply by combining their resources. They did so, according to the recollections of one participant, to bring "the produce of other lands direct from the producer to the consumer, thereby saving themselves the profits of the middleman."[37] Thus, the middleman was an original antagonist to the co-operative project.[38]

But middlemen did not just sit back and take these jibes; sometimes they rose up to defend themselves against co-operators by employing a familiar consumerist strategy: the boycott. For their part, the traders objected to co-operators, who did not pay income tax because co-operative profits were distributed to members in the form of a dividend.[39] When faced with a boycott at the hands of local businessmen, co-operators—both the CWS and the guild—were unified in vociferous opposition. Rather than lead with a working-class identity, however, co-operators insisted on the "un-Britishness" of the boycott. This stance reflected a sense of England, in particular, and Great Britain, in general, as a "free trade nation," with the co-operators as the true British men and women in contrast to the parasitic, unpatriotic middlemen.

Boycotts of co-operative enterprises were a common strategy for associations of traders and shop owners who felt threatened by their co-operative competitors. In the 1890s and 1900s, regional boycotts of co-operatives regularly aroused the ire of co-operators. These boycotts of the co-operative movement were both direct and indirect. Directly, retailers or other salespeople refused to do business with co-operators. Indirectly, they threatened to withdraw business from those who did do business with co-operators. A Scottish butchers' association, for instance, "advised their [United] States and Canadian shippers to refrain from shipping cattle or sheep on board any company's steamers who are carrying cattle or sheep for any co-operative society, or for anyone who deals directly or indirectly with co-operative societies."[40] This was, obviously, an attempt to disrupt the co-operative supply chain. "But . . . the main object of the boycott," declared co-operators, "was to get rid of the co-operative societies in the purchase of American and other foreign stock . . . so as to obtain that cheap foreign meat still more cheaply when relieved from competition by the co-operators."[41] Although these boycotts were often short-lived and proved largely ineffective, the co-operators treated them as a genuine threat. The *Co-operative News* published weekly stories for the duration of several different boycotts in the 1890s and 1900s. Such boycotts were also addressed in regional and national co-operative meetings. In other words, the boycott was not just a threat to a local store but to the very principle of co-operation.

In 1902, traders began to boycott co-operative stores in St. Helens, a municipality in northwest England between Liverpool and Manchester. The 170-member St. Helens Grocers' Association decided to boycott co-operative projects and "everyone who has dealings with the co-operative society [of St. Helens, especially], and tradesmen who work for them, together with bankers, doctors, and even churches, and chapels which have any association with the stores."[42] The St. Helens traders did in fact fire some employees who belonged to or were associated with the co-operative society in St. Helens. Co-operators often pointed to the futility of boycotts from a public relations standpoint. And in doing so, they expounded on the virtues of co-operation: "The audacity of the boycott has appealed to all lovers of liberty, all social reformers, and all who see in co-operation the hope of the working-classes, and, in fact, of the nations."[43] By appealing to "lovers of freedom" and the "hope of nations," the co-operators made a more general political claim—one that could extend beyond the British Isles. At the same time, in the St. Helens boycott, the co-operators did not hesitate to align themselves with the "negative reply of the nation" over and against the traders. In a series of discussions surrounding the St. Helens boycott, co-operators raised concerns about parliamentary politics, taxation, and the (British) nation.[44]

The rhetoric of freedom and liberty conjured a uniquely British legacy of free trade in the nineteenth century. As Frank Trentmann has shown, the British commitment to free trade did not require an uncritical endorsement of competition; rather, it could be joined to a democratic culture of fairness and equity.[45] Co-operators traded on this unique, British commitment to free trade. "The English mind," "free commerce," "free trade" peppered co-operative discussions of traders' boycotts.[46] The secretary of the Co-operative Union delivered an official statement about the boycott:

> The small section of co-operators [in this case, merchants] who seek to stem the ever-growing force of co-operation by what they are pleased to call a "defense" movement object strongly to the term "boycott" being applied to their methods knowing as they well do how repulsive to the English mind both the term and the methods are when shown in their actual form.[47]

Co-operators cemented this quintessentially British identification with free trade by alluding to the public and national interests served by co-operation. George Holyoake published a series of papers dedicated to "the connection of co-operation with public interests."[48] This generic language of public interest, however, often morphed into full-fledged national and imperial identification. The editors of the *Co-operative News* drew an analogy between "Colonials [who] helped Great Britain when once war was unhappily declared in South Africa" and "co-operators outside the menaced districts" who were loyally bound to support their brethren.[49] In effect, co-operators argued that their uniquely British commitment to free trade led them to detest coercive measures like the boycott of co-operative stores. This is why the merchants would have objected to the term.

The non–co-operative merchants clearly sought a hearing with co-operatives in the court of public opinion. In response, co-operators aligned their interests with British national and imperial interests as well as a national culture of free trade. The culture of free trade entailed a commitment to unrestricted commercial exchange; restrictions on trade, for instance, were understood as bad for businesses *and* the general public because they would result in higher prices. In this context, the co-operators were well aware that "boycott" suggested coercion. To avoid such unpleasant connotations in co-operative work, co-operators aligned themselves with the moral project of educating the public as to their responsibilities. Unlike boycotts, education was voluntary. If people joined the co-operative movement upon learning about mutual effort or consumer democracy or even the dividend, they did so freely.[50]

Members of the Women's Co-operative Guild and the Co-operative Wholesale Society, for instance, hosted and advocated conferences in support of free trade policies.[51] In their educational outreach to the British public, both the guild and the CWS emphasized the non-coercive power of knowledge—it was up to individuals to join the co-operative movement. The guild aimed "to spread a knowledge of the *advantages* of co-operation," while the CWS repeatedly raised the issue of co-operative education to "raise the taste of [co-operative] members."[52] At the time of the St. Helens boycott, some co-operators observed, "[T]he question before the country at present is education, and where can there be found a more educational body than among co-operators, each important society having its educational fund, while many keep open both classes and reading rooms."[53] If co-operators were simply doing the hard work of educating the public, they could not be accused of coercing people into co-operation against their will.

When they assailed the traders' joint action as a "boycott," then, co-operators traded on this unfavorable British association of boycotts with coercion. This positioned the co-operators as simultaneously fairer and more British than the coercive traders. The boycott was inimical to "lovers of freedom," an attempt "to compel the public," and groundless "intimidation."[54] While the co-operators were not always explicit about this British culture of free trade, their language resonated entirely with its voluntarism. At the turn of the twentieth century, for instance, co-operators questioned British tax policies. Members of the CWS and the guild campaigned against taxes on sugar, corn, tea, coffee, and other national duties.[55] In a discussion of the 1895 national budget, co-operators called for the reduction or abolition of duties on coffee, tea, dried fruits, and tobacco, concluding that "all measures must be taken into a measure of relief to the poor taxpayer and consumer."[56] But co-operators made this association between boycotts, coercion, and Britishness even more explicit when reflecting on a boycott in 1897: "[T]he newspapers are unanimously of the opinion that the very worst way to fight the battle of the individual trader is the discredited and un-British boycott."[57] Even in the First World War, as the British cultural commitment to democratic and egalitarian free trade began to break apart,[58] co-operators affirmed the importance of non-coercive free trade. "For the best way to make all nations prosperous," wrote one co-operator, "is for each to supply the things that it can make best . . . and get from others the things it can get less easily or not at all."[59]

Thus, when confronted with the agitations of non–co-operative merchants, co-operators became strong British patriots. In doing so, they drew on a common narrative of Britishness supplied by the democratic language of free trade. This qualified the sympathetic consumer as a British consumer, a tension with which co-operators themselves sometimes wrestled. In support of a co-operative shopping week, a member of the Women's Co-operative Guild observed, "It should give us an opportunity of explaining to our children that to be 'All-Co-operative' is a far finer and nobler spirit than to be 'All-British,' for co-operation holds out the hand of fellowship to all kinds and conditions of men and to all nationalities."[60] Regardless, when compared with their labor struggles, the co-operators were substantially more unified in response to traders and non–co-operative merchants.

*   *   *

Ultimately, different features of consumer co-operation took on salience in these clashes with businesses and labor. A conflict with workers, whom they perceived as a friendly foe, drove co-operators' working-class origins to the surface; co-operators marked the sympathetic consumer as a working-class one. Furthermore, labor conflicts converged with gendered issues in co-operation; the Women's Co-operative Guild fearlessly cast their lot with trade unions and, where necessary, against the CWS. These working-class affinities bolstered both the efforts of the Co-operative Wholesale Society and the guild to hold their positions through these conflicts. On the other hand, a conflict with traders, whom co-operators perceived as an intransigent foe, elicited cross-class and gender identification as British. But through it all, co-operative consumer activism remained steady.

The National Consumers' League Conflicts over Business and Labor

The National Consumers' League, too, found that consumer activism could aggravate labor and business. John Graham Brooks located the real obstacles to greater justice in consumers:

> Whether the League . . . succeed or fail, let us at least understand that the responsibility lies, not without us, but in ourselves as consumers, heedless of the power we exercise. Nor is the objection valid that we cannot greatly affect the multitudinous public which chokes the avenues to the last bargain counter. The advocates of a League claim only that a distinct beginning can be made and ways opened for all who really wish to do their duty as buyers.[61]

The "multitudinous public," seeking bargains, were consumers. But at the same time Brooks left open the path to defining the consumer in more particular terms, noting the need to begin with those who wished to "do their duty." NCL members were comfortable with the notion, like the co-operators, that the work of awakening the public to their duty had to begin somewhere. Rather than the working classes, though, the consumers' leagues sought to mobilize well-to-do consumers, first and foremost.

The elevated class position of most members allowed the NCL to adopt a more conciliatory approach to both laborers and businessmen. In short, members downplayed their class positions to embody a middle way between the warring interests of capital and labor. Brooks assured businesses, "[T]he whole purpose of the League . . . need not antagonize one legitimate interest of trade."[62] They were not interfering with "legitimate" commerce, only the degrading and super-exploitative kind. But at the same time, the NCL naturally favored labor. It sought to improve conditions in retail shops "by recommending those which offer good conditions to their employees" and "indirectly to improve conditions under which goods are produced by increasing and by formulating the demand for those produced under proper conditions."[63] Even with its attenuated focus on consumers, the stated purpose was not to support business. Given this ambiguity, NCL claims to nonpartisanship could not smooth over the conflicts with business and labor. In fact, this steadfast desire to stand above class conflict exacerbated tensions between the NCL and the trade unions.

But it was not just class that played into these tensions: Gender, too, was crucial. The organizing strategy of many trade unions, including the American

Federation of Labor, traded on the leverage and legitimacy afforded by "manly" trades. The AFL leadership, in particular, worried that the inclusion of women and children would undermine its narrow, simple focus on greater wages and shorter working days. As an upper-middle-class organization of women, the NCL drew on its feminine and maternal authority to navigate tensions with labor and business groups. It embraced gendered authority to push for sympathetic consumption, labor laws, and access to workplaces. These explicitly maternalistic positions led the NCL to organize against the Equal Rights Amendment and the National Women's Party.[64] League members worried that the movement for gender-blind equity would undermine gender-based legal restrictions on working hours and conditions, many of which the NCL fought to secure. Thus, the NCL was quite comfortable with gender as an organizing principle.

In conflicts with labor and business, these gender and class characteristics enabled the NCL to maintain a rhetorical commitment to the sympathetic consumer. But these same characteristics affected the practical course of their advocacy, including the NCL's decision to abandon the label in 1918.

Working around labor: The NCL and the American Federation of Labor

When the NCL was founded, it addressed an "oversight" on the part of trade unions—women and child laborers. Many trade unions looked askance at the prospect of organizing women and children, who were perceived as defenseless; they appeared as more of a burden than a boon to union power.[65] Thus from the beginning, the NCL defined the scope of their activism on terms set by trade and labor unions. In the meetings that led to its formation, Florence Kelley defined the league's prospective work in relation to the trade union label: "the fact that the Union Label, does not ensure sanitary conditions in manufactures, and that there are no unions in the manufactures of women's and children's white underwear."[66] The first drafted constitution positioned the league's work as an extension, both in breadth and depth, of the trade union label.[67]

At the same time, the NCL resolved to avail itself of the information collected by trade unions; but the standards for awarding the label were not trade union standards. In the initial meetings on the label, representatives voted to award labels to manufacturers whose goods were made exclusively on the premises and paid a fair wage, both of which were to be confirmed by a factory inspector.[68] A manufacturer could, therefore, meet those standards without employing trade unionists. The NCL would not withhold the label from an employer who employed non-union labor at a fair wage. Ultimately, before launching its label, the NCL dropped the wage standard because it was unable to settle on a wage scale that pleased unions and addressed regional variation.[69]

Consequently, the NCL was charting its own course on trade union terrain; this led to periodic disputes. By its own admission, the NCL focused on "weaker" workers in particular—that is, women and children.[70] In 1916, New York proposed a canners' bill that permitted the employment of women over eighteen to work 12 hours a day and 72 hours a week during parts of the canning season. The labor unions supported the bill. Pauline Goldmark, a member of the Consumers' League of New York City, remarked, "[I]t had been found impossible to co-operate with the labor unions, who supported Commissioner Lynch absolutely . . . [and] there was a tendency for the employers to unite against the reformers who represent the interests of women and unorganized labor, as well as the public."[71] For strategic reasons, most likely, the unions were cautious about advocating on behalf of women workers. But many rank-and-file activists, as well as women's trade unions, were wholeheartedly opposed to the canners' bill. Eventually, the bill was vetoed by the New York Governor Charles Whitman.[72] Regardless, this conforms to a broader pattern of masculine union advocacy and feminine NCL support for less manly workers.

The NCL also took care not to draw labor's ire. For instance, a member of the Consumers' League of Kentucky described a campaign for child labor laws: "Our child labor committee, therefore, gave up their part of the work in order not to interfere with the work of the unions."[73] In this instance, the Consumers' League of Kentucky may have had a legitimate need not to duplicate the efforts of labor unions, which were involved in the investigation of conditions in factories. There were other instances where the NCL tiptoed around labor. For instance, the Consumers' League of Massachusetts consulted with Florence Kelley about providing a label to Hecht, a manufacturer of boys' knickerbockers (baggy, knee-length pants). The NCL agreed to do so on the condition that it was not found to antagonize the trade union label.[74] The point is, in this case as in many others, the NCL deferred to labor or clashed with them in its efforts to protect women and children workers.

While the NCL may have desired to avoid union reprobation, it employed a central strategy—product labeling—destined to antagonize trade unions. NCL members were aware of this. In a 1903 meeting of the labeling committee, members voted on whether to field a presentation from Mary Kenney O'Sullivan of the Union Label League. O'Sullivan "violently" opposed the consumers' league label, which she claimed the league had "stolen from the Unions."[75] While this did not yet deter the league in its labeling efforts, the dispute augured the conflict that would bring about the label's end fifteen years later. In 1911, the league considered pursuing a label in the field of knitted underwear; the label committee recommended "that as there is already a Union in the trades making knitted underwear and hosiery, the Consumers' League shall not go into this field."[76] Furthermore, NCL members were attuned to the ways that apparent competition between the National Consumers' League and trade unions, whether genuine or superficial, could benefit the aims of labor unions and consumers' leagues. As Frederick Stimson—legal counsel for the NCL— argued, "The value of the Consumers' Leagues [is] in supporting good labor conditions, etc. we cannot join with them [unions] on account of diversity of other objects, and really it is advantageous for both to work in harmony if in apparent competition."[77]

The NCL label periodically aggravated trade unionists throughout the first two decades of the league's existence. Often, the NCL had to insist that the label was not a trade union label. In 1910, for instance, the NCL's label committee resolved,

> That the Label Committee be given power to endorse from time to time (and also to withdraw such endorsements) the label of any Union which may seek such endorsement, in any industry related to the work in which the Consumers' League is engaged, provided that this label covers in its requirements the requirements established for the use of the label of the National Consumers' League.[78]

The NCL would endorse union labels, but only in the event that the workplace in question conformed to its standards. Of special concern were health and safety standards and protections for women. Given their distinct goals and strategies, there was no guarantee that a workplace that earned trade union approval would meet the NCL standards and vice versa.

By the second decade of the twentieth century, trade unions began to complain that businesses were using the National Consumers' League label as a cover for shady bargaining tactics. A business could employ the NCL label to ward off public scrutiny, while simultaneously hiring replacement workers during strikes and negotiating in bad faith. In 1916, the NCL responded to trade union complaints by changing the label contract. This revised contract included guidelines for employers who were authorized to display the label on their garments: "That there shall be inserted in the contract after due notice to the manufacturers, a clause stating in substance that where a strike occurs and arbitration is refused by employers, the contract is automatically cancelled."[79] This change was a temporary measure, and even members of the league recognized it as such. Consequently, members began to question the viability of a labeling strategy that granted owners undue leverage over workers and that exacerbated lingering tensions with the unions. The executive committee members suggested that the label problem was "so big" that they should consider a plan "which might supersede the work of the Label Committee."[80]

Early in 1918, shortly after this incident, Florence Kelley issued a "Memorandum on the Label" that laid out the problem in greater detail.[81] She cited new opposition from the American Federation of Labor to the continued use of the NCL label. Two years prior, Kelley recounted, there was a trade union strike at a factory that also had the approval to use the NCL label. A representative of the striking workers communicated to the consumers' leagues, "[U]nless the strike was immediately settled favorably to the union or, failing that, unless the NCL withdrew its label, the factory, label, and all would be subjected to a boycott." Even more troubling, Kelley reported, the AFL began to attack the consumers' leagues, "stating that employers hostile to unions affiliated with the Federation can and do use the Consumers' League label as a cloak for their hostility." Given that the NCL had no way of ascertaining whether employers who rejected the union label were using the NCL label, Kelley remarked, "[O]ur position is obviously untenable as friends of labor, if we persist in pushing our label as a rival to the label of the AFL, against the protests of union officials." Here Kelley admitted that the status of the league label was in question. But she also owned up to the implicit antagonism between trade union and the NCL labels.

Perhaps most telling, Kelley's letter acknowledged the NCL's affinity for *and* difference from labor with the phrase "friends of labor." Unlike co-operators, who could identify *as* working-class laborers, the National Consumers' League had no such option. Moreover, as friends of labor, the NCL needed to work with them and conceded that its label could antagonize trade unions. Recall that co-operators could claim to truly represent the interests of workers by pursuing their consumer activism and the co-operative brand. The Co-operative Wholesale Society, in particular, pointed to rank-and-file trade unionists who claimed, in the face of trade union opposition, that the co-operative label "ought to be sufficient for every man or woman in the society."[82] By contrast, if the NCL insisted on the value of the label in the face of sustained resistance from labor, it would have had to rescind its claim to be a friend of labor.

The juxtaposition of the NCL with the co-operators brings out the role of class politics in the eventual demise of the league label. After Kelley's memorandum, the NCL continued with the label for several months until a special meeting, which sealed its fate. After consulting the league attorneys and the executive council, Florence Kelley reported that the NCL had agreed to jettison the label within ninety days.[83] On March 18, 1918, ten days after that meeting, the NCL composed a letter to manufacturers, whom the league had furnished with a template for reproducing and affixing the label to their manufactured goods. The letter began with the following assertion:

> The Consumers' League finding that its label does not now perform the service for which it was originally devised, and believing that the aims of the League can best be promoted through other means, has for several months been considering its discontinuance.[84]

The letter celebrated the rising legal standards for industrial production as another reason for abandoning the label. And while the NCL did, in fact, continue to pursue legal means of improving working conditions, the letter declined to mention the increasingly vociferous protestations from trade unions. In November of 1918, the NCL struck the following clause from the constitution: "It shall be the special object of the National Consumers' League to secure adequate investigation of the conditions under which goods are made, in order to enable purchasers to distinguish in favor of goods made in the well-ordered factory."[85] Thus, even as it shifted away from a labeling strategy that directly antagonized labor unions, the league retained its wary, subterranean relationship with labor—especially before the eyes of businesses.

Despite losing the label to the unions, however, the league reaffirmed its commitment to its founding principles one year later in 1919. In particular, it affirmed, "Employers who are under the stress of competition are virtually helpless to maintain a high standard as to hours, wages, and working conditions, unless sustained by the cooperation of consumers."[86] Thus, the NCL remained committed to the vision of the sympathetic consumer set forth at its founding. What changed was the manner in which consumers were to make their concerns and influence known. In a sense, then, by dismantling the label, the league lost out to labor with respect to its main consumer-oriented tactic. Furthermore, when it reaffirmed the commitment to consumers as change agents, the NCL reaffirmed its commitment to a disinterested middle way between the partisan interests of capital and labor. This reflected, in part, the

NCL's upper-class constituency and was a common limitation of progressive politics.[87] In its conflict with the more working-class and masculine unions, then, the NCL actually shifted its practical work away from sympathetic consumer strategies and reaffirmed its class identification as disinterested bourgeois reformers vis-à-vis labor.

Placating manufacturers

The NCL found itself in an equally complex yet respectful relationship with manufacturers and business owners. But there was another reason for the NCL to preserve cordial relations with businesses: Namely, it needed to solicit the co-operation of manufacturers in disseminating the label. The league depended on manufacturers who would consent to allow investigators into their factories and affix the label to their products. Consequently, the NCL often mediated between competing businesses—those who felt that they were unfairly denied a label and those who felt that other businesses were unfairly awarded one. The conflicts with businesses were less vociferous and more particular than the labor conflicts. They were also less significant to the development of the NCL's practical work with one obvious exception: The initial decision to solicit the co-operation of higher-status manufacturers in the labeling campaign. Given the upper-class character of the NCL, members would have been comfortable addressing manufacturers and businesses as relative equals.

Early on, the NCL made strategic decisions about the kind of goods to target and the kinds of firms to approach. Of the 1898 meetings to plan for a labeling campaign, Kelley reported: "Our work would thus begin with more reputable firms—who should be put under legal bonds, in the use of our label."[88] To establish the label, league members decided to approach firms that produced higher-end goods. There were times when the members worried about the quality of the goods bearing the league label. As one member of the committee on advertising reported, "[An] investigation . . . showed that the goods endorsed by our League are mostly of inferior quality such as do not appeal to the class of people from which we have, as yet, largely recruited our membership."[89] Thus, the NCL planned to approach high-end firms in a way that would match the class character of their membership.

To get the label off the ground, NCL members needed to persuade such businesses to adopt it. Many businesses were hesitant to adopt first, especially without prior knowledge of the National Consumers' League as an organization. In 1898, the Consumers' League of Massachusetts sent a letter to Boston firms to prepare manufacturers for a national label. In the letter, the Massachusetts league reassured manufacturers and businesses that the league was an unthreatening presence. At the same time, the letter slyly invoked the power that could be wielded by a sympathetic public of consumers: "As encouragement in this undertaking we have the support of economists and the awakened social conscience of our time. Both of these forces recognize that trade is a matter of supply and demand, and that the demand of purchasers may be powerfully influenced by motives of justice and fairness."[90] Like the co-operators, the letter writers were attuned to the unsavory connotations of consumer activism as "coercive." They noted, "It is not in a spirit of interference or coercion, but for the purpose of educating a great body of shoppers to a better and keener sense of personal responsibility, and to a more intelligent use of their influence."[91] In addition to ideological concerns, there were practical issues to address. Among other things, manufacturers were asked to consent to periodic inspections by league members as well as to the implicit expense involved in labeling the products themselves. As NCL members throughout the country approached businesses and manufacturers, they did so with similar caution and anticipated a wary reception.

On the whole, the NCL needed to escape from a vicious circle for the label to take hold. None of the manufacturers cared to use the label unless demand warranted, and, further, none had confidence in the demand being stable— even if the league presented letters signed by consumers. At the same time, the league needed to sustain interest in the label among consumers, which would dissipate if consumers did not expect to encounter labels while shopping. Kelley described how, in the first few years of the labeling campaign, one firm's decision to adopt the label saved the campaign:

> At this discouraging moment, the George Frost Manufacturing Company undertook to use license No. 1, and proceeded to attach labels to garments sent out from their factory. The high standing of this firm rendered it comparatively easy to enlist other manufacturers.[92]

The league members had the difficult task, therefore, of asking manufacturers to take on a risky proposition, without any clear benefit in line for the first movers.

Even after some initial businesses consented to inspections and to receive the label, the NCL continued to confront resistance. Florence Kelley visited Boston, for instance, to convince a factory owner that he could stamp the label on a box rather than pin the label on each article.[93] Some manufacturers looked for reasons not to adopt the label. Kelley reported that some manufacturers refused, "because their owners are not yet convinced that the constituency of the League is sufficiently stable and persistent to justify them in undertaking the slight expense involved in printing and attaching the label."[94] By the end of the third year of soliciting and inspecting factories, the league had convinced thirty-eight manufacturers across twelve states to adopt the league label. That number increased slowly throughout the first decade of the new century.[95]

Manufacturers could also take offense at any apparent preference shown toward trade unions. One manufacturer, F. B. Hastings, wrote a letter "[p]rotesting against our [the league's] becoming identified with trades unions as exemplified by our taking part in the industrial exhibit."[96] The skittishness of manufacturers reinforced the NCL's class-inflected desire to stand apart as mediators in the war between capital and labor. Newton Baker, the league president in the 1910s, wrote as much to Samuel Gompers, head of the American Federation of Labor. Baker rejected the "natural" or "biological" antagonism between workers and employers: "To me, industrial relations, in the U.S., have for the last twenty-five years, been a war—a civil war, a class war—for which the respective sides are constantly preparing."[97] Such preparations, he reasoned, thwarted a more harmonious social order. In order to be brokers of a peace between workers and employers, the NCL deferred to both parties, seeking not to alienate either one. In interactions with trade unions, league members insisted on maintaining a position of neutrality. When John Manning, an organizer for a laundry union, solicited the NCL's help, members gladly furnished him with literature. But they were careful to preserve their "neutral attitude in the Trades Union question."[98]

While the relationship with manufacturers did not induce the league to change course, it presented obstacles in their dealings with firms on a case-by-case basis. Manufacturers did not organize in public against the NCL, but the NCL had to court individual firms to join its cause. This placed the league in a deferential relationship with manufacturers, one that was encouraged by and encouraged its class-inflected commitment to transcending the rift between owners and workers. As the NCL ended its labeling campaign, Florence Kelley told manufacturers, "For all the help you have given, the League will remain lastingly grateful."[99] While hardly revealing on its own, this statement captures the extent to which the league needed to ingratiate itself to manufacturers just for the opportunity to label goods. At the same time, the NCL supported labor in spite of their different class positions and thus depended on labor's good graces to preserve the label. Ironically, because it depended on labor and capital alike—a consequence that followed from both its class character as well as organizational structure—the NCL appeared as a neutral intermediary between two warring factions.

The Vagaries of History

What are we to make of these conflicts with business and labor? It will not do to insist either (a) that the sympathetic consumer was irrelevant to these clashes or (b) that nothing mattered save for the sympathetic consumer. These conflicts clearly depended on activists' efforts to encourage sympathetic consumption. But specific aspects of group identity and structure informed the development and resolution of these conflicts. A brief comparative summary brings out several overarching themes: organization, class and gender, and national identity.

For one, we can see how organizational form and context mattered. Distinct organizational structures may help to explain why these activists either caved to various demands of labor and business or stood their ground.[100] The Co-operative Wholesale Society operated stores. As such, its existence depended on people becoming members of the stores and spending money there. The CWS needed people to consume. Thus, the CWS depended on consumers in a unique and direct manner; it had a "natural" investment in them. When challenged by labor in particular, the CWS leaned on this organizational imperative to support its broad identification as a consumers' movement. Despite some members' assertions that "something is wrong with the co-operation that is not prepared to give an equal guarantee to that given [to labor] by private makers," the CWS stood firm.[101] In contrast, the Women's Co-operative Guild had more organizational flexibility than its wholesale counterparts. Committed though the guild was to consumer co-operation, it was not beholden to consumers in the same way. This flexibility was on display as the guild sided with trade unions when the latter came into conflict with the CWS, especially conflicts over unionizing co-operative employees. Though not beholden to consumers in the same way, the NCL depended on both labor and business. Ironically, this organizational weakness may have reinforced the NCL's embrace of consumers as peaceful mediators between capital and labor. But this did not preclude legal advocacy, which offered the NCL a fallback not explicitly directed toward consumer mobilization.

Another comparison reveals how social identifications like class and gender mattered. In the CWS, the conflicts with trade unions elicited unapologetic appeals to co-operators' own working-class authority. Co-operators' identified themselves as working-class *consumers* above all else. But this established the CWS as supporters of working-class improvement. This identification as working class actually reinforced the consumerist tactics of the CWS while simultaneously qualifying its bolder systemic vision of the sympathetic consumer. These same conflicts exposed the working-class character of the Women's Co-operative Guild. But rather than identify as working-class *consumers*, guild women identified as *working-class* consumers. To fully understand this consequence, we need to recall co-operative gender dynamics. Given the significant but unappreciated roles that women played in the co-operative movement as both employees and as consumers, the conflicts with trade unions offered the opportunity to improve the station of women. It was also an opportunity to challenge many co-operators' assumptions that co-operation was a masculine endeavor. Thus, these conflicts brought out the guild's working-class backgrounds and highlighted co-operative gender dynamics.

Analogous conflicts underscored the classed and gendered character of the National Consumers' League, too. Labor and business conflicts encouraged the NCL to embrace its maternal role as protector of workers whom major trade unions often ignored. At the same time, these conflicts reinforced the class distance between the NCL and the labor unions. They also elicited class-based attempts to identify with the business owners, whom the NCL needed to enroll in its labeling campaign. Ultimately, the conflicts with business and labor had an inverse effect on the National Consumers' League and the Co-operative Wholesale Society: For the NCL, these conflicts reinforced the systemic vision of the sympathetic consumer, while they qualified its consumerist tactics; for the CWS, these conflicts qualified the systemic vision of the sympathetic consumer, while they reinforced its consumerist tactics.

Finally, we can see how national culture mattered. Co-operators and merchants jockeyed for better standing in the court of public opinion. Rather than accentuate their working-class bona fides as they did in conflicts with workers, the struggle with other merchants led co-operators to accentuate their Britishness. In particular, they arrayed free, British co-operation against the merchants' coercive and un-British boycotts. These strategic appeals traded on the common British association of free trade with freedom and protectionism with slavery. The National Consumers' League sometimes worried about the association between "preferential dealing" and coercion. But the NCL did not find itself in truly antagonistic conflicts with business that drew members into debates over national belonging. Where the co-operators treated business as a threat, the National Consumers' League needed them as potential allies. Perhaps because the NCL depended on both business and labor, it rarely antagonized them openly. This could have diminished any incentive to shift disagreement onto the terrain of national belonging. Further, without an established sense of the United States as a "free trade nation," such a conflict perhaps could not have shifted to such terrain.

A Capitalist Culture

With these observations in mind, we arrive at one plausible description of how a capitalist culture can work: People encounter phenomena like commodity-exchange; they interpret these phenomena in ways that build upon available conventions and ideas as well as the qualities of the phenomena in question; as people develop and elaborate on such interpretations through their actions, the sense and coherence of these interpretations comes to depend on those phenomena—it can appear as if the interpretations issue from the phenomena themselves; finally, these interpretations orient people as they engage with the world. To people who share in them, these interpretations will not dictate or determine what they do. Rather, the interpretations present, emphasize, discourage, or rule out possible strategies, as when the NCL pursued a product labeling strategy that vexed trade unions or the CWS challenged trade unions over the principle of a closed shop. Such interpretations both depend on capitalist social conditions *and* remain open to more contingent influences. In the face of challenges from labor and business, the visions and practices of the sympathetic consumer shifted in significant ways. Such shifts reveal the capaciousness of this particular cultural pattern of interpretations and social conditions—the sympathetic consumer does not appear to command fealty, but only makes it possible. As such, no one had to become a sympathetic consumer. The activists' received no mandates from this capitalist social order to feel, reflect on, and act in the world as sympathetic consumers. Nevertheless, it would be folly to insist that the sympathetic consumer did not depend on certain capitalist phenomena like commodity fetishism. In this way, the interpretations that belong to a capitalist culture can appear, at once, to follow from *and* to produce conditions in a capitalist social order.[102]

7

Whither the Sympathetic Consumer?

I CAN NOW OFFER a more precise account of the sympathetic consumer as a coherent pattern of interpretations and social conditions that emerges from a capitalist social order. It manifests in visions, practical strategies, and moral arguments wherein the consumer plays a vital functional and ethical role in the world. In this role, the consumer "feels with" those who produce goods and makes purchasing decisions on the basis of those sympathies. The sympathetic consumer highlights certain ways that people make sense of commodity-exchange as well as the social conditions that make it possible—efforts that have recurred in distinct phases of capitalist development. Consequently, the sympathetic consumer depends on a capitalist social order for its coherence. Without those interpretations *in* and *of* commodity-exchange—and without the institutional order that undergirds those interpretations—the sympathetic consumer, if it could even exist, would make a very different kind of sense. A world characterized by commodity fetishism makes the sympathetic consumer possible.

Just as important, while activists in different times and places have promoted sympathetic consumption, these times and places informed the consequences and evolution of their activism. This tells us, moreover, that to speak of the sympathetic consumer and a capitalist culture does not require anyone to ignore or suppress difference; these patterns must necessarily work through difference.[1] Thus, to discuss the sympathetic consumer does not preclude other ways of making sense of capitalist phenomena—even other partially conflicting patterns that arguably belong to a capitalist culture like *homo economicus*, the utility-maximizing individual. As such, the sympathetic consumer can coexist alongside many other patterns of interpretation and social conditions specific to a capitalist culture. In fact, the sympathetic consumer calls attention to a long, tangled history of capitalism, liberalism, and sympathy; it shares in the tragic virtues and drawbacks of many humanitarian projects spawned throughout this history.[2] Such attentiveness to difference reminds us, further, that the sympathetic consumer is not a mere expression of technical laws of capitalist development.

Yet the sympathetic consumer is almost uniquely bound to capitalist development. Its advocates seek to conjure the world that stands behind commodity-exchange—to dispel the fog of dreams, anxieties, schemes, habits, needs, and values that motivate our purchases. Further, these advocates insist that the world behind these motives and anonymous goods deserves special consideration and requires self-conscious imagination to discern. This does not establish the sympathetic consumer as the one, true meaning of consumption in capitalist societies. But it does indicate a unique interpretation of consumption—one arrived at by journeying back through a commodity's systemic conditions of possibility. This journey vests the interpretation with a structure—in thought and practice—that mirrors the world out of which it has evolved. The vision of the consumer organizes a range of practices and necessitates moral arguments in defense of the consumer. And this vision, these practices, and moral arguments reflect the capitalist social order through which they have emerged. The sympathetic consumer is, in this sense, both a condition and a consequence of specific aspects of a capitalist social order. In other words, the interpretations make possible many kinds of consumer activism and commodity-exchange, even as those interpretations are made possible by commodity fetishism, depersonalized labor, and the spread of commodification.

But what about the sympathetic consumer today? There are, at a glance, some obvious places to look for possible contemporary manifestations. Recall Fashion Revolution's "social experiment" with the two-euro t-shirt, which revealed the sweatshop labor behind that low price. All manner of goods can be purchased or certified fair trade—food, clothing, handicrafts, and more. Many animal products on the market involve claims about the conditions of production that sound familiar: "cage free," "free range," "sustainably grown." There are endless opportunities for "green" purchasing and eco-tourism. Farther afield, there are guides to socially responsible investing that cater to various political tastes. The world of humanitarianism allows people to invest in suffering communities, who labor to demonstrate that their suffering is worth humanitarian aid.[3]

Fortunately, we don't need to speculate wildly about the sympathetic consumer of today. We can look for three crucial features: (1) the vision of the consumer, (2) the repertoires of practices used to encourage sympathetic consumption, and (3) the moral assumptions in arguments for the sympathetic consumer. In what follows, I trace some obvious parallels between fair trade and earlier versions of consumer activism, especially to the integrated movement of consumer co-operatives. But I also reflect on what we might discover when we look beyond consumer activism to business rhetoric, particularly the self-described "worldwide movement" called *conscious capitalism*—a business-centered approach to leading lives of purpose and changing the world.[4] This will, in turn, help to highlight what we can learn from the sympathetic consumer and a capitalist culture.

The Vision of the Sympathetic Consumer

I showed, first, how abolitionists and turn-of-the-twentieth-century activists shared a vision of the sympathetic consumer—one that questioned the taken-for-granted nature of commodity-exchange. In this vision, the sympathetic consumer stood at the heart of a capitalist system of production, distribution, and exchange. Further, the consumer had a responsibility to feel with invisible laborers along these circuits of commerce. By abstaining from the wrong goods and choosing the right ones, activists claimed, consumers could make their sympathies felt.

This vision turns up in many fair trade organizations. Equal Exchange—for profit, worker-owned purveyors of fair trade coffee, tea, sugar, bananas, avocados, cocoa, and chocolate—describes its mission:

> [T]o build long-term trade partnerships that are economically just and environmentally sound, to foster mutually beneficial relationship between farmers and consumers, and to demonstrate, through our success, the contribution of worker co-operatives and Fair Trade to a more equitable, democratic, and sustainable world.[5]

When consumers buy the right kinds of things and avoid the wrong kinds, they contribute to an "equitable, democratic, and sustainable world." "Consumers,"

Equal Exchange writes, "do have the power to change the way supermarkets do business."[6] Throughout its report, Equal Exchange appeals to "citizen consumers," a reminder of the responsibility that consumers have to purchase with intention and to foster social well-being.[7] The imperative to sympathize, too, remains evident. In a picture on the cover of the 2018 *Equal Exchange Annual Report*, a Peruvian cacao farmer grins as she shows an Equal Exchange employee "how to graft, prune, harvest, and extract" cacao beans.[8] Equal Exchange writes of the desire to "humanize the food system"[9] and to reveal the challenges and successes of laborers throughout the supply chain. We are asked, as consumers, to "feel with" those involved in food production. In these descriptions of a humane food system, the vision of the sympathetic consumer is alive and well.

But these visions migrate beyond the world of fair trade and worker co-ops, though sometimes appearing as in a funhouse mirror. Whole Foods CEO John Mackey and business professor Raj Sisodia, missionaries for "conscious capitalism," ask people to "think of a business that cares profoundly about the well-being of its customers, seeing them not as consumers but as flesh-and-blood human beings whom it is privileged to serve."[10] They define conscious capitalism as "an evolving paradigm for business that simultaneously creates multiple kinds of value and well-being for all stakeholders: financial, intellectual, physical, ecological, social, cultural, emotional, ethical, and even spiritual."[11] The key word here is "stakeholder." Mackey and Sisodia promote "stakeholder integration" as one of conscious capitalism's main tenets. Stakeholders are "all the entities that impact or are impacted by a business," including the customers, suppliers, employees, investors, community, environment, and company.[12] The conscious capitalist recognizes "that [among these stakeholders] customers are the reason the business exists."[13] Even as they take a corporate perspective, the businesses ostensibly serve the customer—which suggests that, in this vision, consumers regulate this ecology of "stakeholders." Where others have trumpeted the need for consumers to sympathize, Mackey and Sisodia elevate the need of the business to sympathize with consumers: "We have to satisfy . . . customers in terms of what they want in the moment, while steering them toward better choices over time."[14] This requires consumers, or customers, to trust the corporation. In the case of Whole Foods, Mackey claims this trust can help consumers navigate a minefield of unhealthy, processed foods.[15] Although the conscious capitalists displace ethical responsibility onto corporations rather than consumers, they still manage to sing a familiar refrain. "Ultimately," they admit, "our customers 'vote with their money' every time they shop."[16] This language of consumer citizenship returns us to the basic image of the consumer at the heart of capitalist commerce.

In the world of conscious capitalism, the question of consumer sympathy appears to be, at least in some senses, flipped. It is the benevolent corporation that "feels with" the consumer. As usual, sympathy reveals the work of power—Whole Foods "feels with" consumers to build and retain a share of the market. Consumers, for their part, sympathize with a company's "higher purpose" as much as the workers behind the goods. Further, there is a more elaborate ecology of "stakeholders" into which consumers have been fitted. At the same time, it would be a mistake to overlook the persistence of these familiar ideals. Whatever their reasons, advocates of corporate responsibility pay obeisance to the consumer who feels, who commands, who cannot be escaped.

Ways of Seeing

Early consumer activists employed strategic ways of seeing to cultivate sympathetic consumption. Consumers needed enriched and expanded ways of seeing to penetrate commodities and the obfuscations that grew around them—anonymous goods and labor, manias for cheapness, thoughtless purchasing, advertising, selfishness. Imaginative ways of seeing joined consumers to producers with detailed descriptions of the conditions behind the production, distribution, and exchange of commodities. Prose and poetry engaged imaginations by aestheticizing the suffering and toil underlying consumer goods. Sensuous ways of seeing joined consumers to producers with images that consumers could see with their eyes and products they could touch, smell, and taste. Product labels, artwork, photography, exhibitions, and demonstrations placed goods in a new context, one that rendered those unseen chains of dependence sensible. These ways of seeing taught consumers to understand their purchases in terms of the conditions that made them possible and the consequences of their manufacture.

Such ways of seeing appear in fair trade purchasing schemes and advocacy. As one might expect, sensuous ways of seeing, in particular, have proliferated. The annual reports of Equal Exchange feature dozens of pictures of farmers, fields, and distributors—all along the length of the supply chain.[17] The story is the same for the Fair Labor Association, Fashion Revolution, Ten Thousand Villages, and many other organizations devoted to supply chain transparency.[18]

Scan the packages of chocolate bars, coffee, and tea, and you will often find fair trade labels and pleasing images of farmers and other agricultural laborers. Self-described ethical clothing purveyors like Everlane allow you to peek inside factories on four different continents via its website.[19] Tech-savvy groups like Fashion Revolution encourage viral online campaigns where consumers can demand transparency and fair labor practices from brands by asking them #whomademyclothes. Workers, too, can share pictures of themselves holding signs that read "I made your clothes."[20]

And, in almost all of these cases, sensuous ways of seeing are accompanied by imaginative ones. As with earlier activists, their literature focuses on the equitable and healthy conditions of labor along fair trade supply chains, with added concerns about ecological and environmental sustainability. Equal Exchange sketches an equitable picture of banana production:

> In Ecuador, we brought the entire supply chain together from farmer to exporter to importer to ripener to distributor to store. In a conventional supply chain, these different players all operate in their own spheres, doing what they do best. . . . During this week long trip, all the participants came together as equal partners, sitting together at the same table, to share their successes, challenges, and realities with each other.[21]

Everlane's portrayal of its supply chain includes a summary of the factory history and character. Of a factory in Ho Chi Minh City, Everlane writes,

> We always issue a strict compliance audit to account for ethical practices on-site—and our Nylon Bag Factory got one of the highest scores we've seen yet. Employees here make above the local minimum wage and enjoy a number of benefits, like an on-site cafeteria, a soccer field, and a special gift on every birthday.[22]

Coupled with many intimate pictures, these descriptions personalize the laborers and their lives in and around the factory. All of this should be quite familiar by now.

With their focus on the corporation, conscious capitalists gesture obliquely toward sympathetic ways of seeing. Beginning with consumers, Mackey and Sisodia detail "the higher purpose of marketing." In the words of former Trader Joe's president Doug Rauch,

> Since conscious businesses are purpose-driven organizations that are aligned with their stakeholders, they do not need to use marketing as a way to stimulate

or create interest that otherwise wouldn't be there. They can honestly share what's true about their product or service. They don't try to create demand artificially and temporarily; they just authentically communicate and connect with people around their common values.[23]

There aren't any evident ways of seeing here. These businesses foreground the responsibility of the business over the consumer. Earlier movements, especially the co-operative movement, emphasized the responsibility of the consumer. Thus, when discussing suppliers, conscious capitalists present businesses as mediators between suppliers and consumers: "Whole Foods Market is in direct and daily communication with our customers, and we can give feedback to our suppliers network regarding exactly what our customers like or don't like about their products."[24] In one sense, then, a business like Whole Foods provides images of the consumer to the producer who can't see them—effectively reversing the process described in this book.[25]

Yet, in another sense businesses like Whole Foods build their brands on the backs of suppliers who foster ways of seeing for consumers. The suppliers to Whole Foods package products that often suggest wholesome origins. If consumers buy those products, Whole Foods—which "is in direct and daily communication" with consumers—reports back to the suppliers. For their part, Whole Foods can simply stock fair trade goods bearing labels, images, and other sensuous strategies for sympathetic consumption. When they do so, Whole Foods becomes the brand that reliably stocks fair trade and organic goods. As such, Whole Foods becomes a trusted curator of virtue; consumers can see and imagine their relations to those invisible laborers and the whole systemic infrastructure by means of the corporate brand.[26] This parallels the strategy of the Co-operative Wholesale Society. The CWS wanted its brand to stand for quality and justice. Thus, co-operators fretted over events that tarnished the brand such as the discovery of sweatshop goods in co-operative stores. In this way, conscious corporate branding works as an imaginative and sensuous way of seeing that promotes the "conscious customer"—a clear descendent of the sympathetic consumer. It is as if the sympathetic consumer has been refigured with language drawn from a dictionary of late twentieth century marketing and self-help buzzwords.

There are even moments where conscious capitalists employ ways of seeing explicitly. In their discussion of the "environment" as a stakeholder, Mackey and Sisodia outline the Whole Foods approach to seafood sustainability: "We label all of our seafood with MBA [Monterey Bay Aquarium], BOI [Blue Ocean

Institute], and MSC [Marine Stewardship Council] ratings, using a color-coded system based on the degree of sustainability."[27] There is, at the same time, pervasive rhetoric about value-creation throughout the supply chain, from suppliers and consumers to the community and environment. Conscious capitalism "aims to generate multiple kinds of value for all its stakeholders," which only occurs when one finds a higher purpose that "transcends making money."[28] This nebulous language of shared value-creation encourages various participants, including consumers, to form rosy images of the "complex, adaptive" systems of which businesses are the linchpin.[29] Mackey and Sisodia propose that, "[T]o build a great conscious company, leaders need to intentionally shape their culture from the beginning—a culture that reflects, supports, and leverages the full humanity of all its stakeholders."[30] Unlike the consumer activists, there is no painstakingly rendered imagery of the labor process. In fact, labor more or less dissipates into the ether of good feelings. When paired with the corporate brand and labeling practices, this language of value-creation and shared humanity loans consumers a feel-good image of the labor behind their goods. If the company cares about the humanity of all its stakeholders, then must not the supply chain be humane? The sympathetic consumer has been folded into a corporate branding project.

Once again, there are obvious continuities between fair trade practices and earlier consumer activists. The tools evolve with the technology, but the basic repertoire of tactics for seeing centered around the sympathetic consumer remain familiar. When, as in the framework of the conscious capitalists, the sympathetic consumer becomes one "stakeholder" among many, these ways of seeing become the task of specific "suppliers" or appear in the form of corporate branding. The sympathetic consumer recedes into the background, only coming into focus when we fix our gaze on the relevant "stakeholder" relationships.

Moral Justifications and Arguments

Third, along with these ideals and practices, the sympathetic consumer entailed distinct moral background assumptions. These justifications and arguments came to depend on claims about the consumer's place in capitalist production, distribution, and exchange. By tracing the consumer's links to others, especially the nameless and faceless laborers along the supply chain, activists laid the foundation for their interpretations of consumption and, in particular, their arguments about the consumer's moral obligations.

In contemporary fair trade, we can see this sensitivity to the institutions and networks entailed in capitalist production. The moral arguments for ethical purchasing develop almost exclusively via the elaboration of supply chains—the harms of a mainly profit-seeking system and the virtues of one in which goods are traded fairly. Equal Exchange describes the "value chain" of smallholding, cooperative producers and distributors that deliver coffee to consumers. This includes threats to the livelihood of these producers and distributors: "climate change, political violence, migration, market consolidation, and dominance by transnational capital."[31] To help farmers ward off such systemic threats, Equal Exchange asks for "three easy things": "[S]end us good energy, drink coffee, contribute to the DAF [Donor Action Fund]."[32] Such a recommendation foregrounds the role that consumers play in this supply chain, as purchasers of goods and as donors.

Stories of the supply chain enable consumers to read the rising or falling prices of commodities as signs that communicate system dynamics. Supply issues in the world of chocolate, for instance, speak to the "real impact of climate change" on smallholding cacao farmers.[33] The moral arguments unfold via accounts of the harms attendant to a "corporate controlled food system."[34] The citizen consumer has a responsibility to contribute to a "social economy" that forestalls exploitation and ecological destruction. These arguments and justifications suffuse other fair trade projects as well. Fashion Revolution describes a supply chain characterized by ecological degradation and exploitation, as well a culture that motivates the dysfunction: "[E]ncouraging students, educators, and the wider public to understand the provenance of clothing and to connect with the stories of the people who make them, is fundamental in creating an emotional attachment to the clothes we wear, and in challenging the unsustainable culture of throwaway fashion."[35] This statement places commodification at the heart of an "unsustainable culture." After all, it suggests that the depersonalization of goods thwarts our ability to build emotional attachments to our clothing. And the antidote to such a morally decadent culture lies in personalizing those goods. The argument for a fashion revolution, then, requires one to identify the consumer's place within a network of production, distribution, and exchange.

In the world of conscious capitalism, the arguments and justifications depend similarly on capitalist social institutions—depersonalized goods, voluntary exchange, supply chains, the modern corporation. This is clearest in what Mackey and Sisodia call the "Win^6" approach to "stakeholder integration."

"Conscious businesses," they elegize, "engage the limitless power of human creativity to create win-win-win-win-win-win . . . solutions that transcend those conflicts and create a harmony of interests among the interdependent stakeholders."[36] The idea that everybody in the orbit of a conscious business wins—the consumers, suppliers, the local community, environment, employees, and investors—also requires that one imagine the links between these distinct stakeholders. A workbook includes strategies for the conscious capitalist to identify stakeholders and map their needs, with the goal of "creating shared value" for all involved.[37] Bill George, a business school professor and former CEO, depicts the "interdependent nature of a company's stakeholders" with the idea of a virtuous circle: "[I]t starts with the company's purpose and values, which serve to attract and inspire the right team members. This leads to innovation and superior customer service, which then leads to improved market share and higher revenues, profits, and eventually shareholder value."[38]

Compared to contemporary fair trade advocates and their predecessors, the details of these links in the chain are more abstract. Stakeholders can approach their relations with the other stakeholders in one of two ways: competitive or constructive. The constructive, everybody wins approach stands in stark contrast to the competitive, zero-sum one. What Mackey and Sisodia refer to as "stakeholder cancer," or lack of cooperation between stakeholders, commonly results from selfish pursuits of various stakeholders—in the book, they single out shareholders, management, and "team members" (that is, employees—unsurprisingly, unionized ones are especially selfish).[39] But to recognize this proposed truth about the capitalist world—stakeholder interdependence—requires "holistic systems intelligence."[40] Such intelligence arises when one can see the "living relationships" between the stakeholders in a business and by mapping the relations between them.[41] While these "living relationships" are little more than glittering generalities, the phrase bears a hefty moral and analytical load. When one takes measure of these living relationships, the moral choice becomes obvious—everyone should win. What kind of monster would want some stakeholder to lose? In this way, the moral argument in favor of conscious capitalism evolves out of an ironically lifeless and sterile picture of a capitalist world as a complex adaptive system.

The capitalist supply chain—its structure and dynamics—works its way into these moral arguments and justifications for fair trade and conscious capitalism. The consumer's moral role is revealed, as before, via an elaboration of the system that joins consumers to producers (or, in the argot of conscious capitalism, joins various stakeholders). The sympathetic consumer, therefore, takes stock of her world and appreciates the relationships that make it all possible. In so doing, the right course of action becomes clear. Unlike previous accounts, however, contemporary justifications less frequently devolve onto explicitly articulated moral foundations. Christian and even rights-based deontological grounds give way to a lightly worn consequentialist argument about the greater social good that results from ethical purchasing and business. There is plenty of room for the consumer to read their preferred moral reasons into such generic notions of the social good. Further, the personal moral urgency on display in earlier forms of consumer activism more or less evaporates. Where the earlier advocates of the sympathetic consumer spoke an uncompromising language of grand moral imperatives, these contemporary advocates cast such imperatives aside. Rather, they lead the consumer to the desired conclusion as if nervously laying out a trail of breadcrumbs.

Beyond the Advocates

Propelled to the foreground by activists since the late eighteenth century, the sympathetic consumer is evident in three centuries of capitalist development. To be sure, this figure has evolved with the times and places where it has become a public issue. As its advocates have shifted, new and different features have come into relief. It is, as I just mentioned, difficult to imagine the "thought leaders" behind conscious capitalism summoning any of the moral urgency that inspired many earlier consumer activists. But the basic, patterned elements of the sympathetic consumer remain. The visions, practices, and assumptions of fair trade advocates or conscious capitalists still convey the consumer's distinct moral role.

Yet the sympathetic consumer does not depend on advocates alone. It depends just as much on the materials through which the sympathetic consumer has been, and continues to be, constructed: the vehicles and people that bear goods to stores and homes; the markets many pass by and through regularly; the depersonalized goods many pick up and put down in those markets; the money with which we purchase these goods; the reflections on commodity-exchange that, sometimes, alight on the other people and places these goods have seen. These phenomena aren't uniquely available to advocates of the sympathetic consumer or even to those who can afford the luxury of paying more for "ethical" goods. The intoxicating power of this vision relies on intuitions that make sense because of the way exchange works in a capitalist society. This vision appeals to thoughts that you or someone you know have very likely had—regardless of whether those thoughts stayed with you or whether you have had the luxury to buy ethically sourced goods. It arises through our efforts to make sense of a world where commodity-exchange can be taken for granted.

Consequently, we don't simply impose a vision of the sympathetic consumer onto the world in which we find ourselves; just as our eyes bear the imprints of the light reflecting around us, this moral vision bears the impressions of our world. Too often, many critics of capitalism laugh off these efforts to make business or "economic life" moral as pure fantasy or delusion. There is no morality and no capitalist culture but the effort to maximize profit, they might claim. They suggest that the banal world of capitalist economic life is hostile to everything but self-deluding moral sentiment or bad faith. But if we are to understand the workings of capitalist societies, we must realize—whatever their efficacy or plausibility or even virtue—that distinct moral visions make sense within these societies.[42] These moral visions depend on and gain their appeal from phenomena that are anything but exclusive to the advocates and zealots who take up these causes. Even if we question the relevance or efficacy of sympathetic consumption, and indeed we should, we must recognize that it makes a kind of sense—not only as a feature of liberal ideology and belief, but through the everyday phenomenon of depersonalized goods in exchange. This is the profound lesson of commodity fetishism.

Possibilities and Limits of Consumer Activism

Taking in the trajectory of the sympathetic consumer from the eighteenth century to the present, there is an opportunity to make some informed observations about the possibilities and problems of consumer activism. I offer these not as falsifiable historical or sociological judgments, but as a matter of broader public concern. Whatever its virtues, to the extent that activism unfolds via the purchase of goods by consumers, it will have certain limitations. After all, to return to the matter of commodity fetishism, consumer activism assumes the very thing that it seeks to overcome—the fundamental anonymity of commodities and labor to consumers in the marketplace.[43] This is true whether the activism in question focuses on the labor conditions in and along the supply chain or, more generally, on issues related to the origins, production, safety, and value of goods.[44] Thus, these movements and activism, to the extent that they work alone, can only weakly address issues that are connected to fundamental features of capitalist societies: alienation and labor domination, climate change, globalized racial and class hierarchies, to start.

But this does not mean that consumer activism of some kind has absolutely no place in movements that seek to address such things. Others have written extensively about the contributions of consumer activism to legal transformations, movements for civil and social rights, the creation of international organizations to monitor labor and environmental conditions, and some changes in specific corporate practices.[45] Consumerist tactics have contributed to anti-imperial and anti-colonial campaigns, as well as pro-imperial and pro-colonial ones. They have served nationalist and internationalist movements. Abolitionist consumer advocacy helped to popularize the antislavery campaigns and a model of humanitarian advocacy on behalf of distant strangers. Turn-of-the-twentieth-century consumer activists aided in the push for legal wage protections, early welfare state institutions like the Food and Drug Administration, and official oversight of workplaces. Moreover, these groups—both abolitionists and turn-of-the-twentieth-century activists—established networks of like-minded advocates across nations and continents.

To the extent that they contributed to these changes, consumer activists engaged in collective advocacy—as public pressure groups and activists. They expected that people would not simply play their role as consumers. This consumer activism was tied to the development of mass political and social movements, to collective education projects, and to direct action against offending parties. On this score, there is a stark contrast between earlier iterations of the sympathetic consumer and many of my contemporary examples. The former chart ways for people to participate in public, political life, while the latter focus more on people's consumer choices as politics. Abolitionists and turn-of-the-twentieth-century activists carried out public research, investigated workplaces, participated in organizational meetings, and petitioned political bodies. They advocated consumer activism as members of activist groups. They sought, in a sense, to de-privatize consumption by embedding it in public activism. By way of contrast, many contemporary advocates of sympathetic consumption have shrunken, if not eliminated, that space for activism. To the familiar claims that such shifts resulted from the neoliberal devolution of politics to personal choice, we might also point to the growing scope, scale, and complexity of capitalist production.[46] It is simply more difficult to pull off that kind of work from the perspective of the consumer now. In this light, claims about the democratic nature of contemporary marketplace activism appear less convincing.[47]

It stands to reason that, if it is to contribute to more profound social changes, consumer activism must display a more robust collective and political character. But my account of the sympathetic consumer reveals a less appreciated possibility as well as problem: how consumer activism encourages people to think systemically. If the problems addressed by consumer activists issue from a system of terrifying complexity, almost incomprehensible in scale and scope, then creating an image of that system will be a crucial part of figuring out where the problems, weaknesses, or possibilities for change lie—whatever politics and strategies one endorses. We have seen, repeatedly, how advocates of the sympathetic consumer encouraged people to imagine the relations of production in which they were wittingly or unwittingly enmeshed. To build this imagination, they depicted the invisible chains that linked consumers to the faceless people and nameless places through which commodities traveled. With these depictions of commodity chains, activists advanced unsparing moral arguments. These arguments were unsparing because once these links in the chain became visible, it was easy to imagine that commodities conveyed ultimate responsibility for workers' suffering to consumers in a capitalist system.

In many ways, despite activists' arguments to the contrary, these arguments and imaginative raw materials point people beyond consumer activism. That image of the sympathetic consumer puts all of us purchasers in a state of dependence on things that we would otherwise struggle to endorse. When it tempted consumers with a two-euro t-shirt in Berlin, Fashion Revolution played on precisely this struggle. Of course, it strains credulity to indict consumers as primary agents of the many harms that result from such a terrifyingly complex system, even if we confine ourselves to the world's wealthiest people and nations. After all, the consumers are also, as Horkheimer and Adorno noted, products of this complex capitalist system. But indict these images do. Through these portrayals of consumer power and complicity, people learn to imagine the capitalist social order: its contours, tendencies, and essential features. These portrayals may also motivate or amplify one's concern for the suffering that this social order produces and allows. Ironically, then, the sympathetic consumer hints that there is much more to do than buying the right things. This is what I mean when I say that consumer activists' imaginative tools transcend their relatively narrow range of strategies and tactics.

For these very reasons, this image of the sympathetic consumer harbors a seductive, twofold danger. Taken literally, this moral picture of the consumer's role in a capitalist society can lead merely to consumerism. If the way out of exploitative or expropriative relationships, entrenched social hierarchies, and even ecological destruction goes through the consumer, then we can simply buy more and more of the right things, while we drift away from other forms of collective, political engagement. This moral picture recalls the sober-minded mysticism of the liberal political economists, whom Marx derided in his account of commodity fetishism. The differences between the sympathetic consumer of early activists and its contemporary cousins certainly suggests that this fear of seductive consumerism is not misplaced—though we should be careful not to attribute these developments to the moral picture of the consumer alone. After all, this picture depends at least as much on the capitalist tendencies, social relations, and phenomena that lend it credibility. Taken figuratively, the sheer weight and complexity of this moral picture may court a kind of nihilism. One who contemplates the vast cosmos of capitalism bearing down upon her in all of its immobilizing weight and overwhelming complexity could surely succumb to despair. She could, quite plausibly, lose the will or ability to imagine alternatives.[48] To existing worries that consumer activism defuses or co-opts mobilization, we should add these concerns about despair and fatigue.

Thus, the question is whether these moral arguments can promote systemic thinking and channel these consumer-centered intuitions toward other types of collective political action or struggle. Otherwise, such arguments and tactics risk deforming political and moral questions into mere matters of consumer choice. In all, to the extent that the sympathetic consumer asks us to enlarge our understanding of the world in which we live and does so through a very common phenomenon, it seems like a vision worth taking seriously—even if, or perhaps especially if—the vision leads us astray.

Beyond the Sympathetic Consumer

There are, of course, many questions that have arisen that this book does not address. Some will require us to elaborate on the sympathetic consumer and seek out further examples or comparisons across space and over time. Other questions look beyond the sympathetic consumer to the matter of a capitalist culture.

Many people have advocated sympathetic consumption since the eighteenth century. Yet many more have rarely, if ever, thought to advocate for such consumption, in spite of ever more insistent demands to live one's life through the market. In the last half of the nineteenth century, markets for grains (e.g., wheat, rice, rye, and oats, among others) and stimulants (e.g., tobacco, sugar, coffee, tea, and chocolate) were global through and through.[49] We should recall, too, that domestic production for sale on markets was similarly elaborate, as the co-operators and National Consumers' League demonstrated. Advances in manufacturing and technology facilitated global trade and waves of mass consumerism over the course of the twentieth century.[50] Until the 2008–2009 global financial crisis, the length of global production chains, not to mention intra-national production chains, increased consistently. Since then, the global growth of production chains has decreased slightly, though it remains to be seen whether the trend will persist. Even so, just about 20 percent of global GDP derives from international trade and production.[51] Between 2000 and 2014, the average number of stages in the production process ranged from just below two, for pure domestic production, to over five, for complex globally produced goods.[52] Even excluding secondary markets for used goods and informal markets in licit or illicit products, the intensification and expansion of commodification means that many people around the world have opportunities to engage in some kind of capitalist commodity-exchange.

Consequently, we can raise comparative questions—over the last three centuries up to the present—about the sympathetic consumer, particularly in places that have come to rely on mass consumerism. If this form can be identified in public debates and advocacy, then we should compare the visions, practices, and moral assumptions that comprise it. If the sympathetic consumer cannot be identified, then we should look into the reasons for its absence. One wonders whether, for instance, concerns about depersonalized goods rise to the level of public discussion variously in what world-systems analysts sometimes call the "semi-periphery" and "periphery" as opposed to the core. Such questions point to the systemic structure and operations of power and sympathy. An answer to these questions will require us to attend to the ways that people talk about and make sense of the goods that enter their lives—something that scholars of consumption grasp well already. But aside from these well-documented consumer and material cultures, we should look into the ways that people make sense of the institutions and practices that make their goods possible. Where do markets, supply chains, sellers, laborers, and others behind our goods fit into people's observations and worldviews? These things pass through our everyday lives but frequently evade our attention. It would be helpful to know if there are ways that they shape or affect our attentions, as well as how these processes vary.

If one can feel with others through consumer goods, then it stands to reason that one could also feel against. We might call this the unsympathetic consumer—a pattern of repulsion and resentment, wherein people feel against those unseen workers and civilizations behind commodities. An unsympathetic consumer may imagine the consumer in capitalist circuits of commerce as the last defense against foreign enemies and conquering hordes. Or she might shamelessly and unapologetically consume goods that, in some way or another, degrade, exoticize, or trivialize the producers. Such visions of consumer goods as Trojan horses or rituals of domination have existed as long as the sympathetic consumer, if not longer. While the abolitionists lamented slave labor, some contemporaneous essays in British periodicals cautioned against the emasculating and enervating effects of Chinese tea on the national temper.[53] These patterns have been replicated throughout the world, from boycotts of Japanese goods in the United States in the 1940s and 1980s to Chinese boycotts of French retailer Carrefour in the leadup to the 2008 Beijing Olympics. As a counterpart to the sympathetic consumer, we should expect to find interpretations of commodity-exchange that foreground racism, xenophobia, and anti-modernism. Investigations into an unsympathetic consumer could shed light on the relevance of popular revulsions to the sympathetic consumer as well. Beyond the consumer, even, we could begin to explore the worker as the object of sympathy, as well as the possibility that the worker could sympathize with the consumer. This was, after all, a matter of special concern for the cooperators, who were proud of their working-class background.

The question of a capitalist culture, further, points beyond the sympathetic consumer. Max Weber famously presented the anxious, ascetic Protestant as the accidental harbinger of the capitalist spirit. But he was less concerned to demonstrate the path through which the "cloak" of Protestant spirituality became an "iron cage" of capitalist acquisitiveness and industriousness. C. B. Macpherson found the "possessive individual" in the market societies of seventeenth century Europe. But he identified the capitalist marketplace mainly in the political theories of Hobbes and Locke.[54] If we seek to trace the various elements comprising a capitalist culture, we should look to the ways that people encounter and understand the everyday phenomena of capitalist societies.

I have done this by rethinking and investigating commodity fetishism. Commodity fetishism helps to describe the phenomenon of commodity-exchange in capitalist societies, the various conditions upon which the phenomenon rests, and the interpretations that people make of these phenomena and conditions. Yet commodity fetishism obviously may apply to many circumstances that don't involve consumer activism. And what of other phenomena in a capitalist social order? For instance, what of those associated with financialized exchanges? What of those associated with the production and reproduction of wage labor? What of ownership? What of unremunerated household labor? What of the separation of humans from other animals and our natural environs? What of the state and the nation? What of sociocultural differences like religion, sexuality, ethnicity, and race? We should seek to clarify if and how these phenomena relate to basic features of a capitalist social order. Obviously, such work is already underway.[55] The trick will be to bring these accounts of interpretation, capitalism, and difference into conversation without losing either precision or vision.

Michael Berman's work on interfaith chaplains in Japan offers a provocative illustration of where such questions might lead. In the wake of Japan's devasting earthquake and tsunami in 2011, Berman followed the efforts of some Buddhist priests to sustain withering religious communities and tend to the victims of the tragedy. These priests, along with other religious clergy, trained to serve as interfaith, non-denominational chaplains. Yet to engage in this public ministry, they had to suppress their Buddhist background and attend only to suffering. This constructs a general form of religion—a balm to suffering—that is distinct from Buddhist work and traditions. The interfaith chaplaincy, further, established no ties between Buddhist traditions and this ministry to those suffering. As one priest observed, "I think interfaith chaplaincy is an important way for us to connect with society, and it's a way for me to pay back the community for all the years that they supported us with donations for funerary services, but it doesn't bring in new parishioners or money."[56]

Consequently, this split between general religion and particular traditions further corroded the foundations of the latter. We might think of this religion in general as another possible pattern in a capitalist culture, one that converges with the sympathetic consumer around questions of suffering. Such work could help us to chart the contours of a capitalist culture. How does a capitalist culture cohere? When is it more or less like ideology? This work could lead us, further, to account for the empirical—not just the logical—relations between these distinct patterns. This isn't, after all, a "pristine culture of capitalism";[57] it draws at least some coherence from the messy realities of life in capitalist societies.

But if a capitalist culture depends on ordinary capitalist phenomena and the conditions that make such phenomena possible, what happens when these are in crisis? Marx observed that the "regulative law" of capitalist value would make itself felt, as with gravity, "when a person's house collapses on top of him."[58] What happens when the supporting conditions wither away or collapse? What happens when they simply ossify or are replaced? Can a capitalist culture persist as the materials through which it has been fashioned are transformed or disappear? What happens to the sympathetic consumer when the markets and supply chains through which it has been elaborated no longer exist? Periods of crisis—market failures or collapse, wars and revolutions, political tumult, global pandemics, and ecological disasters—may threaten the coherence of the sympathetic consumer or even much of a capitalist culture. Alternatively, such periods may simply offer the chance to christen the world newly capitalist once again. Such questions also remind us to examine the bounds and limits of a capitalist culture. We must be attuned to interpretations that coexist with but do not depend on tendencies, social relations, and phenomena central to a capitalist social order. Furthermore, we should also look out for interpretations that challenge and point beyond such tendencies, social relations, and phenomena.

Wherever these questions lead, they can help us clarify the workings of a capitalist social order. A capitalist culture does not simply stand apart from this order, periodically intervening or shaping the economy; it is threaded throughout as people seek to make sense of their lives and surroundings. And should we desire to understand, let alone transform, this mysterious and unruly patchwork world, we must be aware of these patterns of interpretation and social conditions—those that repeat as well as those without precedent. The sympathetic consumer, I have argued, is one such repeating pattern. It sheds light on the places where the world of ordinary commodity-exchange, including the sense that people make of this phenomenon, meets the chains of labor, ownership, extraction, toil, and suffering upon which this world depends. If we, like centuries of activists and thinkers before us, look for these points of contact between interpretations and social conditions, then we may discover other patterns and seek their sources.

Back to the Origins

"It appears," observed William Fox, in the opening lines of his 1791 *Address to the People of Great Britain*, "that though claiming for ourselves the most perfect freedom, we have been imposing upon others a slavery the most oppressive; and that, whilst enjoying a degree of felicity unequalled in any age or country, we are traveling the earth to increase the misery of mankind."[59] Focused only on the sugar and rum that traveled from the slave plantations of the British West Indies, he sensed that this world turned him and his fellow Britons into hypocrites. But they weren't just accidental hypocrites: "We have planted slavery in the rank soil of sordid avarice: the produce has been misery in the extreme."[60] Not only did the happiness of Britons depend on a "most oppressive" slavery—slavery was their produce. Where others cultivated wheat or barley or sugar cane, the death-dealing Britons cultivated misery, suffering, and destruction—all to enrich themselves at the expense of the faraway worlds and people upon whom their everyday lives depended.

Fox and his fellow abolitionists brought those distant worlds and people home. To do so, they latched onto a very simple fact: that the sugar now common in British marketplaces and diets concealed the ghastly circumstances of its origins. In sugar they found a "magic mirror" that revealed, however obliquely, horizons beyond their own. Sugar demonstrated that these horizons—of the enslaved Africans, British settlers, the slave-traders, and other agents of empire—weren't separate and self-standing from those of metropolitan Britons; they were all, in fact, inextricably linked. A single commodity could bring home the institution of chattel slavery and the network of people, organizations, and things from whence it came. This scrutiny of sugar presaged an interpretation of consumption that would later envelop all manner of commodities, from food, cotton, and spices to cars, cell phone providers, and even financial instruments.

In 1921, Margaret Llewelyn Davies, the leader of the Women's Co-operative Guild, lamented,

> Under present-day Capitalism, with its profit-making basis, the long-suffering "consumer" is being continually overlooked and sacrificed. . . . In their gigantic distributive and productive business, covering one-third of the population of Great Britain, [co-operators] recognise this central fact, that industry and trade have resulted from the fundamental need of consumption, and they base their

economic theory and practice on consumption as the most universal, vital and human interest.[61]

In just over one century, the abolitionist intuition of the sympathetic consumer had blossomed into an all-encompassing vision of consumer sovereignty. The commodity became the lens through which activists could view central institutions of capitalist life—labor, exchange, profit, and property. It was also the means of overcoming its central contradictions. Now, not only was the producer sacrificed—as in merchant capitalist chattel slavery or in the satanic mills of industrial capitalist production—but the consumer was as well. The sympathetic consumer expanded in scope and scale with a capitalist social order. In proliferating consumer goods, the co-operators discovered many more magic mirrors that could, from the right angle, disclose horizons beyond horizons—horizons of distant workers and others that were, once again, linked inextricably to their own.

As we look back on these abolitionists and co-operators, the former's narrow focus on sugar may seem quaint, while the latter's grandiose visions of consumer sovereignty may seem naive. However, these activists hardly deserve our condescension. Their interpretations, stripped by time of certain idiosyncratic blinders, remain with us. When advocates tell us why we should care about what we buy, they refer to the chains and networks of commerce through which these goods enter our lives; they promote ways of seeing into the conditions that obtain in these chains and networks; and they imagine consumers as the pulsing, moral heartbeat of capitalism. This interpretive pattern remains not only because of the quirks and desires of the advocates themselves, but because they advocate with common materials—the flotsam and jetsam of a capitalist social order that drift into our lives.

Of these common materials, the most humble and strange is the commodity. Marx described a lowly wooden table, which "as soon as it emerges as a commodity . . . evolves out of its wooden brain grotesque ideas far more wonderful than if it were to begin dancing of its own free will."[62] These grotesque and wonderful ideas, like the sympathetic consumer, haunt our encounters with goods in capitalist marketplaces. Yet there are surely other ideas that haunt phenomena crucial to capitalist societies. Only once we have taken stock of such patterns of interpretation and social conditions will we begin to comprehend the workings of a capitalist culture. This project, I hope to have shown, directly concerns those of us who seek to describe and explain aspects of a capitalist social order. It may also be familiar to those who, after making a purchase, have found themselves reflecting on what they have done and on the kind of world that made it possible. In the end, the search for a capitalist culture is nothing more and nothing less than an effort to explain why this world makes the strange kind of sense that it does.

Notes

Chapter 1

1. "The 2 Euro T-Shirt—A Social Experiment," https://www.youtube.com/watch?v=KfANs2y_frk

2. *Annual Report of the National Consumers' League* 1903-1904, pp. 18-23.

3. *Considerations Addressed to Professors of Christianity of Every Denomination, on the Impropriety of Consuming West-India Sugar and Rum, as Produced by the Oppressive Labour of Slaves* (London: M. Gurney, 1792), p. 2.

4. Ibid., p. 4.

5. Ibid.

6. Ibid., p. 8.

7. See Biernacki 2005; Haydu 1998; Mahoney and Rueschemeyer 2003; Skocpol and Somers 1980.

8. Throughout, I will use "depersonalized" and "depersonalization" to indicate the condition in which labor appears as abstracted, or as that which renders commodities equally valuable, in capitalist commodity-exchange. I will use "anonymous" and "anonymity" to stress the participant's interpretation of abstract labor and goods as both banal and strange in exchange. In other words, "anonymity" and "anonymous" indicate how people interpret depersonalized goods.

9. Rutherford 2018, p. 59.

10. Dauber 2013; Muehlebach 2012; Pearson 2011; Rai 2002; Rutherford 2018.

11. Rutherford 2018, pp. 55-81.

12. See, for example, Hochschild 2003; Jasper 1997; Summers-Effler 2010; Turner and Stets 2005.

13. Fennell 2015, p. 24.

14. Horkheimer and Adorno 2002; Weber 1930.

15. Abend 2014a; de Vries 2008; Fourcade and Healy 2007; Storr 2013; Thompson 1971; Trentmann 2016; Wherry 2012; Zelizer 2011.

16. Karl Polanyi (2001) referred to these dynamics as a "double movement," evident in struggles over regulation and deregulation across the nineteenth and twentieth centuries.

This perspective, along with the associated idea of "embeddedness," has been enormously influential in political and economic sociology (see, especially, Block 2018; Krippner 2011; Somers and Block 2005). The consumer activists discussed in this book, undoubtedly, fit this general scheme, seeking as they did to regulate markets through the mobilization of consumer sympathy. But I find Polanyi less helpful than Marx for two main reasons. First, although he recognizes the unique emergence of laissez-faire liberalism in the eighteenth and nineteenth centuries, Polanyi tends to characterize the dynamics of market embeddedness as a generic sociological problem. As a result, it remains unclear whether or to what extent such "double movements" refer to specific features of a capitalist social order. Second, the notion of a "double movement" cannot account for the precise character of these efforts to regulate "disembedded" markets—whatever the source and substance of such regulatory efforts may be. My interest is not only in the fact that people have attempted to regulate markets—something that a motley crew of activists, politicians, technocrats, and even capitalists across this period have variously attempted—but in the precise features of these attempts. The book will show that commodity fetishism can account for specific features of consumer activism that have recurred from the late eighteenth century to the present. Thanks to Zach Levenson for helping me clarify these points.

17. Miller 2006, pp. 11, 161–219.

18. Konings 2015; Wherry 2014.

19. Zelizer 1994; see also, Abend 2014a; Haskell and Teichgraeber 1996; Miller 2006. One notable exception is Alexander 2006.

20. Biernacki 1995.

21. Consider, for instance, the immense literature that examines neoliberalism as a distinct historical formation: Ascher 2016; Brown 2015; Comaroff and Comaroff 2001; Konings 2015; Mirowski and Plehwe 2009.

22. See, for example, Eichengreen 2011; Shaikh 2016.

23. Banet-Weiser 2012; Boltanski and Chiapello 2018; Chin 2016; Mokyr 2018; Stamatov 2014.

24. Althusser 1971; Engels 2010; Federici 2014; Habermas 1989; Hobsbawm and Ranger 1992; Wallerstein 1983.

25. My point is not that there are no meaningful differences between some things that we call "economic" and some that we call "cultural." It is simply that such a distinction does not capture those differences well. Laura Miller (2006) and Lyn Spillman (2012) make related points about the ways that culture makes possible or constitutes economic life. Yet both seem to accept, implicitly, an understanding of a capitalist culture as oriented fundamentally around "self-interested exchange," rationalization, and profit (see Miller 2006, pp. 197–229; Spillman 2012, pp. 6–7). Spillman sees capitalist cultures, not a capitalist culture, that depend on the solidaristic work of business organizations and other institutions that make self-interested, capitalist activity possible.

26. Arrighi 2010; Cooper 2017; Dörre, Lessenich, and Rosa 2013; Fraser and Jaeggi 2018; Rosa 2013; Sewell 2008; Wallerstein 1983.

27. That said, I seek to avoid any unfounded assumptions about the relations between these varied features of a capitalist social order—the vexed question of cause.

When the abolitionist writes "[W]ithout [consumers] the slave-trade . . . must soon cease," he argues, in effect, that a transformation in the consciousness of consumers will transform relations all along the British imperial supply chain. Here culture dictates how the economy works. Others have argued the opposite. These are exactly the kinds of assumptions about causal relationships that I aim to avoid. It is more important for me to chart the ways that activists' interpretations develop through specific aspects of a capitalist social order. Thus, I focus on the ways that the sympathetic consumer evolves in relation to commodity-exchange, supply chains, religious and moral frameworks, and conflicts with labor and business organizations—not mainly on questions of first cause. As such, I do not take a position on the longstanding debate about culture and the origins of capitalism. My sense is that this debate assumes exceedingly narrow understandings of culture and causality. Though mentioned here, this question surely merits a more sustained discussion elsewhere.

28. Hudis 2013; Postone 1993; Sraffa 1975; Wallerstein 1983.

29. For this reason, to talk of the people who consume without the intent to produce as consumers in general is misleading. It elides all of the consumption that occurs for the sake of production throughout the supply chain—what Marx called "productive consumption" (1973, p. 90). To avoid confusion about the referent and for the sake of rhetorical parsimony, throughout the book I will use "consumer" in the presently accepted sense—to refer to the private person who withdraws a good from circulation without any intent to use it, directly, to produce further wealth. But it would be more accurate to think of such consumers as contributing only to a portion of the total consumption in a society at any given time. Thus, perhaps a phrase like "private consumers" would communicate this more accurately. They are my intended referent. Some may object that there is no consistent way to distinguish "private" and "productive" consumption. I disagree. There are certainly borderline cases that cannot be decided upon in advance, but that hardly discredits the distinction. There are entities that consume vast amounts of resources in the process of production, and our notion of consumption should aim to include and distinguish these from private consumers. In any case, my purpose is simply to remind that private consumers are a specific subset of consumers in general. On other elisions in talk of consumption, see Graeber 2011.

30. Fraser and Jaeggi 2018, pp. 18–19; Shaikh 2016, pp. 259–326.

31. Weber 1930; Sombart 1967; see also Campbell 1987; Jaeggi 2014; Rosa 2019.

32. Arrighi 2010; Harvey 2010; Krippner 2011; Luxemburg 2003; Marx 1991.

33. Marx 1935; this is, needless to say, not the only relevant social division in a capitalist society, but it is a central one.

34. See, for example, Beckert 2015; Coclanis 2018; Johnson 2013.

35. Hodgson 2015; Pistor 2019.

36. *Considerations Addressed to Professors of Christianity of Every Denomination,* p. 4.

37. Bhattacharya 2017; Hochschild and Machung 1989.

38. Esping-Andersen 1990.

39. Beckert 2015; Inikori 2002; Mintz 1985; Robinson 1983.

40. Clelland 2014; Gray 2014; Ribas 2015.

41. *Considerations Addressed to Professors of Christianity of Every Denomination*, p. 4.

42. For recent overviews in sociology, see Patterson 2014; Spillman 2019.

43. On matters of culture and interpretation, especially with reference to that which we commonly call the "economy," see Alexander 2003; Biernacki 1995; Miller 2006; Sewell 2005; Spillman 2012; Weber 1930; Wherry 2012; Zelizer 2011; Zukin 2004.

44. To say that these interpretations are necessary for social phenomena is not to say that these interpretations are unconditioned by the world within which they emerged. In Chapter 5, I describe how certain moral background conditions for the sympathetic consumer came to depend on a capitalist social order.

45. Abend 2014b; see also Krause 2014; Spillman 2012. Isaac Reed (2011) makes a related argument when he claims that theories supply landscapes of meaning within which certain practices, understandings, and institutions become intelligible. Yet he re-inscribes this argument about conditions of possibility into a more familiar action-oriented analytic framework (pp. 123–162).

46. To "make sense" is not necessarily to be empirically correct. One's reasoning may be coherent and have some empirical basis without being demonstrably true. Whether the consumer is the wellspring of all production may not, for instance, be strictly true, but it can make sense with regard to specific features of a capitalist world *as well as* other propositions about the world.

47. For example, people have engaged in cultic behaviors toward goods for much of human history. Thus, that tendency is not unique to capitalism. But one can show that a particular form of cultic behavior such as mass consumerism depends, in some nontrivial way, on mass production or wealth-producing private property or other institutional features of capitalist life. More conceptual and empirical work is surely required to treat these issues with the seriousness they deserve.

48. Bagchi 2008; Gereffi, Spener, and Bair 2002; Harootunian 2015; Wood 1991.

49. Louis Althusser (1971) provides a classic conceptual exposition of this argument in the essay on ideological state apparatuses. See also his essay on "overdetermination" (Althusser 2005).

50. One could also imagine, with Antonio Gramsci (1972), a "war of position" where some struggle to establish an alternative common sense that could compete with a capitalist culture.

51. It is this interest in a more general capitalist culture, therefore, that has been insufficiently developed in other clearly related research. Ellen Meiksins Wood's essay on English capitalism proposes some components of a capitalist culture—namely, individualism, ahistoricism, and the fragmentation of the social world (1991, pp. 81–93). These are remarkably suggestive, but I see no reason why such a culture must exclude their opposites. As such, there may be non-individualistic and historical tendencies within a capitalist culture. James Livingston (1997) describes the rise of a particular, flexible notion of self or subjectivity in the United States in the context of the political economy of corporate capitalism. This is another plausible element of a capitalist culture (see Rosa 2003). From an apologetic perspective, Deirdre McCloskey (2006) traces the emergence and character of the bourgeois virtues in a capitalist social order; however, she makes a

general argument about the ways that capitalism reinforces seven classical virtues: prudence, justice, love, faith, hope, temperance, and courage (pp. 303–306).

52. Berman 1988; Marx and Engels 1978; Polanyi 2001; Schumpeter 1950.

53. William Sewell (2008, p. 527) describes capitalism as "hypereventful" and "monotonously repetitive," while Klaus Dörre, Stephen Lessenich, and Hartmut Rosa (2017, p. 53) refer to "dynamic stabilization." See also Postone 1993.

54. Thus, while I am broadly sympathetic with Martijn Konings's (2015) effort to unravel the ethics and "emotional logic" of neoliberal capitalism, I think such a project can look beyond the more limited temporal horizons of the last century. Of course, a capitalist culture will surely encompass novel forms that emerge in particular phases of capitalist development. I claim only that we should include longer-haul continuities in the study of a capitalist culture, not that we should exclude novelty. Eva Illouz (2007) describes the making of "emotional capitalism" in terms of a similar arc.

55. Jennifer Silva's (2013) research on working-class adulthood presents one such image—of people who come to distrust public and collective projects in response to their experiences in the labor market and schools. Daniel Fridman (2016) demonstrates how people learn to become capitalist subjects through a comparative investigation of financial self-help groups in Argentina and the United States.

56. The classic conceptual statement on this matter is Georg Lukács (1971); for a discussion of how egalitarian possibilities can arise in and through workplaces, see Katherine Sobering (2019).

57. Michael Taussig's (1980) excellent ethnographic study of rural people's experience of capitalist relations of production is one of the only works of empirical social science to employ commodity fetishism for analytical purposes. I discuss one more recent work that does so by Elizabeth Chin (2016). For work on the politics and culture of food consumption, see Bowen and Gaytán 2012; DeSoucey 2016; Gray 2014; Jordan 2015; on commodification, see Cook 2004; Healy 2006; Zelizer 2011.

58. Marx 1977, p. 165.

59. Zukin 2004, p. 268; see also: Lyon 2006, p. 459; Zelizer 2011, pp. 95–96.

60. Stillerman 2015, pp. 7–8.

61. Guthman 2009, p. 192.

62. Pitkin 1987, p. 270; see also Guthman 2009, p. 198.

63. Cohen 2001; Taussig 1980.

64. Chin 2007, p. 335. See also: Billig 1999; Chin 2016; Duncombe 2013; Torrance 1995; Trentmann 2016, p. 113.

65. On the problem of authenticity in consumer culture, see Banet-Weiser 2012; Lears 1981; Nielsen and Skotnicki 2019, pp. 125–129.

66. The following sections summarize one of the arguments in Skotnicki (2020). In that paper, I distinguish between three ways that scholars have traditionally characterized commodity fetishism: cognitive error, ideological illusion, and capitalist subjectivity. Having already mentioned error and illusion in the main text, I should add that Georg Lukács (1971) established the template for approaching commodity fetishism as subjectivity (p. 87; see also Amariglio and Callari 1989). While these approaches touch

on important aspects of commodity fetishism, I argue that they are ill suited to account for aspects of Marx's own description. Moreover, they obscure possible analytical uses of commodity fetishism. This book explores some of the analytical possibilities that I could only propose or hint at in the article.

67. Adams and Raisborough 2008; Bourdieu 1984; Campbell 1987, 2004; Chin 2016; Douglas and Isherwood 1979; Johnston, Rodney, and Szabo 2012; Miller 1987, 1997; Stillerman 2015; Wherry 2006; Zukin 2004; on the conceptual argument for severing production from consumption, see Jean Baudrillard (1975, 1998). Baudrillard argues, in short, that consumption can be understood in terms of signifying activity in a manner analogous to that of language. We come to understand consumption, in other words, as part of a system of meaningful activity that envelops our purchase and use of commodities—other goods, marketing, relationships, places, feelings, and so forth. Typically, this has been taken to demonstrate that production, so far removed from these more immediate contexts of consumption, can be safely ignored when considering the significance or meanings of purchasing.

68. DeSoucey 2016; Gray 2014; Jordan 2015; Trubek 2008.

69. Marx 1977, p. 163.

70. Katy, "Shopping," *Co-operative News*, 11 June 1892, pp. 638–639.

71. It is likely that a healthy percentage of co-operative women worked for wages. At the same time, it is also worth remembering the important reproductive role of women's domestic labors. In ways both direct and indirect, then, women would have traded "thought and toil and weariness" for money.

72. Ibid.

73. Ibid.

74. Marx 1977, p. 163.

75. Ibid.

76. Ibid.

77. Marx writes, famously, that the "analysis" brings out "metaphysical subtleties" and "theological niceties." Ibid.

78. Ibid., p. 165.

79. Ibid.

80. Ibid, pp. 157–163.

81. Max Horkheimer and Theodor Adorno understood this well. At the close of their essay on the culture industry, they describe consumers, the objects of mass culture, as helpless, cynical participants in their own degradation: "The most intimate reactions of human beings have become so entirely reified, even to themselves, that the idea of anything peculiar to them survives only in extreme abstraction: personality means hardly more than dazzling white teeth and freedom from body odor and emotions. That is the triumph of advertising in the culture industry: the compulsive imitation by consumers of cultural commodities which, at the same time, they recognize as false" (2002, p. 139). This is not, as the typical reading goes, a picture of consumers as simply hoodwinked. Rather, it is a picture of powerlessness. What option is there but to buy in? See also Postone 1993, pp. 166–171. William Roberts (2017, pp. 82–94) offers an important

clarification of fetishism as domination: It is social domination that occurs through the medium of commodities, not necessarily abstraction *per se* that is at issue.

82. Katy, "Shopping."

83. Ibid.

84. Ibid. (italics in original)

85. I am indebted, in particular, to Diane Elson's brilliant essay, "The Value Theory of Labour" (1979), Slavoj Žižek's classic, *The Sublime Object of Ideology* (1989), and Moishe Postone's *Time, Labor, and Social Domination* (1993), which reject the assertion that commodity fetishism is only errant or delusional. See also Peter Hudis (2013), William Roberts (2017), and David Andrews (2018), who arrive at similar conclusions. I took a first and, to my mind, insufficient pass at this issue (Skotnicki 2017, pp. 621–623).

86. Marx 1977, p. 168.

87. Ibid. (italics added)

88. Ibid., p. 169.

89. I am not claiming—nor, I would argue, was Marx—that labor is the "true" source of value for all time, as opposed to demand or use. This value form is, rather, a way to describe how labor appears in capitalist societies. The tendency to rely on private wage labor is a necessary condition of capitalist commodity-exchange—though all labor in such a society need not occur as wage labor. To the British worker buying sugar in the late-eighteenth century, the difference between free-labor and slave-labor produce would have been no more apparent in exchange than it would have been to the British worker buying cocoa at the turn of the twentieth century. My point is not that the differences between slave labor and free labor are of no consequence. Rather, it is that the value form necessarily obscures the differences—even slave labor can appear as free labor in commodity-exchange.

90. Katy, "Shopping."

91. Ibid.

92. Ibid. It is no coincidence, I think, that Katy and Marx, when characterizing depersonalized goods and their consequences, resort to visual metaphors—magic mirrors, an "impression made by a thing on the optic nerve" (Marx 1977, p. 165).

93. Katy, "Shopping."

94. Drescher 1987, pp. 82–83; this estimate refers to the early phase in 1792. The numbers in the 1820s and 30s were greater than 1 million.

95. Literary scholar Charlotte Sussman is an exception. She has an exemplary study of the politics of consumption in the British empire during the eighteenth and early nineteenth centuries (1994, 2000). In her work, Sussman figures the significance of consumer activism in the abolitionist movement, particularly in terms of gender and colonial politics.

96. Glickman 2009, pp. 2–3.

97. Beckert 2015, pp. 29–82; Mintz 1985, pp. 19–73; Patel and Moore 2017, pp. 95–110.

98. Trentmann 2016, pp. 78–118.

99. Arrighi 2010, pp. 50–52; Tilly 1990, pp. 82–83.

100. Stamatov 2013, pp. 159–160.

101. Smith 2003; on free trade and the British empire, see Semmel 1970.

102. Hall and Schwarz 1985; Sklar 1995b, 1998; Trentmann 2008.

103. Cohen 2003; Hilton 2003.

104. Rappaport 2000, p. 142–177; Sklar 1988.

105. Curtis 1991; Joyce 1991; O'Day 1979.

106. Ralph and Singhal 2019; Robinson 1983.

Chapter 2

1. *Considerations Addressed to Professors of Christianity of Every Denomination, on the Impropriety of Consuming West-India Sugar and Rum, as Produced by the Oppressive Labour of Slaves* (London: M. Gurney, 1792), p. 4.

2. Throughout the book, I use phrases like "capitalist circuits of commerce" and "systems of production, distribution, and exchange" as synonyms. Unlike Viviana Zelizer (2011, pp. 303–343), I do not emphasize the different meanings that arise within these circuits. This is not because I deny their existence, but because I am tracing how activists understood the consumer's role in a capitalist system. Thus, these phrases allow me to describe how activists envisioned the consumer in capitalist networks of commodification.

3. See, for example, Blackburn 2011, pp. 145–169; Brown 2006, pp. 33–101; Davis 1975, pp. 213–254; Drescher 1987; Rediker 2017; Sinha 2016, pp. 9–33; Stamatov 2013, pp. 97–124.

4. Blackburn 1998; Bradley and Cartledge 2011; Davis 1966; McCusker and Menard 2010; Patterson 1982.

5. As David Brion Davis notes, the history of slavery has been riven with contradictions (1975, pp. 39–41). Las Casas certainly recognized them and ultimately advocated against slavery in principle and practice. But the broader point is that people were used to living with those particular contradictions. On Las Casas, see Blanchard 2010; Stamatov 2013; Wagner with Parish 1967.

6. There was an ongoing discussion about the profitability of slavery, one prompted by Eric Williams's *Capitalism and Slavery* (1994). Williams argued that slavery was ultimately incompatible with capitalist profit-making and thus declined in the nineteenth century. Subsequent critiques (Cateau and Carrington 2000; Drescher 2010) challenged Williams's argument about the demise of slavery in Great Britain. At this point, the consensus is that slavery was profitable and that one must seek alternatives to the argument that, strictly speaking, slavery was incompatible with capitalist profit-seeking imperatives. For a summary, see Coclanis 2010.

7. Richardson 1987; on the history of sugar in the British empire, see Mintz 1985, and on ordinary diets in Europe, see Braudel 1992.

8. The series of treaties or Peace of Utrecht—signed by Spain, Portugal, France, the

Dutch Republic, Savoy, and Great Britain between 1713 and 1715—resulted in British control of formerly Spanish ports in the Mediterranean as well as the license (*asiento*) to the slave trade in Spanish colonies in the Americas.

9. Within Europe, enslavement of fellow Christians fell out of favor through conflicts with Muslim empires. Faced with the threats from Muslims in northern Africa, Spain, and the Levant, the idea that master and slave should not hail from the same race or religion gradually took hold. See Blackburn 1998, pp. 42–44.

10. Blackburn 1998, p. 111; Fernández-Armesto 1982.

11. Sinha 2016, p. 11.

12. Frederickson 1988, pp. 189–205; Rana 2010, pp. 47–48; Reed 2020, pp. 127–135; the association of blackness and slavery developed in Islam in the fourteenth and fifteenth centuries, when enslaved people from northern Africa were exported to the Levant for the purpose of cultivating sugar. There are significant debates about the extent to which these modern racial ideologies motivated chattel slavery in the European empires from the beginning, or whether such racial ideologies evolved out of chattel slavery. For a version of the former argument, see Robinson 1983. For the latter, see Lockley 2010.

13. As we will see, racist ideologies could coexist easily with abolitionist sentiment. However, to assign Black Africans to a subhuman caste certainly made it easier to justify the atrocities of chattel slavery.

14. Roger Anstey (1975) made the strongest claims for the ideological role of Christianity in abolition. While his arguments about Christianity and abolition may be overstated, historians of slavery and abolitionism have been unable to ignore the ways that Christian universalism and ethical principles nurtured antislavery sentiment. But as Peter Stamatov shows, the role of Christianity may have been as much sociological and organizational as ideological. In the context of imperial expansion, conflicts internal to specific religious confessions such as Catholicism and Quakerism may have created places for pro-indigenous and antislavery sentiment to flourish within dissenting fractions of these religious communities. See Stamatov 2013, pp. 36–40.

15. Stamatov 2013, pp. 45–72; Peter Stamatov chronicles the emergence of a network that published information about slavery and petitions on behalf of those suffering distant atrocities to relevant political authorities.

16. On Quakerism and its history, see Braithwaite 1955; Dandelion 2007; Ingle 1994; Kunze 1994.

17. Brycchan Carey (2012) traces the history of this internal debate, which sometimes spilled over into demands on Quakers in specific communities to divest from slavery; see also Aptheker 1940; Brown 1988.

18. Quoted in Carey 2012, pp. 31–32.

19. Marcus Rediker (2017) retells this story, as well as the rich life of Benjamin Lay (pp. 1–2); see also Holcomb 2016, pp. 13–35.

20. Slaughter 2008; Thomas Haskell (1985b) situates Woolman's antislavery attitudes in the context of expanding markets. Many Quakers were successful business-

people and, as such, very familiar with contracts. Haskell argues that these contracts entailed promises that held across time and space, thus enabling people to imagine themselves as responsible for distant actions.

21. David Brion Davis stresses both of these intellectual trends in addition to the "evangelical faith in instantaneous conversion and demonstrative sanctification" and the literary image of the noble savage. The former was wholly compatible with a demand to commit oneself to God and demonstrate one's piety by means of immediate renunciation of slave-holding. The latter provided an alternative antislavery rationale. See Davis 1975, pp. 45–48.

22. On the role of sympathy in the Enlightenment more generally, see Frazer 2010; Luc Boltanski (1999) demonstrates the relevance of sympathy to distant suffering in a mass-mediated culture. The ability to identify with the suffering of distant strangers gained force throughout the eighteenth century, especially on the heels of Las Casas and the pro-indigenous movement in the Spanish empire.

23. While the portrayals of the earthquake, which occurred in 1755, did not open up any way for people to intervene on behalf of the people of Lisbon, it enabled people to extend sympathies to those whom they would never know or encounter otherwise. See Sliwinski 2011, pp. 35–56.

24. Carrington 1987, p. 135.

25. Davis 1975, pp. 52–53; Stinchcombe 1995.

26. In the classic, *Econocide*, Seymour Drescher argued that historians of slavery needed to look beyond explanations for abolition grounded in the simple claim that slavery was no longer profitable; they needed to take political and ideological matters more seriously. See Drescher 2010.

27. Breen 2004; Brown 2006; Glickman 2009.

28. For a detailed account, see Brown 2006, pp. 333–462.

29. Wyman-McCarthy 2018.

30. Lynn Hunt (2015) stresses the role of democratic revolutions—especially the English, American, and French—in establishing a language of human rights. As we will see, this language certainly appears in abolitionist writing of the late eighteenth century.

31. John Churchman, *An Account of the Gospel Labours, and Christian Experiences of a Faithful Minister of Christ, John Churchman, Late of Nottingham, in Pennsylvania, Deceased* (London: James Phillips, 1781).

32. On the life of Anthony Benezet, see Jackson 2009; Rossignol and van Ruymbeke 2016.

33. Anthony Benezet, *Some Historical Account of Guinea, Its Situation, Produce, and the General Disposition of Its Inhabitants with an Inquiry into the Rise and Progress of the Slave Trade, Its Nature, and Lamentable Effects: A New Edition* (London: James Phillips, 1788 [originally published 1767]), pp. 109–110.

34. This paragraph draws from Peter Stamatov (2013), who highlights the political innovations of Benezet's advocacy (pp. 115–124, 129–133); see also Morgan 2010.

35. Stamatov 2013, p. 128.

36. Ibid., pp. 162–164; Van Cleve 2010.

37. "Repertoires of contention" refer to the learned and shared strategies for making public demands. Charles Tilly uses the notion to characterize the cultures of social movement activism or, in his preferred nomenclature, contentious politics. See Tilly 1995, pp. 41–42, and Tilly 2006; on the character of these repertoires, see Tilly 1995, pp. 45–46. See also Calhoun 2012, pp. 249–281.

38. Seymour Drescher (1987) stresses the role of petitions in the antislavery movement. For a general discussion of abolition as a social movement, see Leo d'Anjou (1996). Peter Stamatov (2013) describes how the abolitionists codified a form of long-distance advocacy, including the publication of information and the cultivation of activist networks. David Richardson (2007) observes the significance of public demonstration as a means of pressuring Parliament in the early efforts to abolish the slave trade. For a helpful overview of the rhetoric of abolitionist consumer activism, see Charlotte Sussman (2000). On the role of free Blacks in England in the abolitionist thought and campaigns, see Kaplan and Oldfield 2010; Swaminathan 2009; Thomas 2000. Adam Hochschild (2005) captures the significance of antislavery imagery like the diagram of the *Brookes*, which depicted the inhuman stacking of Africans in the hold of a ship bound for the Americas.

39. Ashworth 1987; Davis 1975; Turley 1991; Karl Polanyi (2001, p. 35) adapted William Blake's phrase to emphasize the depredations of life and liberty to which industrial workers of the eighteenth and nineteenth centuries were subjected.

40. *Manchester Herald,* 28 April 1792, cited in Drescher 1987, p. 245 fn87.

41. Drescher 1987, pp. 127–132.

42. Quirk and Richardson 2010, pp. 271–272.

43. See Seymour Drescher (2009), for estimates of abolitionist participation and Martin J. Daunton (1995, p. 574) for estimates of UK populations across these periods. The numbers run from one-tenth to one-fifteenth of the population.

44. For some crucial work on the demographic, political, and cultural role of women in abolition, see Midgley 1992; Twells 2011; Whelan 2011. Charlotte Sussman (2000) demonstrates the profound significance of gendered understandings of sympathy to the rhetoric of abolition. This created a space for women to develop a unique, gender-specific role in the development of the movement.

45. Whelan 2009, pp. 398–400.

46. Sussman 2000, pp. 124–127; Sussman underscores the significance of feminine virtues in presenting an alternative form of consumption in the poetry, literature, and advocacy of the early 1790s. See also, Midgley 1992, pp. 9–40.

47. Hochschild 2005, pp. 324–325; Midgley 2011. On the influence of Elizabeth Heyrick's call for immediate abolition, see Lasser 2011 and Sinha 2016.

48. Blackburn 2011; Drescher 1987; Gilroy 1993; Goodrich 2014; Linebaugh and Rediker 2000; Scott 2019; Walvin 1986.

49. The subsequent wrangling over the best logical and rhetorical interpretation of Lord Mansfield's decision in the case does not diminish the historical claim that, at that time, the decision was understood to outlaw slavery on English land. See Cotter 1994; Drescher 1987, pp. 25–49; Fryer 1984, pp. 203–207.

50. On the influences from outside of England proper, see Drescher 1987, pp. 97–110; Linebaugh and Rediker 2000; on the revolution in Haiti and its consequences for abolition, see Dubois 2004; Fick 1990; on the consequences for the sugar campaign, see Davis 1975, pp. 435–436; Sussman 2000, pp. 37–38.

51. Historians tend to divide the early abolitionist movement into two distinct phases: the 1780s and early 90s, and the 1820s and 30s. This reflects the cessation of public abolitionist advocacy by the middle of the 1790s until the middle of the 1810s. In a panic induced by the French Revolution, the British Parliament introduced an array of sedition acts that curtailed public activism. This hobbled the abolitionist movement, which began again in earnest in the early 1820s as it became clear that the abolition of the slave trade would not address the issue of slavery.

52. Black 2012, pp. 27–52; Brown 2006, pp. 451–462; d'Anjou 1996, pp. 169–198; Davis 1975, pp. 82–83; Drescher 2009, pp. 245–252.

53. Black 2012, p. 31.

54. Drescher 2009, pp. 220–221.

55. Anstey 1975; Farrell 2007; Hochschild 2005.

56. It may be historically inaccurate to insist that abolition occurred for narrowly economic reasons, but the relationship between capitalism, humanitarianism (especially abolitionism), and slavery has remained a relevant question. I take this up, particularly the relationship between capitalism and humanitarianism in Chapter 5.

57. On the strategic and institutional legacies of abolition, see Drescher 1987; Kurasawa 2014; Stamatov 2013.

58. Colley 1992; Drescher 2009, pp. 248–266; Midgley 1992, pp. 60–62.

59. See, for example, the "Minutes of the Anti-Slavery Society," 29 September 1824, p. 139; "Letter to the Society of Friends," 26 May 1825; "Report of the Society for Mitigating and Gradually Abolishing Slavery Throughout the British Dominion," 9 February 1825; *Ladies' Anti-Slavery Associations* (Liverpool: 1827), pp. 1–15. All of these disparate organs report campaigns to encourage the purchase of free labor goods. These campaigns continued, with minimal observable impact on the persistence of slavery, into the period of the American Civil War, 1861–1865.

60. Craton 1982; Morgan 2007, pp. 173–198; Scott 2019.

61. On emancipation, see Blackburn 2011; Draper 2010; Morgan 2010; Stinchcombe 1995, pp. 175–200.

62. See Morgan 2007, pp. 184–194.

63. *Considerations Addressed to Professors of Christianity of Every Denomination,* 1792, p. 3.

64. There is, I think, a fourth element that I alluded to in Chapter 1 that requires a distinct analytical treatment to do justice to its complexity: the question of difference and the sympathetic consumer. This includes, but is not limited to, racism, ethnocentrism, and xenophobia. Charlotte Sussman (2000) has address this matter with respect to colonial consumption and abolition, where the discourse around West Indian sugar reduced enslaved Africans to bearers of pollution. A broader comparative approach may clarify how consumer encounters with depersonalized goods either facilitate or depend

on fears and fantasies of difference, as well as the racialized character of the sympathetic consumer.

65. Walsh 1995; White 2013.

66. Mokyr 1988.

67. On sugar in the British diet, see Berg 2004; Mintz 1985, pp. 75–150.

68. Stobart 2013, p. 131.

69. McKendrick 1982; Walker 1973.

70. Rappaport 2017, pp. 51–55; Stobart 2013, pp. 170–175.

71. Glickman 2009, pp. 35–49; Walsh 2014, pp. 49–52.

72. On the standard of living in Britain in the late eighteenth and early nineteenth centuries, see Taylor 1975.

73. On the circulation figures, see Whelan 2009, p. 402.

74. William C. Fox, *An Address to the People of Great Britain, on the Propriety of Abstaining from West India Sugar and Rum*, 24th ed. *(London: M. Gurney,* 1791), pp. 2–3.

75. Ibid., 6th ed., pp. 3–4.

76. Ibid., 6th ed., p. 4.

77. Thomas Cooper, *Considerations on the Slave Trade; and the Consumption of West India Produce* (London: Darton and Harvey, 1791), p. 14.

78. *Considerations Addressed to Professors of Christianity of Every Denomination*, p. 4.

79. *A Second Address to the People of Great Britain Containing a New, and Most Powerful Argument to Abstain from the Use of West India Sugar*, 2nd ed. *(London: M. Gurney,* 1792), pp. 6–7.

80. *An Address to Her Royal Highness the Duchess of York Against the Use of Sugar* (London, 1792), p. 13.

81. *Strictures on an Address to the People of Great Britain on the Propriety of Abstaining from West-India Sugar and Rum*, 2nd ed. (London: T. Boosey, 1792), p. 6; "the System of the author" refers to that of William Fox, the author of the *Address to the People of Great Britain*. Thus, critiques of consumer hypocrisy arose in conjunction with the ideals of the sympathetic consumer. Abolitionists countered these claims by either (a) asserting the strategic significance of sugar or (b) accepting the point and turning it against their critics, asking whether the charge of hypocrisy actually negated the force of their argument. See, for instance, Richard Hillier, *A Vindication of the Address to the People of Great-Britain on the Use of West India Produce: With Some Observations and Facts Relative to the Situation of Slaves: In Answer to a Female Apologist for Slavery* (London: M. Gurney, London, 1791); Cooper, *Considerations on the Slave Trade*, pp. 15–16.

82. William Allen, *The Duty of Abstaining from the Use of West India Produce, a Speech, Delivered at Coach-Maker's Hall, Jan.* 12, 1792, 2nd ed. (London: T. W. Hawkins, 1792), pp. 8–9 (italics and capitalization in original). Strikingly, Allen further applied this reasoning to public charities: "This Connection might also have been illustrated by a reference to the *Principle* upon which PUBLIC CHARITIES are supported—An *individual Subscriber* to a Benevolent Institution, cannot have a more *direct* concern in the GOOD thereby effected, than a *Consumer* of West India Produce has in the EVIL at-

tendant on the Slave Trade!" Thus, he offers an expanded ethical vision of the consumer that people typically associate with humanitarianism and socially responsible investing in contemporary capitalism. See, for example, Krause 2014.

83. *A Short Sketch of the Evidence Delivered Before a Committee of the House of Commons for the Abolition of the Slave-Trade*, 3rd ed. (London: M. Gurney, 1792), p. 21.

84. Fox, *An Address to the People of Great Britain*, 6th ed., p. 5.

85. Some critics of the sugar campaign accepted this vision of consumer power, while others challenged it. For the former, see *Strictures on an Address to the People of Great Britain*, pp. 7–8. For the latter, see *A Vindication of the Use of Sugar, the Produce of the West-India Islands. In Answer to a Pamphlet Entitled Remarkable Extracts, &c. &c.*, 2nd ed. (London: T. Boosey, 1792).

86. Cooper, *Considerations on the Slave Trade*, pp. 13–14; Fox, *An Address to the People of Great Britain, 24th ed.*, p. 1.

87. Allen, *The Duty of Abstaining*, p. 12.

88. An Act of the People, *No Rum!—No Sugar! Or, the Voice of Blood, Being Half an Hour's Conversation Between a Negro and an Englishman Shewing the Horrible Nature of the Slave Trade and Pointing out an Easy and Effectual Method of Terminating It* (London: L. Wayland, 1792), pp. 18–23.

89. Davis 1975, p. 436.

90. "Minutes of the Anti-Slavery Society," 29 September 1824, p. 139.

91. Advertisement, *East India sugar basins*, B. Henderson, China Warehouse, Rye-Lane, Peckham.

92. *Appeal to the Hearts and Consciences of British Women* (Leicester: A. Cockshaw, 1828), p. 6.

93. *Ladies' Anti-Slavery Associations* (Liverpool: 1827), p. 1; *The Ladies Association of Liverpool and Its Neighbourhood in the Aid of Negro Emancipation* (Liverpool: G. Smith, 1828), p. 1; *Rules and Resolutions of the Dublin Ladies' Anti-Slavery Society, with Lists of the Distinct Treasurers, Committees, and Secretaries, and of the Subscribers* (Dublin: R. Napper, 1828), p. 6.

94. Humanitas, *To the Society of Friends*, 26 May 1825; Mercator, "View of Some of the Advantages of the Tropical Free-Labour Company," *New Times*, 28 March 1825.

95. "There Is Death in the Pot!" (Newcastle: R. Ward, 1848).

96. Midgley 2007, p. 57.

97. Holcomb 2016, pp. 104–105; Stobart 2013, p. 46.

98. Julie Holcomb (2016) details the complicated influence of Black abolitionists, among others, on the free labor produce movement in Great Britain and the United States.

Chapter 3

1. Redfern 1913, p. 181.

2. Redfern 1946, pp. 31–42.

3. "Constitution: Article III," *Records of the National Consumers' League,* 1899.

4. Bandelj and Wherry 2011; DeSoucey 2010; Fairbrother 2014; Fourcade 2009, 2011; Lamont and Thevenot 2000.

5. Bendix 1977; Biernacki 1995; Moore 1966; Skocpol 1979; Tilly 1995.

6. The most consistent exponents of an alternative perspective tend to stress either local variation or monotonous cultural homogeneity (see, e.g., Appadurai 1986; Lechner & Boli 2005). This strikes me as a false choice. In Chapter 6, I illustrate that we can discuss the sympathetic consumer in a way that remains sensitive to local and regional variation. This desire is evident in a range of different works on racial capitalism, the capitalist world-system, and some ambitious projects in cultural sociology and aesthetics. What is needed, I think, is more work that seeks to specify how to identify and justify general cultural tendencies empirically. See Alexander 2006; Arrighi, Hopkins, and Wallerstein 1989; Bernstein 2018; Illouz 2007; Krause 2014; Ngai 2012; Ralph 2015.

7. Maddison 2007, pp. 73–74.

8. Fields 2004; Schivelbusch 2014.

9. Bair 2009.

10. Malm 2016.

11. Abrams, Li, and Mulligan 2013; Sklar 1995a; Wiebe 1967; immigration from east and south Asia also began to increase in the second half of the nineteenth century, though the United States restricted immigration from China in 1882.

12. Osterhammel 2014; Rosenberg 2012; Wallerstein 1983.

13. Engels 1993; Taylor 1975.

14. Booth 1903; Residents of Hull House 1895.

15. Grant 2005.

16. Robins 2012.

17. Joyce 1980; Rodgers 1978; Wright 1990.

18. de Grazia 2005; Livingston 1997; Sklar 1988.

19. Pugh 1999, pp. 122–123.

20. Blaszczyk 2008, p. 20; Schneirov 2006, pp. 207–208.

21. Glickman 1997.

22. Gurney 1996, pp. 17–18.

23. Clemens 1997; Rappaport 2000.

24. Pelling 1968; Powell 1992.

25. Jones 1974.

26. There is considerable debate about the extent to which we can say that these industrial transformations cause or are caused by shifts in consumer culture. To adjudicate such claims is not my purpose. Moreover, this debate often gives the impression that we can and should understand the economy and culture as separate spheres. For that reason, I leave the technical question about the different relations between production and consumption, supply and demand, to the side. The answer to such a question is important, but also would benefit from more context as well as analysis than I can provide here. For both context and analysis, the interested reader can see Lears 2009; Livingston 1997; Martin 1999; Mukerji 1983; Wilmers 2017.

27. Breen 2004; Bushman 1992; McKendrick, Brewer, and Plumb 1982; Trentmann 2016; Weatherill 1996.

28. Benson 1986; Bowlby 1985; Crossick and Jaumain 1999; Hetherington 2007; Leach 1993; Richards 1990.

29. Glickman 1997; Hobsbawm 1974.

30. "'Shop Window Rantin,' A Popular Institution in West Yorkshire Factory Circles," *Co-operative News*, 6 July 1912.

31. Ibid.

32. Crary 2000; Ewen 1976; Ohmann 1996; Rappaport 2000.

33. Benson 1981, p. 2; Leach 1993, p. 123. Jon Stobart (2017) cautions against assuming that all department stores operated strictly with fixed prices, though many certainly did.

34. On the counter, see Stobart 2017, pp. 833–844.

35. Benson 1981; Crossick and Jaumain 1999.

36. Blaszczyk 2008; Porter 1971; Stobart 2017.

37. Lancaster 1995; Miller 1981; on the use of shopping to create publics in late Victorian London, see Rappaport 2000.

38. Benson 1986; Opler 2018.

39. Bowlby 1985; Leach 1993.

40. Parker 2019, pp. 15–53.

41. Kelley 2016.

42. Kelley 1998; McGovern 2006, pp. 23–61; Schwarzkopf 2015; Trentmann 2008, pp. 125–130.

43. Baldasty 1992; Brown 1985.

44. Calder 1999; Gordon 2012; O'Connell 2009.

45. Enstad 1999; Johnson 1983; Yates and Hunter 2011.

46. Rappaport 1996.

47. Glickman 2009, pp. 61–90; Holcomb 2016.

48. Haydu and Skotnicki 2016, p. 348.

49. Gurney 2015; on free trade and the peculiarity of British modernity, see Gunn and Vernon 2011.

50. Ruskin 1903, p. 93.

51. Ibid., p. 103; see also Craig 2006.

52. Grimmer-Solem 2003; Stapleford 2009; Taylor 1975.

53. These campaigns often had profoundly exclusionary consequences for women and non-white workers; see Glickman 1997, pp. 108–128, 133–146.

54. *National Union of Boot and Shoe Operators, Monthly Report,* January 1908, p. 13; however, the trade union label or stamp was not publicized until late 1910 or early 1911. More on this trade union in Chapter 6.

55. Trentmann 2016, pp. 146–160.

56. Jevons 2013, p. 39.

57. Cited in Trentmann 2016, p. 153.

58. Horowitz 1985; Williams 1982, pp. 276–321.

59. First Meeting of the Conference of the Federation of Consumers' Leagues, 16 May 1898; while sometimes used by local leagues after 1899, white lists were largely superseded by the development of the label. See Wiedenhoft 2008, p. 286.

60. Sklar 1995a.

61. Du Bois 1966, p. 99.

62. Hofstadter 1955; McGerr 2003; Painter 2008; Rodgers 1998.

63. *Annual Report of the National Consumers' League* 1900–1901.

64. Sklar 1998; Storrs 2000, p. 26.

65. For example, see Kelley 1901.

66. There is some irony in the league's influence on continental Europe. The Consumers' League of New York City adopted its name from the Consumers' League of London, an organization that existed for a few years and about which little information remains. But, by the late 1890s, the London group had long since disappeared as the founder, Clementina Black, turned her attention toward trade unions. More on this issue later in the chapter.

67. For histories of the Co-operative Wholesale Society during this period, see Briggs and Saville 1971; Cole 1944; Gurney 1996; Redfern 1913; Webb 1930.

68. *Co-operative People's Yearbook* 1950, cited in Wilson, Webster, and Vorberg-Rugh 2013, p. 68.

69. Gurney 1996, pp. 19–20.

70. "Report of the Central Board," *Forty-Sixth Annual Co-operative Congress*, 1914, p. 80.

71. E. C. Sharland, "Talks on Co-operation," 1898, p. 11.

72. Scott 1998.

73. Cited in Scott 1998, p. 42. For a survey of Davies's life, see Scott 1998, pp. 35–66, and Oldfield 1998.

74. The Co-operative Union was a federated body that included representatives of the English and Scottish Co-operative Wholesale Societies, a range of distributive societies, and associations of producers owned by the CWS. In contrast to the CWS, which concentrated on retail and funded co-operative productions, the Co-operative Union was the "propagandist" wing of the co-operative movement. While not directly engaged in politics, this group used its power to support the co-operative cause. It played a controversial role in doing so. In either case, the CWS was by far the largest member of the Co-operative Union and thus shaped the bulk of its advocacy. On this issue, see Webb 1904.

75. *Thirty-second Annual Report of the Women's Co-operative Guild*, May 1914–1915, p. 3.

76. First Meeting of the Conference on the Federation of Consumers' Leagues, 16 May 1898.

77. Second Meeting of the Conference on the Federation of Consumers' Leagues, 17 May 1898.

78. "Constitution," *Annual Report of the National Consumers' League* 1900–1901, p. 3.

79. "Letter to Myrta," 18 September 1915, in Kelley 2009, p. 204.

80. "Report of 1914," *Consumers' League of New York Membership Pamphlet.*

81. Kelley 1899, p. 290.

82. "Constitution," *Annual Report of the National Consumers' League* 1900–1901, p. 3.

83. *Annual Report of the National Consumers' League* 1902–1903, p. 38.

84. List of Manufacturers Using This Label, 1916. The NCL wavered from referring to the consumer in the abstract, often with masculine "universal" pronouns to explicit allusions to women as consumers. It strikes me that the league rhetoric grasps at the arguable universality of the consumer's position vis-à-vis labor and capital, while recognizing that, in practice, women were often the shoppers.

85. Hobson 1938.

86. Nathan 1926, p. 23.

87. Hobson 1901, p. 368.

88. Ibid., p. 370.

89. Ibid., p. 372.

90. Hobson 1898, p. 218.

91. Brooks 1900, p. 3.

92. Ibid., p. 19.

93. See, for instance, "First Plans for CWS" in Percy Redfern's *The Story of the C.W.S.* (1913, pp. 405–413). This plan focused on wholesale purchasing and establishing stores. It made no claims for the consumers or buyers, as such, even though the consumer is, as Redfern suggests, largely implicit.

94. "Consumers' v. Producers' Co-operation," Editorial, *Co-operative News,* 4 December 1920.

95. The middlemen—people who operated for-profit shops to sell goods made elsewhere—were great villains in the co-operative world. They represented the worst of competitive, capitalist society. For more on the conflict between co-operators and middlemen, see Chapter 6.

96. This was also true of the National Consumers' League. In a 1919 letter to American Federation of Labor leader Samuel Gompers, Newton Baker—the second league president—observed: "[O]ver these two groups [labor and capital] and including them both stands the great public, which has specialized itself into all sorts of activities to carry on the business, preserve the health, promote the education and recreation, and minister to the higher aesthetic and artistic needs of a modern society."

97. Redfern 1946, p. 155.

98. "Problems for Co-operators. How Consumers are Becoming Slaves of Private Producers," *Co-operative News,* 23 September 1911, p. 1216.

99. Ibid., p. 1216. (italics added)

100. For instance, "Sweating and Some Remedies," *Co-operative News,* 5 October 1889, p. 1089; "The Duty of the Store to the Wholesale," *Co-operative News,* 4 July 1891, p. 678.

101. "Worker, Consumer, and Capitalist," *Co-operative News,* 8 March 1890, p. 231; all of the towns mentioned were sites of co-operative manufacturing.

102. "Employment of Women in Shops," *Co-operative News*, 8 September 1884, p. 1030.

103. "The Taint of the Sweater," *Co-operative News*, 26 May 1906, p. 584.

104. "Mancunian," "Workmen as Producers and Consumers," *Co-operative News*, 8 December 1900, p. 1383.

105. Ibid., p. 1383.

106. "The Sweating System," *Manchester & Salford Equitable Society Monthly Herald*, August 1902, vol. 14, no. 165, pp. 132–133. Beatrice Potter (later Webb)—no relation to Beatrix Potter, the writer and conservationist—was a social reformer and researcher who helped to establish the London School of Economics and played a significant role in the Fabian Society, an organization of British socialists founded at the end of the nineteenth century.

107. "The Revolt of the Consumer," *Co-operative News*, 28 September 1912, p. 1214.

108. "All Women Should Vote," *Bolton Co-operative Record*, March 1908.

109. For example, Percy Redfern, "The Store Movement and the Wholesale Society," Committee of Enquiry into Control of Industry, Barrow House Conference, 1913.

110. "The Women's Corner," *Co-operative News*, 6 January 1883.

111. "Objects of the Women's Co-operative League," Women's Corner, *Co-operative News*, 12 May 1883, p. 396.

112. Webb 1927, p. 18.

113. Annie M. Bacon, "The Art of Dress," *Co-operative News*, 1894, p. 1130; "Educating the Purchaser," *Co-operative News*, 1898, p. 802; "How to Do the Impossible," *Co-operative News*, 7 March 1903, p. 274; "Our Duties as Consumers," Editorial, Women's Corner, *Co-operative News*, 20 January 1912; "Shopping and How to Do It," *Co-operative News*, 9 April 1892.

114. "Store discipline" referred to consistent shopping at co-operative stores, rather than seeking deals at non–co-operative shops. See "The Store Discipline," Editorial, *Co-operative News*, 12 March 1898, p. 278.

115. "Educating the Purchaser," Women's Corner, *Co-operative News*, 1898, p. 802.

116. Geraldine Hodgson, "Papers on the Growth and Acquisition of Wealth: Paper V.—The Consumer," *Co-operative News*, 11 January 1890, p. 44.

117. M. C. Spooner, "The Co-operative Store: Paper I. Committees, Members, & Employes," n.d., *Women's Co-operative Guild*, p. 3. (italics in original)

118. Margaret Llewelyn Davies, "Our Duties as Consumers," *Co-operative News*, 20 January 1912, p. 78.

119. Ibid.

120. Ibid.

121. "The Woman with the Basket," *Co-operative News*, 2 January 1909, p. 22.

122. Ibid., p. 23.

123. Barbara Blaszak offers a comprehensive discussion of the gendered politics of co-operation. In particular, she notes that male co-operators advocated an "active" brand of consumption that flattered their image of masculinity. As I will show, we need not ignore the gendered character of consumption in the co-operative movement to il-

lustrate certain ways that male and female co-operators articulated a common vision of the consumer. On gendered co-operation, see Blaszak 2000, p. 1–24.

124. Many British historians assume that the idiosyncratic strength of free trade ideology in the British empire is sufficient to draw clear distinctions between the two. American historians are more likely to ignore England entirely. See, for example, Hilton 2003, p. 51; Trentmann 2008, p. 17; on free trade, see Grampp 1987; Howe 1997. One notable exception is Ian Mitchell (2015), who argues that the Christian Social Union—an organization of reform-minded Anglicans founded in Oxford at the end of the nineteenth century—took up the mantle of the failed Consumers' League in London. The CSU certainly fit into this tradition as well, though they did not foreground the consumer like other turn-of-the-century activists. Their penchant for "white lists" of righteous shops and organized buying campaigns were but one element of a broader project to bend a secular economy to Christian principles. I discuss them briefly in Chapter 5.

125. "The Working Women's Society," *New York Times*, 10 November 1889.

126. Hilton 2003, p. 51.

127. Ibid., pp. 47, 51.

128. Vincent 2006, p. 38.

129. In an early article promoting the National Consumers' League, Florence Kelley noted the kinship between consumer co-operation in Great Britain and the consumers' leagues in the United States: "All factory legislation is enacted in recognition of the fact that the human relations of supply and demand are susceptible of beneficent modifications; the coöperative movement is a further witness to the same fact; the Consumers' League, latest comer in this field, aims at still another demonstration of this truth" (Kelley 1899, p. 295).

130. Breen 2004; Cohen 2003; Glickman 2009; de Grazia 2005; Hilton 2003; Maclachlan 2006; Strasser, McGovern, and Judt 1998; Trentmann 2008; Yates and Hunter 2011. Frank Trentmann's (2016) global history of consumption since the fifteenth century both breaks with and conforms to this pattern. While tracing the emergence of a world of consumers, he judiciously examines the many varied regional meanings that consumption has taken.

131. Loveman 2014; Mudge 2018; Paschel 2016.

Chapter 4

1. William C. Fox, *An Address to the People of Great Britain, on the Propriety of Abstaining from West India Sugar and Rum*, 24th ed. (London: M. Gurney, 1791), pp. 2–3; for an account of the literary and sociopolitical history of abolition, see Charlotte Sussman (2000, p. 43). She describes the ways that antislavery activists equated sugar and rum with the bodily secretions of the enslaved people who produced them. These equations implied that consumers were cannibals. It is worth noting that Marx also satirizes the consumer as a cannibal in *Capital*. On this, see Sutherland 2008.

2. Fox, *An Address to the People of Great Britain*, 24th ed., pp. 2–3.

3. Ibid., 24th ed., p. 3.

4. Katy, "Shopping," *Co-operative News*, 11 June 1892, pp. 638–639.

5. Ibid.

6. Berger 1977.

7. Fox, *An Address to the People of Great Britain*, 24th ed., p. 5.

8. Thomas Cooper, *Considerations on the Slave Trade and the Consumption of West Indian Produce* (London: Darton and Harvey, 1791), p. 4.

9. Elihu Burritt, "*Twenty Reasons for Total Abstinence from Slave-Labour Produce*" (1853).

10. *The Case of Our Fellow-Creatures the Oppressed Africans, Respectfully Recommended to the Serious Consideration of the Legislature of Great-Britain by the People called Quakers* (London: James Phillips, 1783).

11. Andrew Burn, *A Second Address to the People of Great Britain Containing a New, and Most Powerful Argument to Abstain from the Use of West India Sugar by an Eye Witness to the Facts Related* (London: M. Gurney, 1792), p. 4.

12. Ibid., p. 4.

13. Sussman's work explores the rhetorical work of abolitionists and, especially, the gendered dynamics of abolitionist consumer activism in her excellent *Consuming Anxieties* (2000). For examples of poetry, see Cowper's *A Subject for Conversation and Reflection at the Tea Table* (London, 1788), pp. 1–4.

14. "The Sugar-Plums," *The Abolitionist: or Record of the New England Anti-Slavery Society*, 1833, p. 33.

15. *Birmingham Female Society for the Relief of Negro Slaves, First Report*, cited in Sussman 2000, p. 141.

16. *The Ladies Association of Liverpool and Its Neighbourhood*, 1827, p. 6.

17. George Thompson, *Substance of an Address to the Ladies of Glasgow and Its Vicinity upon the Present Aspect of the Great Question of Negro Emancipation: Delivered in Mr. Anderson's Chapel, John-St., Glasgow, on Tuesday, March 5th, 1833* (Glasgow: D. Robertson, 1833).

18. Benjamin Franklin, *Memoirs of the Life and Writings of Benjamin Franklin* (London: Henry Colburn, 1818), p. 542; paraphrased in Fox, *An Address to the People of Great Britain*, 6th ed., p. 3, as: "a French writer observes, 'That he cannot look upon a piece of sugar without conceiving it stained with human blood' and Dr. Franklin adds, that had he taken in all the consequences 'he might have seen the sugar not merely spotted, but thoroughly dyed scarlet in grain.'"

19. Burn, *A Second Address to the People of Great Britain*, p. 7.

20. William Allen, *The Duty of Abstaining from the Use of West India Produce, a Speech, Delivered at Coach-Maker's Hall, Jan. 12, 1792*, 2nd ed. (London: T. W. Hawkins, 1792), p. 10.

21. "*There Is Death in the Pot!*" (Newcastle: R. Ward, 1848).

22. For an account of the visual iconography of the antislavery movement, see Fuyuki Kurasawa (2014).

23. Stamatov 2013, pp. 159–160.

24. Kurasawa 2014, pp. 9–18.

25. *Ladies' Anti-Slavery Associations* (Liverpool: 1827).

26. Advertisement, East India sugar basins, B. Henderson, China Warehouse, Rye-Lane, Peckham.

27. Advertisement at the close of Burritt, "*Twenty Reasons for Total Abstinence from Slave-Labour Produce,*" p. 4.

28. "*There Is Death in the Pot!*" p. 4.

29. Ibid., p. 1.

30. Ibid.

31. "The Charity Side of the Labor Problem," *Annual Report of the National Consumers' League* 1904, pp. 17–18.

32. "Sweating Evil," February 1908, vol. 20, no. 231, p. 24.

33. *Annual Report of the National Consumers' League* 1900–1901, p. 14. (italics in original)

34. Ibid., p. 14. (italics added)

35. Redfern 1913, p. 291.

36. "Forward by the President," *The Work of the Consumers' League of the City of New York*, 1915, p. 6.

37. "The Poor Consumer," *Co-operative News*, 17 November 1906, p. 1354.

38. Kelley 1899, p. 303.

39. Florence Kelley, "The Responsibilities of the Consumer," *Annals of the American Academy of Political and Social Science*, 32, suppl. 22 (1908). Child Labor and Social Progress. Proceedings of the Fourth Annual Meeting of the National Child Labor Committee, p. 109.

40. "Report of the Secretary," *Annual Report of the National Consumers' League* 1914–1917, pp. 20–21.

41. Ibid., p. 21.

42. R.,"Time and Trade: Should Co-operative Societies Advertise?" *Co-operative News*, 4 September 1909, p. 1137; on the co-operative struggles with advertising, see Kelley 1998.

43. "Report of the Secretary," p. 12.

44. *Annual Report of the National Consumers' League* 1900–1901, inside front cover.

45. "Committee on Label," *Consumers' League of the City of New York*, 1915, pp. 35–36.

46. Gurney 2017, pp. 111–112.

47. However, local wholesale societies were not required to stock goods exclusively produced in co-operative industries for co-operative stores. This was a common issue that cropped up in discussions of loyalty to the co-operative store. But reports of labeling issues analogous to the kind experienced by the consumers' leagues are scant.

48. "Workmen as Producers and Consumers," The Labor World, *Co-operative News*, 8 December 1900, p. 1383.

49. Ibid.

50. This text comes from a 1916 advertisement for co-operative clothing; see *Co-operative News*, 22 January 1916, p. x. Advertisements for co-operative products appear in many co-operative publications, including the national weekly *Co-operative News*, local monthly papers published by individual co-operative societies, and co-operative journals such as *The Wheatsheaf*.

51. *Thirteenth Annual Report of the Women's Co-operative Guild, April* 1895–1896, p. 5.

52. The article spanned two issues of the *Manchester & Salford Monthly Equitable Society Monthly Herald*, October 1908, vol. 20, no. 239, pp. 206–210, and November 1908, vol. 20, no. 241, p. 228.

53. "The Taint of the Sweater," Editorial, *Co-operative News*, 26 May 1906, p. 583.

54. *Annual Report of the National Consumers' League* 1905–1906, pp. 4, 13, 24, 28, 36, 38, 40, 44, 45, 48, 49.

55. The Consumers' League of the City of New York, *Children Who Work in the Tenements*, March 1908; "Appendix VII," *What the United States Government Says About Child Labor in Tenements*, New York Child Labor Committee, March 1911.

56. See *Manchester & Salford Equitable Society Monthly Herald*, October 1900, vol. 12, no. 143.

57. "A 'Corner' in Biscuits," *Manchester & Salford Equitable Society Monthly Herald*, March 1908, vol. 20, no. 232, p. 47; "Bacon," *Manchester & Salford Equitable Society Monthly Herald*, May 1910, vol. 22, no. 257, p. 93; "C.W.S. Drug Works," *Manchester & Salford Equitable Society Monthly Herald*, September 1910, vol. 22, no. 261, pp. 170–173.

58. Mitchell 1989; Richards 1990.

59. For instance, "On the Trail of the Sweater" described a conference with displays of sweating conditions in the chocolate, confectionary, trade biscuits, jellies, and pickle-making trades. "On the Trail of the Sweater," *Co-operative News*, 14 March 1914; on the significance of exhibitions to the co-operative movement, see Gurney 1996, pp. 79–80.

60. Cited in Gurney 1996, p. 80.

61. *1900 CWS Balance Sheets and Annual Report*, p. 79.

62. "Demonstration at Bolton," *Co-operative News*, 1 February 1902, p. 124.

63. "The Annual Report of the WCG," *Co-operative News*, 23 May 1891, p. 518.

64. On lantern lectures and turn-of-the-twentieth-century humanitarianism, see Grant 2005, pp. 39–78.

65. "Bristol Society: Report of the Women's Guild," *Annual Co-operative Congress*, 1906, pp. 159–160; "Co-operative Production," *Twenty-Seventh Annual Report of the Women's Co-operative Guild, May* 1909–1910, pp. 12–13; *Sixteenth Annual Report of the Co-operative Women's Guild, April* 1898–1899, p. 5.

66. "A Factory Entertains a League," *Annual Report of the National Consumers' League* 1902–1903, p. 15.

67. "Exhibits of Labeled Goods," *Annual Report of the National Consumers' League* 1901–1902, pp. 21–22.

68. "Report of the Committee on Exhibits," *Annual Report of the National Consumers' League* 1914–1917, p. 46.

69. Ibid.

70. "A Factory Entertains a League," *Annual Report of the National Consumers' League* 1902–1903, pp. 15–16.

71. "Exhibitions," *Annual Report of the National Consumers' League* 1906–1907, pp. 17–18.

72. "Sub-Committee on Exhibits," *The Consumers' League of the City of New York,* 1914, p. 26.

73. "Committee on Label," *Consumers' League of the City of New York,* 1915, p. 37.

74. "Workmen as Producers and Consumers," *Co-operative News,* 8 December 1900, p. 1382.

75. "Report of the Executive Committee," *National Consumers' League Archives,* 2 February 1898.

76. While chattel slavery contradicts a common tendency in capitalist societies—the use of free labor—historians acknowledge that slave labor and other forms of coercive extraction have been and continue to be essential to capitalism. Many have challenged the notion that free labor is a defining feature of capitalist societies, emphasizing instead the role of commodification, primitive accumulation, and a broad understanding of labor's role as a commodity (which includes slavery and impressed agricultural labor). On this, see Postone 1993; Robinson 1983; Wallerstein 1976. One crucial question is, What does the relationship between capitalism and slavery tell us about capitalism as a social system? Robin Blackburn (1998) reminds us that the ancient institution of slavery took on novel characteristics with the rise of plantation slavery in the European imperial colonies. Most important, slavery became a fundamentally commercial institution, oriented toward the production of cash crops like sugar, cotton, indigo, rice, and more. Historians disagree about the implications of this development for our understanding of the relationship between slavery and capitalism. For a summary and assessment of ongoing historiographical debates, see Clegg 2020.

77. In this paragraph, I draw on Glickman 2009, pp. 61–89, and Holcomb 2016.

78. Ibid., pp. 73–76.

79. Cited in Glickman 2009, p. 79.

80. Ibid.

81. On the evangelical character of this activism, see Abzug 1994; Bolt and Drescher 1980; Young 2005.

82. Glickman 2009, p. 63.

83. Fox, *An Address to the People of Great Britain,* 24th ed., p. 3.

84. Burn, *A Second Address to the People of Great Britain,* pp. 6–11.

85. Katy, "Shopping."

86. For an elaboration on this argument that compares consumer activism and environmental justice advocacy, see Skotnicki 2019. Caroline Heldman's (2017) account of consumer activism in the contemporary United States illustrates how such contests over the meaning of goods—particularly arguments about how to understand the relations of goods to the conditions of their production, distribution, and sale—shape the politics of consumption.

87. For more systematic discussions of the limits of focusing on consumers, see Robins 2012; Szasz 2007; for more conceptual arguments, see Bauman 2008, pp. 109–193; Žižek 2009, pp. 52–55.

88. *The Work of the Consumers' League of the City of New York,* 1915, pp. 35–36.

Chapter 5

1. William Bell Crafton, *A Short Sketch of the Evidence Delivered Before a Committee of the House of Commons for the Abolition of the Slave Trade,* 3rd ed. (1792), p. 21. (italics and capitalization in original)

2. Ibid., p. 21.

3. "Constitution: Article III," *Records of the National Consumers' League,* 1899.

4. Abend 2014a.

5. "Report of Committee on Advertising," *National Consumers' League Archives,* 27 January 1904; on the Union Label League, see Plumb 1951, pp. 13–14.

6. "Minutes of the May Meeting of the Massachusetts Consumers' League," May 1908.

7. Abend 2014a, p. 30.

8. Ibid., pp. 33–52.

9. Ibid., pp. 18, 33.

10. Ibid., p. 362.

11. Abend observes that the categories of the moral background are different kinds of things than phenomenal experiences. Following Kant, he writes, "[T]he categories are prior to and condition experience" (2014a, p. 53); that is, moral phenomena depend on moral categories. Without the latter, the former becomes unintelligible. Thus, the reasoning goes, because many of us classify sharks and humans as different kinds of things (one may be a godless killing machine and the other may not be, though who can say which is which), we will arrive at different moral judgments when they harm ocean swimmers. Without such a priori classifications, often made implicitly, we would be unable to understand let alone assess these events. In this way, the moral phenomenon of judging a human or a shark responsible for such harms incurred depends on the categories of the moral background—most often implicit judgments about the nature of morality, not the moral values, judgments, and actions themselves. One need not adjudicate Abend's claim about the origins of morality to inquire whether the phenomena and circumstances about which people render moral judgments can condition moral background categories. It is reasonable to inquire into the historical development and elaboration of these background categories as they are applied in the realm of phenomenal experience. Were a category like "consumer" or "citizen" to become an established means of thinking about sharks, then it would stand to reason that there would be an associated shift in our moral judgments of the harms visited upon ocean swimmers. Further, it would be well worth asking what about the world may have contributed to this innovation in moral background categories.

12. *Thoughts on the Slavery of the Negroes* (London: James Phillips, 1784), p. 6.

13. Ibid., pp. 6–7.

14. Ibid., pp. 18–19.

15. I am grateful to Tien-Ann Shih for insisting on this point.

16. William Dillwyn and John Lloyd, *The Case of Our Fellow-Creatures, the Oppressed Africans* (London: James Phillips, 1784), pp. 3, 10.

17. Ibid., pp. 11–12.

18. C. B. Wadström, *Observations on the Slave Trade and a Description of Some Part of the Coast of Guinea, During a Voyage, Made in 1787 and 1788* (London: James Phillips, 1789), pp. iv–v.

19. Ibid., p. v; in addition to the allusion to Adam Smith's *Wealth of Nations*, one can also sense the author's dismay that commerce could benefit particular individuals at the expense of the common good. Wadström wrote, "This detestable abuse may be considered as proceeding from a degenerate love of *dominion*, and of possessing the property of others, which instead of diffusing the genial influence of benevolence and liberty, produces, in their state of inversion, all the horrors of tyranny and slavery." On the discourse of the civilizing nature of commerce, see Hirschman 1977.

20. Dillwyn and Lloyd, *The Case of Our Fellow-Creatures*, p. 10.

21. Wadström, *Observations on the Slave Trade*, p. 49.

22. James Ramsay, *Objections to the Abolition of the Slave Trade, with Answers* (London: James Phillips, 1788), p. 16.

23. Ibid., p. 29.

24. The rather anodyne term "seasoning" came from the settlers and plantation owners. It referred to the first two years of chattel servitude, when enslaved Africans were especially likely to die in the brutal plantation conditions of life and labor. Thomas Cooper, *Considerations on the Slave Trade and the Consumption of West Indian Produce* (London: Darton and Harvey, 1791), p. 13. (italics in original)

25. Ibid., p. 13.

26. Ibid., pp. 14–15; Cooper included a footnote that explains the strategy for focusing on sugar: "It is the cultivation of sugar-cane alone which supports the trade; the other articles, such as cotton, pimento, indigo, &c. requiring comparatively little attention."

27. My point is not that abolitionists invented such syllogistic moral reasoning or that such reasoning is capitalist. Obviously, that would be nonsense. I want to demonstrate only that their particular moral reasoning, focused on the guilt of the consumer, depends essentially on their account of British imperial commerce.

28. Andrew Burn, *A Second Address to the People of Great Britain Containing a New, and Most Powerful Argument to Abstain from the Use of West India Sugar by an Eye Witness to the Facts Related* (London: M. Gurney, 1792), p. 7.

29. *An Address to Her Royal Highness the Duchess of York Against the Use of Sugar* (London, 1792), p. 21.

30. Ibid., pp. 16–17. (italics in original)

31. *An Address to Her Royal Highness,* p. 12.

32. William Allen, *The Duty of Abstaining from the Use of West India Produce, a Speech, Delivered at Coach-Maker's Hall, Jan. 12, 1792, 2nd ed.* (London: T. W. Hawkins, 1792), p. 8.

33. Ibid., pp. 9–10.

34. Cooper, *Considerations on the Slave Trade,* pp. 15–16.

35. William C. Fox, *An Address to the People of Great Britain, on the Propriety of Abstaining from West India Sugar and Rum,* 10th ed. *(London: M. Gurney,* 1791), p. 14. (italics in original)

36. *An Address to Her Royal Highness,* p. 10.

37. Ibid., p. 15.

38. Ibid., p. 16.

39. Ibid., p. 17.

40. *West India Sugar* (London: Bagster and Thoms, 1826/1827), p. 1. (capitalization in original)

41. Elizabeth Heyrick, *An Appeal to the Hearts and Consciences of British Women (London: A. Cockshaw,* 1828), p. 9.

42. Committee on Slavery Minutes, Public Meeting, Freemason's Hall, 30 April 1825, pp. 20–21. As British manufacturing grew and the empire shifted toward liberal, free trade policies in the late 1820s and 1830s, the position of the plantation owners became more tenuous; see, for example, Ryden 2012; Williams 1994.

43. Fox, *An Address to the People of Great Britain,* 10th ed., p. 13.

44. Cooper, *Considerations on the Slave Trade,* p. 14. (italics in original)

45. Florence Kelley, "The Responsibility of the Consumer," *Annals of the American Academy of Political and Social Science,* 32, suppl. 22. (1908). Child Labor and Social Progress. Proceedings of the Fourth Annual Meeting of the National Child Labor Committee, p. 108.

46. "The Next Budget," *Co-operative News,* 19 January 1895, pp. 60–61.

47. *Twenty-Five Years of the Consumers' League of the City of New York,* 1916, p. 14.

48. Kelley, "The Responsibility of the Consumer," p. 108.

49. "Labor and Consumption," Editorial, *Co-operative News,* 1 October 1892.

50. Brooks 1900, p. 4.

51. Ibid., pp. 108–109.

52. *Annual Report of the National Consumers' League* 1900–1901, p. 11–12.

53. Ibid., p. 11.

54. Ibid., p. 12.

55. Kelley, "The Responsibility of the Consumer," pp. 108–109.

56. Ibid., p. 109.

57. Ibid., p. 111.

58. "Educating the Purchaser," *Co-operative News,* 12 March 1898, p. 278.

59. "The Sweating System," *Co-operative News,* 13 October 1906, p. 1214.

60. "The Taint of the Sweater," *Co-operative News,* 26 May 1906, p. 583.

61. Ibid., p. 584.

62. Geraldine Hodgson, "Papers on the Growth and Acquisition of Wealth: The Consumer," *Co-operative News*, 11 January 1890, p. 44.

63. "Ethical Side of Democracy," *Co-operative News*, 15 August 1905, pp. 266–267.

64. The manufacturing sites named in the letter refer specifically to co-operative productions—that is, industries collectively owned by the Co-operative Wholesale Society—though they were run separately as co-operative productions. Joseph Tyldesley, "Letter," *Co-operative News*, 8 March 1890, p. 231.

65. Redfern 1913, p. 81.

66. Maud Nathan, "First Meeting of the Conference on the Federation of Consumers' Leagues," 16 May 1898.

67. "Educating the Purchaser," p. 802.

68. George Holyoake, "Anti-Boycott Papers V: The Distinction Between the Shop and the Store," *Co-operative News*, 13 December 1902, pp. 1415–1417.

69. Ibid., p. 1415.

70. "The Poor Consumer," *Co-operative News*, 17 November 1906.

71. Redfern 1913, p. 111.

72. Davies's "Introduction" in Webb 1927, p. 12.

73. "The Revolt of the Consumer," *Co-operative News*, 28 September 1912, p. 1214.

74. "Educating the Purchaser," p. 802.

75. See, for instance, George E. Colpus, "Should We Advertise?" *Co-operative News*, 7 September 1907, p. 1130; R., "Time and Trade: Should Co-operative Societies Advertise?" *Co-operative News*, 4 September 1909, p. 1137.

76. An outfit called Nelson's offered "pension tea," which was advertised to women and sold well above market value. They promised to deliver a pension to these women later in life, particularly in the event that a woman became a widow. In 1905, before paying out a single "pension," the company was declared insolvent. See "The Co-operative Conscience," *Co-operative News*, 25 February 1905, p. 226.

77. "The Bogus of 'Bonus' Tea," *Co-operative News*, 8 September 1906.

78. "The Co-operative Conscience," p. 226.

79. "Credit in the Stores," Women's Corner, *Co-operative News*, 24 December 1898, p. 1452. This concern with credit was heightened by the legal status of women in late Victorian England, who were frequently unable to buy on credit without a husband's permission or without rendering the husband legally responsible for his wife's debts. See Rappaport 1996.

80. Kelley 1899, p. 294.

81. "Constitution: Article III," *Records of the National Consumers' League*, 1899.

82. "Protection for Women," *Buffalo Express*, 30 September 1901.

83. *Annual Report of the National Consumers' League* 1900–1901, p. 10.

84. "Committee on Publicity," *The Consumers' League of the City of New York*, 1914, p. 25.

85. "Luxuries," *Co-operative News*, 11 August 1894. (italics added)

86. Mitchell as quoted in Redfern 1913, p. 203.

87. *Eleventh Annual Report of the Co-operative Women's Guild*, p. 33.

88. Kelley 1899, p. 289.

89. "Article I, II, II," *Annual Report of the National Consumers' League* 1900–1901.

90. Davies 1904, p. 65.

91. Nash, "The Duties of Women as Consumers," cited in ibid., p. 68. (italics in original)

92. Redfern 1920, p. 8.

93. Davies 1904, pp. 68–69.

94. Kelley 1899, p. 289; John Graham Brooks adduced observations from whole swathes of economists to validate his claim that the consumer was responsible for the conditions of production. See Brooks 1900, pp. 4–10.

95. Brooks 1900, p. 24.

96. Kelley 1899, p. 299.

97. Ibid., p. 301.

98. Letter quoted in Davies 1904, p. 18.

99. "Experiments in Morals," *Co-operative News*, 15 April 1916, p. 400.

100. See, for instance, "Citadels of Thrift," *Co-operative News*, 10 February 1900, p. 138; "Employment of Women in Shops," *Co-operative News*, 8 September 1894, p. 1030; "A Homely Chat to Homely Folk," *Manchester & Salford Equitable Society Monthly Herald, November* 1908, vol. 20, pp. 242–251.

101. "The Duty of the Store to the Wholesale," *Co-operative News*, 4 July 1891, p. 673.

102. *Manchester & Salford Equitable Society Monthly Herald*, October 1900, vol. 12, no. 143, p. 148.

103. On Christian socialism in general, see Curtis 1991; Jones 1968; Norman 1987; on the relationship between co-operation and Christian socialism, in particular, see Backstrom 1974. Edward Vansittart Neale helped to compile a pamphlet called "Foundations: A Study in the Ethics and Economics of the Co-operative Movement," originally prepared in 1879 and republished in 1916. The first chapter addresses the relationship between co-operation and Christian faith.

104. There were many advertisements around Christmas and Easter in co-operative publications. These advertisements did not explicitly celebrate the theological significance of Christmas or Easter. Rather, they reinforced the observation that active co-operators may have been more publicly committed to Christian principles than the typical working-class consumer. For example, see the *Manchester & Salford Equitable Society Monthly Herald*, December 1906, vol. 18, no. 217. On the working class and Christianity, see Joyce 1980, pp. 176–179.

105. "Letter to Nicholas Kelley," 18 August 1904, in Kelley 2009, pp. 124–126.

106. "Letter to Katherine Lucy Trevett," in Kelley 2009, pp. 106–107.

107. Ely, a professor of economics at the University of Wisconsin, was also an active member of the Christian Social Union in the United States. John Graham Brooks, too, was affiliated with Christian socialism as a Unitarian minister and wrote extensively on labor issues.

108. *Annual Report of the National Consumers' League* 1904–1905, pp. 21–22.

109. *Annual Report of the National Consumers' League* 1903–1904, p. 8.

110. Ibid., p. 9.

111. See, for instance, "Brooklyn Auxiliary," *The Work of the Consumers' League of the City of New York,* 1915, p. 19.

112. *Annual Report of the National Consumers' League* 1903–1904.

113. For example, see the records of Florence Kelley's travels at the end of every annual report, which involved attending numerous meetings at churches, religious institutions, and affiliated organizations.

114. *Annual Report of the National Consumers' League* 1906–1907, p. 23.

115. Florence Kelley, "The Consumers' League," *American Journal of Nursing,* vol. 1, no. 9 (1901), p. 649.

116. Henry Scott Holland, "The Ground of Our Appeal," September 1907, found in the Christian Social Union archives at the Pusey House in Oxford.

117. "Morals of Political Economy," *Co-operative News,* 14 April 1888, p. 348; see Weber 1946, pp. 323–359.

118. I mentioned another difference at the end of the previous chapter: The abolitionists took a broader "transnational" or imperial approach to their activism, in contrast to the more narrowly circumscribed national activism at the turn of the twentieth century. But one must also bear in mind that any shift toward national consumer politics at the end of the nineteenth century occurred in the face of a trend toward even more observably global supply chains throughout the nineteenth and twentieth centuries. The transnational emphasis of the fair trade movement since the 1950s reflects this trend; see, for example, Keith Brown (2013). Thus, even these differences make sense in light of tendencies in capitalist development.

119. It is, I suppose, possible that someone could arrive at an argument about consumer responsibility to distant persons without establishing the consumer's power over merchants, producers, production, and other elements of these circuits. However, the method of argument would likely differ. There would be no need to follow the links in the chain that connect consumers to producers. An argument for responsibility could skip right to the scene of suffering and not bother to trace out any empirical links between the user and sufferer. Knowledge of suffering related to an object of use would be sufficient cause. Moreover, such an argument would have no evident reason to focus on consumers to address this issue as opposed to, say, workers or citizens or humans who have been made aware of otherwise invisible suffering. Thus, my claim that moral arguments for the sympathetic consumer *depended* on a capitalist social order is both warranted and nontrivial. In other words, this claim does not simply reflect the fact that the activists lived in a capitalist society; rather, as this chapter has shown, the claim picks out how specific features of a capitalist society played into and affected these moral arguments.

120. Davis 1975, p. 41.

121. Ibid., pp. 249–254.

122. Davis 1992, p. 308.

123. Haskell 1985b, p. 559. See also Haskell 1985a.

124. Haskell 1987, p. 852; others, like Seymour Drescher (1987), presented a case for the practical relevance of class, but not class hegemony. He argued that abolitionism grew up within industrial towns in England, relying on support from industrialists, artisans, and miners.

125. Brown 2006, pp. 391–450.

126. Stamatov (2013, pp. 73–96) illustrates, further, the logic of radicalization within the "organizational field of religion." In short, conflicts within religious confessions and sects nurtured humanitarian critiques of exploitative practices within the Spanish and British empire.

127. Ibid.; for another, related perspective on the religious origins of humanitarianism, see Dromi 2016.

128. See, for example, Brown 2006, pp. 20–22; Stamatov 2013, pp. 182–184, and Stamatov 2014.

129. Davis 1987, p. 798. (italics in original)

Chapter 6

1. I say "not necessarily" because there are, as I described in Chapter 4, some strategies that follow quite closely from inflexible interpretations *in* commodity-exchange. For the most part, though, the sympathetic consumer does not force or select but rather forms or limits. On forming and forcing causes, see Reed 2011, pp. 123–162; on selecting and limiting causes, see Wright, Levine, and Sober 1992, pp. 129–175. It may be reasonable to ask whether "cause" is the appropriate language to use in this instance, though I think this raises much larger questions about explanatory frameworks that I must address elsewhere.

2. "Workmen as Producers and Consumers," *Co-operative News*, 8 December 1900, p. 1383.

3. Redfern 1913, pp. iii–iv.

4. On the discussion of labor and consumption, see, for example, "The Claims of Labour and Consumption," Letters to the Editor, *Co-operative News*, 2 July 1892, p. 683; "Labour and Consumption," *Co-operative News*, 1 October 1892, pp. 1100–1102.

5. *Rules of the Women's Co-operative Guild*, 1894.

6. J. S. Appleby, "Co-operation and Culture," *Co-operative News*, 9 February 1907, p. 149.

7. "The Consumers' God," *Co-operative News*, 11 January 1913, pp. 40–41; the "big dividend" refers here to the rate received by co-operative members for purchasing their goods at the store, while the "women's minimum scale" refers to a recent decision to pay women workers at co-operative stores a minimum wage.

8. Davies 1904; "Ethical Democracy," *Co-operative News*, 9 February 1901, p. 1214; "Workmen as Producers and Consumers," *Co-operative News*, 8 December 1900, p. 1383.

9. "Trade Unionism and Co-operation," *Co-operative News*, 30 September 1911, p. 1258.

10. George Quirk, "The C.W.S. and the Trade Union Label," *Co-operative News*, 30 September 1911, p. 1253.

11. *Report of the Trade Unions Congress*, September 1907, pp. 126–127.

12. Ibid., p. 127.

13. "C.W.S. vs. Label," *Co-operative News*, 23 September 1911, p. 1211.

14. See, for example, ads regarding co-operative clothing: "All Women Should Vote," *Bolton Co-operative Record*, March 1908; "Produced . . . Under the Best Conditions of Labour," *Co-operative News*, 22 January 1916, p. x.

15. "C.W.S. vs. Label," *Co-operative News*, 23 September 1911, p. 1212.

16. "About the Label," *Co-operative News*, 16 September 1911, p. 1192.

17. "Problems for Co-operators: How Consumers Are Becoming the Slaves of Private Producers," *Co-operative News*, 23 September 1911, p. 1216.

18. "C.W.S. and the Trade Union Label," Letters, *Co-operative News*, 23 September 1911, p. 1225.

19. *National Union of Boot and Shoe Operators Monthly Report*, October 1909, pp. 447–448.

20. "C.W.S. v. Label," *Co-operative News*, 23 September 1911, p. 1211; A. H. Gill and James Johnston, *Joint Committee Meetings for Trade Unionists and Co-operators*, 1907, p. 135.

21. *Tenth Annual Report of the Women's Co-operative Guild*, April 1893, p. 18.

22. "Trade Unionism and Co-operation," *Co-operative News*, 30 September 1911, p. 1262.

23. "Indirect" refers here to work not immediately within and for the co-operative movement. So these forms of activism were indirect in relation to the guild's support of co-operation. But the guild also recognized, obviously, that broader social and political reform would entail consequences for the co-operative movement.

24. *Thirteenth Annual Report of the Women's Co-operative Guild*, April 1895–1896, pp. 3–4.

25. The Women's Co-operative Guild received some funding from the Co-operative Wholesale Society. In the years from 1910 on, many guild members advocated divorce law reform, which would have lowered the standards of proof of adultery, cruelty, rape, and other charges for women who sought a divorce. Owing to pressure from Catholic groups, the CWS was hesitant to support, even indirectly, divorce law reform. Thus, the Co-operative Congress, which included the CWS, withdrew its grant to the Women's Co-operative Guild in 1914. See *Thirty-second Annual Report of the Women's Co-operative Guild*, May 1914–1915, p. 1.

26. While I focus on the status of women because this was an explicit issue for the guild, it is important to recall that these conflicts also elicit a distinctively masculine identity and response from the CWS. These gender dynamics were encoded into the organization of co-operative life. This makes their convergence upon a shared ideology, strategies, and moral argumentation all the more remarkable. On this, see Blaszak 2000.

27. Miss R. E. Brown, "The Present Position of Working Women as Co-operators and Citizens," *Co-operative News*, June 1900, pp. 702–703; "Employment of Women in Shops," *Co-operative News*, 8 September 1894, p. 1030.

28. M. C. Spooner, "The Co-operative Store: Paper I. Committees, Members, & Employes," *Women's Co-operative Guild*, n.d., p. 10.

29. Ibid.

30. *Twenty-fourth Annual Report of the Women's Co-operative Guild*, May 1906–1907, p. 13.

31. *Twenty-sixth Annual Report of the Women's Co-operative Guild*, May 1908–1909, p. 5.

32. *Twenty-seventh Annual Report of the Women's Co-operative Guild*, May 1909–1910, p. 1.

33. *Thirty-first Annual Report of the Women's Co-operative Guild*, May 1913–1914, p. 4.

34. Ibid., p. 4. (italics added)

35. "Trade Unionism and Co-operation." Women's Corner, *Co-operative News*, 7 October 1911, p. 1258.

36. Ibid.

37. William Marcroft, as quoted in Redfern 1913, p. 20.

38. For instance, co-operators could reject booksellers as middlemen, or any other traders who "merely" bought and sold goods. See the February 17, 1883, issue of the *Co-operative News*, p. 139. Co-operation entailed shared ownership and therefore, at least in theory, less dependence on the profit motive because all profits were to be redistributed to members in the form of a dividend. Sometimes, co-operators compared the middleman to other morally suspect characters like the gambler or the speculator. "The Middleman Ethically Considered," *Co-operative News*, 16 January 1897, p. 61.

39. "Abeawt This Boycott," *Co-operative News*, 18 October 1902, p. 1268.

40. "The Insolence of the Butchers," *Co-operative News*, 17 July 1897, p. 785.

41. "The Philosophy of the Boycott," *Co-operative News*, 25 December 1897, pp. 1442–1443.

42. "The Boycott in England," *Co-operative News*, 26 July 1902, p. 911.

43. "The Ill-Timed Boycott," *Co-operative News*, 11 October 1902, p. 1241.

44. "Co-operative Crisis and Cost of Provisions," *Co-operative News*, 18 October 1902, p. 1265; "The Heart-Burning Amongst the Traders," *Co-operative News*, 11 October 1902, p. 1242; "The Ill-Timed Boycott," *Co-operative News*, 11 October 1902, p. 1241.

45. Trentmann 2008, pp. 33–80. Peter Gurney (2017) summarizes the debates over liberal consumerism and free trade in the late nineteenth and early twentieth centuries (see pp. 116–131).

46. "Boycott Again," *Co-operative News*, 7 September 1907, p. 1105; George Holyoake, "Anti-Boycott Papers: Traders on the Warpath," *Co-operative News*, 15 November 1902, p. 1365.

47. J. C. Gray, "The Boycott. A System of Inquisition," *Co-operative News*, 23 October 1902, p. 1286.

48. Holyoake, "Anti-Boycott Papers: Traders on the Warpath."

49. "The Waning Boycott," *Co-operative News*, 15 November 1902.

50. Fabian socialists Beatrice and Sydney Webb distinguished between voluntary and involuntary co-operation; the former included consumer co-operation. This voluntary nature of consumer's co-operation, in part, convinced the Webbs that it was necessarily limited in scope, especially in comparison with compulsory forms of collective action and services organized by and through the state (e.g., public utilities, municipal governments, etc.). See Sidney and Beatrice Webb, "Special Supplement on the Co-operative Movement," *The New Statesmen*, 30 May 1914, pp. 33–34.

51. As a guild member wrote, "The guild realised early the importance of the free trade controversy. . . . The strong speeches and unanimous vote at the guild annual congress showed how alive members were to the evils of a protective policy [i.e., a policy that would restrict free trade]." *Twenty-first Annual Report of the Women's Co-operative Guild*, April 1903–1904, p. 10.

52. "Educational Convention," *Co-operative News*, 7 August 1886, p. 799; W. C. Jones, "Co-operative Education," *Co-operative News*, 23 May 1885, p. 445; "Objects of the Women's Co-operative League," Women's Corner, *Co-operative News*, 12 May 1883, p. 396.

53. "The Ill-Timed Boycott," *Co-operative News*, 11 November 1902, p. 1240.

54. "Co-operative Crisis and Cost of Provisions," *Co-operative News*, 18 October 1902; George Holyoake, "The Boycott," *Co-operative News*, 18 October 1902; "The Ill-Timed Boycott."

55. "National and Municipal Affairs," *Twentieth Annual Report of the Women's Co-operative Guild*, April 1902–1903, p. 10; *Nineteenth Annual Report of the Women's Co-operative Guild*, April 1901–1902, p. 4.

56. "The Next Budget," *Co-operative News*, 19 January 1895, pp. 60–61.

57. "The Collapse of the Boycott," *Co-operative News*, 4 September 1897, p. 972.

58. Trentmann 2008, pp. 191–240.

59. "Co-operators and Free-Trade," *Co-operative News*, 6 May 1916, p. 486.

60. "Our Shopping Week," *Co-operative News*, 25 March 1911, p. 373.

61. Brooks 1900, p. 27.

62. Ibid., p. 26.

63. "Letter to Boston Firms from Consumers' League of Massachusetts," 20 January 1898.

64. Sklar 1995b; see also Dirks 1996; Skocpol 1992.

65. On manliness and the AFL, see Greene 1998, pp. 107–108, 138–139.

66. "Second Meeting of the Conference on the Federation of Consumers' Leagues," 17 May 1898.

67. Ibid.

68. Ibid.

69. See the updated standards in Florence Kelley, "The Consumers' League," *American Journal of Nursing*, 1901, p. 649.

70. Brooks 1900, p. 3.

71. Pauline Goldmark, "Report on Wages/Hours of Labor," 1 February 1916.

72. Felt 1965.

73. "Consumers' League of Kentucky," 4 March 1903.

74. "Monthly Executive Meeting," Consumers' League of Massachusetts, 30 January 1902.

75. "1903 Annual Meeting Report," National Consumers' League.

76. "Label Committee Report," National Consumers' League, 19 May 1911.

77. "1903 Annual Meeting Report," National Consumers' League.

78. "Report of the Label Committee," *Annual Report of the National Consumers' League* 1910.

79. "Minutes of Executive Committee," *Seventeenth Annual Meeting of the National Consumers' League* 1916.

80. Ibid.

81. References in this paragraph all from Kelley's "Memorandum on the Label," National Consumers' League, 1918.

82. "C.W.S. vs. Label," *Co-operative News*, 23 September 1911, p. 1211.

83. "Committee on Label," National Consumers' League, 8 March 1918, pp. 35–36.

84. "Letter to Manufacturers," National Consumers' League, 18 *March* 1918.

85. "Council Meeting Minutes," National Consumers' League, 21 November 1918.

86. "Council Meeting Minutes," National Consumers' League, 21 November 1919.

87. Huyssen 2014.

88. "Second Meeting of the Conference on the Federation of Consumers' Leagues," 15 May 1898.

89. "Report of the Committee on Advertising," National Consumers' League, 27 January 1904.

90. "Letter from the Massachusetts League," 8 January 1898.

91. Ibid.

92. "Report of the Secretary," *Second Annual Report of the National Consumers' League*, 3 January 1901, p. 10.

93. "Monthly Meeting, Massachusetts League," 24 May 1900.

94. "Report of the Secretary," *Second Annual Report of the National Consumers' League*, 1 March 1901, p. 7.

95. *Third Annual Report of the National Consumers' League*, 4 March 1902, p. 7; *Eighth Annual Report of the National Consumers' League*, 5 March 1907, p. 14.

96. "Monthly Meeting, Massachusetts League," May 1907 (approx.).

97. "Letter to Samuel Gompers," 1918 (approx.).

98. "Monthly Meeting, Massachusetts League," 8 January 1908.

99. "Letter to Manufacturers," 18 March 1918.

100. On the issue of organizations and social movements, see Bell 2014; Binder 2001.

101. Hy. Brown, "Letter on the C.W.S. and the Trade Union Label," *Co-operative News*, 23 September 1911, p. 1225.

102. As such, I do not find it productive to suggest that the sympathetic consumer simply derives from an objective, intransitive social reality (the world out there) as distinguished from a subjective, transitive one (the world as we interpret it). To do so would suggest that these capitalist phenomena and institutions do not depend on our interpretations of them. But these phenomena and institutions—anonymous goods, the market, competition, private accumulation of wealth—are meaningful. They depend on human sense-making, interpretation, and/or intentions—profit, desire, greed, honesty, duty, and so on. I take this dependence to be an underappreciated implication of commodity fetishism. In this sense, I accept the "cultural" argument that the world comes to us already interpreted and that we should seek to understand such interpretations as part of the project to know how the world works. At the same time, it is crucial to appreciate that the sympathetic consumer seems to depend on these phenomena and institutions. Without the historical conjuncture of the commodity-form, depersonalized goods, industrialization, and capitalist commodity chains, the sympathetic consumer would lose any semblance of coherence. Given this, I think that we should take the claim that capitalism, as a social system, exhibits a persistent, meaningful structure seriously. The sympathetic consumer would be but one example of this persistent, meaningful structure.

Chapter 7

1. Such a claim may be true of culture in general, however one may understand such a phrase. But as I mentioned in Chapter 1, many have been skittish about "a capitalist culture" in the singular, preferring the pluralistic phrase "cultures of capitalism" and its cognates. Moreover, a capitalist social order may involve distinct ways of working through differences. This would be a fascinating matter for comparative historical study.

2. Fennell 2015; Krause 2014; Ticktin 2016.

3. Monika Krause (2014) illustrates how such a situation arises through the organization and provision of humanitarian aid (pp. 39–69).

4. "Worldwide movement" comes directly from Whole Foods CEO John Mackey in a manual on "conscious capitalism." In August 2019, the Business Roundtable, an organization of top US CEOs, issued a statement on the "purpose of a corporation" that echoes the language of conscious capitalism—both in its emphasis on purpose and creating "value" for all "stakeholders." On conscious capitalism as a worldwide movement, see Sisodia, Henry, and Eckschmidt 2018, p. ix; for the Business Roundtable statement, see https://opportunity.businessroundtable.org/ourcommitment/

5. *Equal Exchange Annual Report*, 2018, p. ii.

6. Ibid., p. 3.

7. Ibid., pp. 1, 2, 13, 14; on the notion of citizen consumers, see Brown 2011; Cohen 2003; Lekakis 2013; Lewis and Potter 2010; McGovern 2006; Trentmann 2001.

8. *Equal Exchange Annual Report*, 2018.

9. Ibid., p. 2.

10. Mackey and Sisodia 2013, p. 31.

11. Ibid., p. 32.

12. Ibid., p. 34.

13. Sisodia, Henry, and Eckschmidt 2018, p. 108.

14. Mackey and Sisodia 2013, p. 78.

15. Ibid., p. 78.

16. Ibid., p. 79.

17. See, for example, *Equal Exchange Annual Report*, 2018, 2017, 2016, 2015.

18. *Fair Labor Association Annual Report*, 2017: https://www.fairlabor.org/report/2017-annual-public-report; *Fashion Revolution Impact Report*, 2018: https://issuu.com/fashionrevolution/docs/pdf_highres_fashrev_2018_impactpres/29; *Ten Thousand Villages Canada Annual Report*, 2016: https://www.tenthousandvillages.ca/res/pub/Annual_Reports/AnnualReport2016.pdf

19. https://www.everlane.com/factories

20. For a brief description of the project, see: https://www.fashionrevolution.org/tag/imadeyourclothes/

21. *Equal Exchange Annual Report*, 2017, p. 9.

22. https://www.everlane.com/factories/nylon-bags

23. Rauch quoted in Mackey and Sisodia 2013, p. 81.

24. Ibid., p. 114.

25. This recalls Georg Simmel's description of the division between city and country in his essay "The Metropolis and Mental Life." As many of the resources consumed in the city were produced in the regions outside of it, the producers were unable to see the consumers for whom they were, in effect, producing; see Simmel 1971, p. 327.

26. Obviously, this is the company line and should not be taken at face value. Mackey and Sisodia envision that "[A]s conscious businesses change the parameters of their relationship with suppliers, these changes can have a ripple effect throughout the supply chain. Companies should encourage their suppliers to adopt similar approaches in their relationships with their own suppliers. Similarly, suppliers that start seeing the benefits of a win-win relationship with a conscious customer should take this philosophy to their other customers and educate them" (Mackey and Sisodia 2013, p. 121).

27. Mackey and Sisodia 2013, p. 146.

28. Sisodia, Henry, and Eckschmidt 2018, p. 5.

29. Mackey and Sisodia 2013, pp. 168–170.

30. Ibid., pp. 252–253.

31. *Equal Exchange Annual Report*, 2018, p. 4.

32. Ibid.

33. Ibid., p. 12.

34. Ibid., p. 13.

35. *Fashion Revolution Annual Report*, 2018, p. 45.

36. Mackey and Sisodia 2013, p. 34; in his book on humanitarian philanthropy, journalist Anand Giridharadas (2018) presents the win-win as the dominant way of

thinking among entrepreneurial Silicon Valley figures, billionaire philanthropists, and the "thought leaders" who support them. In mathematical terms, the conscious capitalist "Win^6" involves significantly more winning than the "humble" philanthropic win-win.

37. Sisodia, Henry, and Eckschmidt 2018, pp. 154–155.

38. Mackey and Sisodia 2013, p. 167.

39. Ibid., pp. 171–172.

40. Ibid., p. 169.

41. Ibid.

42. Massengill 2013; Muehlebach 2012; Spillman 2012.

43. The conceit of the co-operative movement was that the capitalist marketplace could be commandeered by co-operatives in the name of the people. But the trajectory of the co-operative movement—from movement to a more conventional business—suggests that, if there is an interest in overcoming capitalism, these consumer co-operatives need to join forces with other movements to counterbalance the imperatives that besiege any business in a capitalist society. On the tensions experienced by anti-capitalist sellers, see Miller 2006; on the history of the co-operatives in particular, see Gurney 1996; Wilson, Webster, and Vorberg-Rugh 2013.

44. These latter forms of consumer activism include the value for money and con-sumer safety advocacy that have resulted in consumer product testing, product guides, legal regulation of industries and products, and lawsuits. Such forms of activism also include food activism, BDS (boycott, divestment, and sanction) movements, and others that seek to leverage consumer power to address a social ill.

45. On these and other related matters, see Barnett et al. 2011; Glickman 2009; Hil-ton 2009; Hyman and Tohill 2017; Micheletti 2003; Rappaport 2017; Stolle and Miche-letti 2013.

46. On the trajectory of consumer activism in the twentieth century, see Cohen 2003; Hilton 2003; Trentmann 2016, pp. 522–605; on neoliberalism and the consumer, see Konings 2015; Olsen 2019.

47. *Pace* Heldman 2017.

48. The previous sentence alludes to Weber's famously fatalistic conclusion in his essay on the Protestant ethic. These have been matters of recurring concern throughout the twentieth and early twenty-first centuries. See Fisher 2009; Lears 1981; Nielsen and Skotnicki 2019, pp. 125–129.

49. Topik and Wells 2012, pp. 688–704, 751–752.

50. Cohen 2003; Gerth 2010; Hilton 2009; Maclachlan 2006.

51. Degain, Meng, and Wang 2017, pp. 42–43.

52. Ibid., p. 52; see also Meng, Ye, and Wei 2017; Timmer, Los, Stehrer, and de Vries 2016. A complex global value chain entails products that cross national borders at least twice on the way to the final, salable product and, as a result, are counted multiple times, as imports and exports, in the GDP of the relevant states.

53. Rappaport 2017, p. 51.

54. Macpherson 1962.

55. See Fraser and Jaeggi 2018, pp. 19–38; see also Ascher 2016; Bahng 2018; Bhat-

tacharya 2017; Dawson and Francis 2016; Foster, Clark, and York 2010; Karataşli 2020; Konings 2018; Malm 2016; Mezzadra and Neilson 2019.

56. Berman 2018, p. 228; for an account that proposes the "creative worker" as a feature of what I would call a capitalist culture, see Biernacki 2015.

57. I have put this phrase from Ellen Meiksins Wood (1991) to a distinct historical, but conceptually related use.

58. Marx 1977, p. 168.

59. William C. Fox, *An Address to the People of Great Britain, on the Propriety of Abstaining from West India Sugar and Rum, 2nd ed. (London: M. Gurney, 1791), p. 2.*

60. Ibid., 2nd ed.

61. Davies 1921, p. 1.

62. Marx 1977, pp. 163–164.

Bibliography

Abend, Gabriel. 2014a. *The Moral Background: An Inquiry into the History of Business Ethics*. Princeton: Princeton University Press.

Abend, Gabriel. 2014b. "Transcendental Sociological Arguments." *Contemporary Sociology* 43(3): 327–331.

Abrams, Burton, Jing Li, and James Mulligan. 2013. "Capital Intensity and US County Population Growth During the Late 19th Century." *Eastern Economic Journal* 39(1): 18–27.

Abzug, Robert. 1994. *Cosmos Crumbling*. New York: Oxford University Press.

Adams, Matthew, and Jayne Raisborough. 2008. "What Can Sociology Say About Fair Trade? Class, Reflexivity and Ethical Consumption." *Sociology* 42(6): 1165–1182.

Alexander, Jeffrey. 2003. *The Meanings of Social Life: A Cultural Sociology*. New York: Oxford University Press.

Alexander, Jeffrey. 2006. *The Civil Sphere*. New York: Oxford University Press.

Althusser, Louis. 1971. *Lenin and Philosophy and Other Essays*. New York: Monthly Review Press.

Althusser, Louis. 2005 [1969]. *For Marx*. New York: Verso Books.

Amariglio, Jack, and Antonio Callari. 1989. "Marxian Value Theory and the Problem of the Subject: The Role of Commodity Fetishism." *Rethinking Marxism* 2(3): 31–60.

Andrews, David. 2018. "Error or Absurdity? A Non-cognitive Approach to Commodity Fetishism." *European Journal of the History of Economic Thought* 25(5): 738–755.

Anstey, Roger. 1975. *The Atlantic Slave Trade and British Abolition, 1760–1810*. Atlantic Highlands, NJ: Humanities Press.

Appadurai, Arjun, ed. 1986. *The Social Life of Things*. New York: Cambridge University Press.

Aptheker, Herbert. 1940. "The Quakers and Negro Slavery." *Journal of Negro History* 25(3): 331–362.

Arrighi, Giovanni. 2010. *The Long Twentieth Century: Money, Power, and the Origins of Our Times*. New York: Verso Books.

Arrighi, Giovanni, Terrence Hopkins, and Immanuel Wallerstein. 1989. *Anti-Systemic Movements*. New York: Verso Books.

Ascher, Ivan. 2016. *Portfolio Society: On the Capitalist Mode of Prediction*. New York: Zone Books.

Ashworth, John. 1987. "The Relationship Between Capitalism and Humanitarianism." *American Historical Review* 92(4): 813–828.

Backstrom, Philip, M. 1974. *Christian Socialism and Co-operation in Victorian England*. London: Croom Helm.

Bagchi, Amiya Kumar. 2008. *Perilous Passage: Mankind and the Ascendancy of Global Capital*. Lanham, MD: Rowman & Littlefield Publishers.

Bahng, Aimee. 2018. *Migrant Futures: Decolonizing Speculation in Financial Times*. Durham: Duke University Press.

Bair, Jennifer, ed. 2009. *Frontiers of Global Commodity Chain Research*. Stanford: Stanford University Press.

Baldasty, Gerald. 1992. *The Commercialization of News in the Nineteenth Century*. Madison: University of Wisconsin Press.

Bandelj, Nina, and Frederick Wherry, eds. 2011. *The Cultural Wealth of Nations*. Stanford: Stanford University Press.

Banet-Weiser, Sarah. 2012. *Authentic™: The Politics of Ambivalence in a Brand Culture*. New York: New York University Press.

Barnett, Clive, Paul Cloke, Nick Clarke, and Alice Malpass. 2011. *Globalizing Responsibility: The Political Rationalities of Ethical Consumption*. Malden, MA: Wiley-Blackwell.

Bauman, Zygmunt. 2008. *Does Ethics Have a Chance in a World of Consumers?* Cambridge, MA: Harvard University Press.

Baudrillard, Jean. 1975. *The Mirror of Production*. St. Louis: Telos Press.

Baudrillard, Jean. 1998. *The Consumer Society: Myths and Structures*. Thousand Oaks, CA: Sage Press.

Beckert, Sven. 2015. *Empire of Cotton: A Global History*. New York: Vintage.

Bell, Joyce. 2014. *The Black Power Movement and American Social Work*. Minneapolis: University of Minnesota Press.

Bendix, Reinhard. 1977. *Nation-Building and Citizenship*. Berkeley and Los Angeles: University of California Press.

Benson, Susan Porter. 1981. "The Cinderella of Occupations: Managing the Work of Department Store Saleswomen, 1900–1940." *Business History* 55(1): 1–25.

Benson, Susan Porter. 1986. *Counter Cultures: Saleswomen, Managers, and Customers in American Department Stores, 1890–1940*. Champaign: University of Illinois Press.

Berg, Maxine. 2004. "Consumption in Eighteenth- and Early Nineteenth-Century Britain." In *The Cambridge Economic History of Modern Britain. Vol. 1: Industrialisation, 1700–1860*, Roderick Floud and Paul Johnson, eds. New York: Cambridge University Press.

Berger, John, with Sven Blomberg, Chris Fox, Michael Dibb, and Richard Hollis. 1977. *Ways of Seeing*. New York: Penguin.

Berman, Marshall. 1988. *All That Is Solid Melts into Air: The Experience of Modernity*. New York: Penguin.

Berman, Michael. 2018. "Religion Overcoming Religions: Suffering, Secularism, and the Training of Interfaith Chaplains in Japan." *American Ethnologist* 45(2): 228–240.

Bernstein, Elizabeth. 2018. *Brokered Subjects: Sex Trafficking and the Politics of Freedom.* Chicago: University of Chicago Press.

Bhattacharya, Tithi, ed. 2017. *Social Reproduction Theory.* London: Pluto Press.

Biernacki, Richard. 1995. *The Fabrication of Labor: Germany and Britain, 1640–1914.* Berkeley: University of California Press.

Biernacki, Richard. 2005. "The Action Turn: Comparative-Historical Inquiry Beyond the Classical Models of Conduct." In *Rethinking Modernity,* Julia Adams, Elisabeth Clemens, and Ann Shola Orloff, eds. Durham: Duke University Press.

Biernacki, Richard. 2015. "The Capitalist Origin of the Concept of Creative Work." In *The Architect as Worker: Immaterial Labor, the Creative Class, and the Politics of Design,* Peggy Deamer, ed. New York: Bloomsbury Academic.

Billig, Michael. 1999. "Commodity Fetishism and Repression: Reflections on Marx, Freud, and the Psychology of Consumer Capitalism." *Theory & Psychology* 9(3): 313–329.

Binder, Amy. 2001. *Contentious Curricula: Afrocentrism and Creationism in American Public Schools.* Princeton: Princeton University Press.

Black, Jeremy. 2012. "Suppressing the Slave Trade." In *British Abolitionism and the Question of Moral Progress in History,* Donald Yerxa, ed. Columbia: University of South Carolina Press.

Blackburn, Robin. 1998. *The Making of New World Slavery: From the Baroque to the Modern, 1492–1800.* London: Verso Books.

Blackburn, Robin. 2011. *The American Crucible: Slavery, Emancipation, and Human Rights.* New York: Verso Books.

Blanchard, Peter. 2010. "Spanish South American Mainland." In *The Oxford Handbook of Slavery in the Americas,* Robert Paquette and Mark Smith, eds. New York: Oxford University Press.

Blaszak, Barbara. 2000. *The Matriarchs of England's Cooperative Movement: A Study in Gender Politics and Female Leadership, 1883–1921.* Westport, CT: Greenwood Press.

Blaszczyk, Regina Lee. 2008. *American Consumer Society, 1865–2008: From Hearth to HDTV.* Hoboken, NJ: Wiley-Blackwell Publishers.

Block, Fred L. 2018. *Capitalism: The Future of an Illusion.* Berkeley: University of California Press.

Bolt, Christine, and Seymour Drescher, eds. 1980. *Anti-Slavery, Religion, and Reform.* Hamden, CT: Archon Press.

Boltanski, Luc. 1999. *Distant Suffering: Morality, Media, and Politics.* Graham Burchell, trans. New York: Cambridge University Press.

Boltanski, Luc, and Eve Chiapello. 2018. *The New Spirit of Capitalism.* London: Verso Books.

Booth, Charles. 1903. *Life and Labour of the People in London.* New York: Macmillan.

Bourdieu, Pierre. 1984. *Distinction: A Social Critique of the Judgment of Taste.* Cambridge, MA: Harvard University Press.

Bowen, Sarah, and Maria Sarita Gaytán. 2012. "The Paradox of Protection: National Identity, Global Commodity Chains, and the Tequila Industry." *Social Problems* 59(1): 70–93.

Bowlby, Rachel. 1985. *Just Looking: Consumer Culture in Dreiser, Gissing, and Zola*. New York: Methuen.

Bradley, K. R., and Paul Cartledge, eds. 2011. *The Cambridge World History of Slavery. Vol. 1: The Ancient Mediterranean World*. New York: Cambridge University Press.

Braithwaite, William C. 1955. *The Beginnings of Quakerism*, 2nd ed. New York: Cambridge University Press.

Braudel, Fernand. 1992. *Civilization and Capitalism, 15th–18th Century. Vol. 1: The Structures of Everyday Life*. Berkeley: University of California Press.

Breen, T. H. 2004. *The Marketplace of Revolution: How Consumer Politics Shaped American Independence*. New York: Oxford University Press.

Briggs, Asa, and John Saville, eds. 1971. *Essays in Labour History, 1886–1923*. New York: Archon Books.

Brooks, John Graham. 1900. *The Consumers' League*. Cambridgeport, MA: The Co-operative Press.

Brown, Christopher Leslie. 2006. *Moral Capital: Foundations of British Abolitionism*. Chapel Hill: University of North Carolina Press.

Brown, Ira V. 1988. "Pennsylvania's Antislavery Pioneers: 1688–1776." *Pennsylvania History* 55(2): 59–77.

Brown, Keith R. 2011. "Interaction Ritual Chains and the Mobilization of Conscientious Consumers." *Qualitative Sociology* 34(1): 121–141.

Brown, Keith R. 2013. *Buying into Fair Trade: Culture, Morality, and Consumption*. New York: New York University Press.

Brown, Lucy. 1985. *Victorian News and Newspapers*. New York: Oxford University Press.

Brown, Wendy. 2015. *Undoing the Demos: Neoliberalism's Stealth Revolution*. New York: Zone Books.

Bushman, Richard. 1992. *The Refinement of America: Persons, Houses, Cities*. New York: Vintage Books.

Calder, Lendol. 1999. *Financing the American Dream: A Cultural History of Consumer Credit*. Princeton: Princeton University Press.

Calhoun, Craig. 2012. *The Roots of Radicalism: Tradition, the Public Sphere, and Early Nineteenth Century Social Movements*. Chicago: University of Chicago Press.

Campbell, Colin. 1987. *The Romantic Ethic and the Spirit of Consumerism*. Oxford: Blackwell.

Campbell, Colin. 2004. "I Shop Therefore I Know that I Am: The Metaphysical Basis of Modern Consumerism." In *Elusive Consumption*, Karin M. Eckstrom and Helene Brembeck, eds. Oxford: Berg Publishers.

Carrington, Selwyn H. H. 1987. "The American Revolution and the British West Indies' Economy." In *British Capitalism and Caribbean Slavery: The Legacy of Eric Williams*, Barbara Solow and Stanley Engerman, eds. New York: Cambridge University Press.

Carey, Brycchan. 2012. *From Peace to Freedom: Quaker Rhetoric and the Birth of American Antislavery, 1657–1761*. New Haven: Yale University Press.

Cateau, Heather, and Selwyn H. H. Carrington. 2000. *Capitalism and Slavery Fifty Years Later: Eric Eustace Williams, the Man and His Work*. New York: Peter Lang.

Chin, Elizabeth. 2007. "The Consumer Diaries, or, Autoethnography in the Inverted World." *Journal of Consumer Culture* 7(3): 335–353.

Chin, Elizabeth. 2016. *My Life with Things: The Consumer Diaries*. Durham: Duke University Press.

Clegg, John. 2020. "A Theory of Capitalist Slavery." *Journal of Historical Sociology* 33(1): 74–98.

Clelland, Donald. 2014. "The Core of the Apple: Degrees of Monopoly and Dark Value in Global Commodity Chains." *Journal of World-Systems Research* 20(1): 82–110.

Clemens, Elisabeth. 1997. *The People's Lobby: Organizational Innovation and the Rise of Interest Group Politics in the United States, 1890–1925*. Chicago: University of Chicago Press.

Coclanis, Peter. 2010. "The Economics of Slavery." In *The Oxford Handbook of Slavery in the Americas*, Robert Paquette and Mark Smith, eds. New York: Oxford University Press.

Coclanis, Peter. 2018. "Review Essay: Slavery, Capitalism, and the Problem of Misprision." *Journal of American Studies* 52(3): 1–9.

Cohen, G. A. 2001. *Karl Marx's Theory of History: A Defense*. Princeton: Princeton University Press.

Cohen, Lizabeth. 2003. *A Consumers' Republic: The Politics of Mass Consumption in Postwar America*. New York: Vintage.

Cole, G. D. H. 1944. *A Century of Co-operation*. London: George Allen & Unwin Ltd.

Colley, Linda. 1992. *Britons: Forging the Nation, 1707–1837*. New Haven: Yale University Press.

Comaroff, Jean, and John Comaroff, eds. 2001. *Millennial Capitalism and the Culture of Neoliberalism*. Durham: Duke University Press.

Cook, Daniel. 2004. *The Commodification of Childhood: The Children's Clothing Industry and the Rise of the Child Consumer*. Durham: Duke University Press.

Cooper, Melinda. 2017. *Family Values: Between Neoliberalism and the New Social Conservatism*. New York: Zone Books.

Cotter, William. 1994. "The Somerset Case and the Abolition of Slavery in England." *History: The Journal of the Historical Association* 79(255): 31–56.

Craig, David Melville. 2006. *John Ruskin and the Ethics of Consumption*. Charlottesville: University of Virginia Press.

Crary, Jonathan. 2000. *Suspensions of Perception: Attention, Spectacle, and Modern Culture*. Cambridge, MA: MIT Press.

Craton, Michael. 1982. *Testing the Chains: Resistance to Slavery in the British West Indies*. Ithaca, NY: Cornell University Press.

Crossick, Geoffrey, and Serge Jaumain, eds. 1999. *Cathedrals of Consumption: The European Department Store, 1850–1939*. Brookfield, VT: Ashgate.

Curtis, Susan. 1991. *A Consuming Vision: The Social Gospel and American Culture*. Baltimore: Johns Hopkins University Press.

Dandelion, Pink. 2007. *An Introduction to Quakerism*. New York: Cambridge University Press.

d'Anjou, Leo. 1996. *Social Movements and Cultural Change: The First Abolition Campaign Revisited*. Hawthorne, NY: Aldine de Gruyter.

Dauber, Michele. 2013. *The Sympathetic State: Disaster Relief and the Origins of the American Welfare State*. Chicago: University of Chicago Press.

Daunton, Martin J. 1995. *Progress and Poverty: An Economic and Social History of Britain, 1700–1850*. New York: Oxford University Press.

Davies, Margaret Llewelyn. 1904. *The Women's Cooperative Guild*. Kirkby Lonsdale, Westmorland: Women's Co-operative Guild.

Davies, Margaret Llewelyn. 1921. *Women as Organised Consumers*. Manchester: Co-operative United Limited.

Davis, David Brion. 1966. *The Problem of Slavery in Western Culture*. Ithaca, NY: Cornell University Press.

Davis, David Brion. 1975. *The Problem of Slavery in the Age of Revolution, 1770–1823*. Ithaca, NY: Cornell University Press.

Davis, David Brion. 1987. "Reflections on Abolitionism and Ideological Hegemony." *American Historical Review* 92(4): 797–812.

Davis, David Brion. 1992. "The Perils of Doing History by Ahistorical Abstraction: A Reply to Thomas L. Haskell's *AHR Forum* Reply." In *The Antislavery Debate: Capitalism and Abolitionism as a Problem in Historical Interpretation*, Thomas Bender, ed. Berkeley: University of California Press.

Dawson, Michael C., and Megan Ming Francis. (2016). "Black Politics and the Neoliberal Racial Order." *Public Culture* 28(1): 23–62.

Degain, Christophe, Bo Meng, and Zhi Wang. 2017. "Recent Trends in Global Trade and Global Value Chains." In *Measuring and Analyzing the Impact of GVCs on Economic Development*. Washington, DC: World Bank.

DeSoucey, Michaela. 2010. "Gastronationalism: Food Traditions and Authenticity Politics in the European Union." *American Sociological Review* 75(3): 432–455.

DeSoucey, Michaela. 2016. *Contested Tastes: Foie Gras and the Politics of Food*. Princeton: Princeton University Press.

de Vries, Jan. 2008. *The Industrious Revolution: Consumer Behavior and the Household Economy, 1650 to the Present*. New York: Cambridge University Press.

Dirks, Jacqueline. 1996. *Righteous Goods: Women's Production, Reform Publicity, and the National Consumers' League, 1891–1919*. Unpublished dissertation.

Dörre, Klaus, Stephen Lessenich, and Hartmut Rosa. 2013. *Sociology—Capitalism—Critique*. New York: Verso Books.

Dörre, Klaus, Stephen Lessenich, and Hartmut Rosa. 2017. "Appropriation, Activation, and Acceleration: The Escalatory Logics of Capitalist Modernity and the Crises of Dynamic Stabilization." *Theory, Culture, & Society* 34(1): 53–73.

Douglas, Mary, and Baron Isherwood. 1979. *The World of Goods*. New York: Routledge.

Draper, Nicholas. 2010. *The Price of Emancipation: Slave-Ownership, Compensation, and British Society at the End of Slavery*. New York: Cambridge University Press.

Drescher, Seymour. 1987. *Capitalism and Antislavery: British Mobilization in Comparative Perspective*. New York: Oxford University Press.

Drescher, Seymour. 2009. *Abolition: A History of Slavery and Anti-Slavery*. New York: Cambridge University Press.

Drescher, Seymour. 2010. *Econocide: British Slavery in the Era of Abolition*. Chapel Hill: University of North Carolina Press.

Dromi, Shai. 2016. "Soldiers of the Cross: Calvinism, Humanitarianism, and the Genesis of Social Fields." *Sociological Theory* 34(3): 196–219.

Dubois, Laurent. 2004. *Avengers of the New World: The Story of the Haitian Revolution*. Cambridge, MA: Belknap Press.

Du Bois, W. E. B. 1966 [1932]. "Du Bois on Florence Kelley." *Social Work* 11(4): 98–100.

Duncombe, Stephen. 2013. "It Stands on Its Head: Commodity Fetishism, Consumer Activism, and the Strategic Use of Fantasy." *Culture and Organizations* 18(5): 359–375.

Eichengreen, Barry. 2011. *Exorbitant Privilege: The Rise and Fall of the Dollar and the Future of the International Monetary System*. New York: Oxford University Press.

Elson, Diane. 1979. "The Value Theory of Labour." In *Value: The Representation of Labour in Capitalism*, Diane Elson, ed. New York: Verso Books.

Engels, Friedrich. 1993 [1885]. *The Condition of the Working-Class in England in 1844*. New York: Oxford University Press.

Engels, Friedrich. 2010 [1884]. *The Origin of Private Property, Family, and the State*. New York: Penguin.

Enstad, Nan. 1999. *Ladies of Labor, Girls of Adventure: Working Women, Popular Culture, and Labor Politics at the Turn of the Twentieth Century*. New York: Columbia University Press.

Esping-Andersen, Gøsta. 1990. *The Three Worlds of Welfare Capitalism*. Princeton: Princeton University Press.

Ewen, Stuart. 1976. *Captains of Consciousness: Advertising and the Social Roots of the Consumer Culture*. New York: McGraw-Hill.

Fairbrother, Malcolm. 2014. "Economists, Capitalists, and the Making of Globalization: North American Free Trade in Comparative-Historical Perspective." *American Journal of Sociology* 119(5): 1324–1379.

Farrell, Stephen. 2007. "'Contrary to the Principles of Justice, Humanity, and Sound Policy': The Slave Trade, Parliamentary Politics, and the Abolition Act, 1807." In *The British Slave Trade: Abolition, Parliament, and People*, Stephen Farrell, Melanie Unwin, and James Walvin, eds. Edinburgh: University of Edinburgh Press.

Federici, Sylvia. 2014. *Caliban and the Witch: Women, the Body, and Primitive Accumulation*. Brooklyn: Autonomedia.

Felt, Jeremy P. 1965. *Hostages of Fortune: Child Labor Reform in New York State.* Syracuse: Syracuse University Press.

Fennell, Catherine. 2015. *Last Project Standing: Civics and Sympathy in Post-Welfare Chicago.* Minneapolis: University of Minnesota Press.

Fernández-Armesto, Felipe. 1982. *The Canary Islands After the Conquest: The Making of a Colonial Society in the Early Sixteenth Century.* New York: Oxford University Press.

Fick, Carolyn. 1990. *The Making of Haiti: The Saint Domingue Revolution from Below.* Knoxville: University of Tennessee Press.

Fields, Gary. 2004. *Territories of Profit: Communications, Capitalist Development, and the Innovative Enterprises of G. F. Swift and Dell Computer.* Stanford: Stanford University Press.

Fisher, Mark. 2009. *Capitalist Realism: Is There No Alternative?* Washington, DC: Zero Books.

Foster, John Bellamy, Brett Clark, and Richard York. 2010. *The Ecological Rift: Capitalism's War on the Earth.* New York: Monthly Review Press.

Fourcade, Marion. 2009. *Economists and Societies: Discipline and Profession in the United States, Britain, and France, 1890s to 1990s.* Princeton: Princeton University Press.

Fourcade, Marion. 2011. "Cents and Sensibility: Economic Valuation and the Nature of 'Nature.'" *American Journal of Sociology* 166(6): 1721–1777.

Fourcade, Marion, and Kieran Healy. 2007. "Moral Views of Market Society." *Annual Review of Sociology* 33: 1–27.

Fraser, Nancy, and Rahel Jaeggi. 2018. *Capitalism: A Conversation in Critical Theory.* New York: Polity Press.

Frazer, Michael L. 2010. *The Enlightenment of Sympathy: Justice and the Moral Sentiments in the Eighteenth Century and Today.* New York: Oxford University Press.

Frederickson, George. 1988. *The Arrogance of Race: Historical Perspectives on Slavery, Racism, and Social Inequality.* Middletown, CT: Wesleyan University Press.

Fridman, Daniel. 2016. *Freedom from Work: Embracing Financial Self-Help in the United States and Argentina.* Stanford: Stanford University Press.

Fryer, Peter. 1984. *Staying Power: The History of Black People in Britain.* London: Pluto Press.

Gereffi, Gary, David Spener, and Jennifer Bair, eds. 2002. *Free Trade and Uneven Development: The North American Apparel Industry After NAFTA.* Philadelphia: Temple University Press.

Gerth, Karl. 2010. *As China Goes, So Goes the World: How Chinese Consumers Are Transforming Everything.* New York: Hill and Wang.

Gide, Charles. 1898. "Has Co-operation Introduced a New Principle into Economics?" *The Economic Journal* 8(32): 490–511.

Gilroy, Paul. 1993. *The Black Atlantic: Modernity and Double Consciousness.* Cambridge, MA: Harvard University Press.

Giridharadas, Anand. 2018. *Winners Take All: The Elite Charade of Changing the World.* New York: Vintage.

Glickman, Lawrence. 1997. *A Living Wage: American Workers and the Making of Consumer Society.* Ithaca, NY: Cornell University Press.

Glickman, Lawrence. 2009. *Buying Power: A History of Consumer Activism in America.* Chicago: University of Chicago Press.

Goodrich, Amanda. 2014. "Radical 'Citizens of the World,'" 1790–95: The Early Career of Henry Redhead Yorke." *Journal of British Studies* 53(3): 611–635.

Gordon, Andrew. 2012. "Credit in a Nation of Savers: The Growth of Consumer Borrowing in Japan." In *The Development of Consumer Credit in Global Perspective: Business, Regulation, and Culture*, Jan Logemann, ed. New York: Palgrave Macmillan.

Graeber, David. 2011. "Consumption." *Current Anthropology* 52(4): 489–511.

Grampp, William. 1987. "How Britain Turned to Free Trade." *The Business History Review* 61(1): 86–112.

Gramsci, Antonio. 1972. *Selections from the Prison Notebooks.* New York: International Publishers.

Grant, Kevin. 2005. *A Civilised Savagery: Britain and the New Slaveries in Africa, 1884–1926.* New York: Routledge.

Gray, Margaret. 2014. *Labor and the Locavore: The Making of a Comprehensive Food Ethic.* Berkeley: University of California Press.

de Grazia, Victoria. 2005. *Irresistible Empire: America's Advance Through Twentieth-Century Europe.* Cambridge, MA: Harvard University Press.

Greene, Julie. 1998. *Pure and Simple Politics: The American Federation of Labor and Political Activism, 1881–1917.* New York: Cambridge University Press.

Grimmer-Solem, Erik. 2003. *The Rise of Historical Economics and Social Reform in Germany, 1864–1894.* New York: Oxford University Press.

Gunn, Simon, and James Vernon, eds. 2011. *The Peculiarities of Liberal Modernity in Imperial Britain.* Berkeley: University of California Press.

Gurney, Peter. 1996. *Co-operative Culture and the Politics of Consumption in England, 1870–1930.* New York: Manchester University Press.

Gurney, Peter. 2015. *Wanting and Having: Popular Politics and Liberal Consumerism in England, 1830–1870.* Manchester: Manchester University Press.

Gurney, Peter. 2017. *The Making of Consumer Culture in Modern Britain.* London: Bloomsbury Academic.

Guthman, Julie. 2009. "Unveiling the Unveiling." In *Frontiers of Commodity Chain Research*, Jennifer Bair, ed. Stanford: Stanford University Press.

Habermas, Jürgen. 1989. *The Structural Transformation of the Public Sphere.* Cambridge, MA: MIT Press.

Hall, Stuart, and Bill Schwarz. 1985. "State and Society, 1880–1930." In *Crises in the British State, 1880–1930*, Mary Langan and Bill Schwarz, eds. Dover, NH: Hutchinson Publishers.

Harootunian, Harry. 2015. *Marx After Marx: History and Time in the Expansion of Capitalism.* New York: Columbia University Press.

Harvey, David. 2010. *The Enigma of Capital and the Crises of Capitalism.* New York: Oxford University Press.

Haskell, Thomas. 1985a. "Capitalism and the Origins of the Humanitarian Sensibility, Part 1." *American Historical Review* 90(2): 339–361.

Haskell, Thomas. 1985b. "Capitalism and the Origins of the Humanitarian Sensibility, Part 2." *American Historical Review* 90(3): 547–566.

Haskell, Thomas. 1987. "Convention and Hegemonic Interest in the Debate over Antislavery: A Reply to Davis and Ashworth." *American Historical Review* 92(4): 829–878.

Haskell, Thomas, and Richard Teichgraeber III. 1996. *The Culture of the Market: Historical Essays*. New York: Cambridge University Press.

Haydu, Jeffrey. 1998. "Making Use of the Past: Time Periods as Cases to Compare and as Sequences of Problem Solving." *American Journal of Sociology* 104(2): 339–371.

Haydu, Jeffrey, and Tad Skotnicki. 2016. "Three Layers of History in Recurrent Social Movements: The Case of Food Reform." *Social Movement Studies* 15(4): 345–360.

Healy, Kieran. 2006. *Last Best Gifts: Altruism and the Market for Human Organs*. Chicago: University of Chicago Press.

Heldman, Caroline. 2017. *Protest Politics in the Marketplace: Consumer Activism in the Corporate Age*. Ithaca, NY: Cornell University Press.

Hetherington, Kevin. 2007. *Capitalism's Eye: Cultural Spaces of the Commodity*. New York: Routledge.

Hilton, Matthew. 2003. *Consumerism in Twentieth Century Britain*. New York: Cambridge University Press.

Hilton, Matthew. 2009. *Prosperity for All: Consumer Activism in an Era of Globalization*. Ithaca, NY: Cornell University Press.

Hirschman, Albert O. 1977. *The Passions and the Interests: Political Arguments for Capitalism Before Its Triumph*. Princeton: Princeton University Press.

Hobsbawm, Eric J. 1974. *Labour's Turning Point, 1880–1900*. Rutherford, NJ: Fairleigh Dickinson University Press.

Hobsbawm, Eric, and Terence Ranger, eds. 1992. *The Invention of Tradition*. New York: Cambridge University Press.

Hobson, J. A. 1898. *John Ruskin, Social Reformer*. Boston: D. Estes and Company.

Hobson, J. A. 1901 [1894]. *The Evolution of Modern Capitalism*, 2nd ed. New York: Charles Scribner's Sons.

Hobson, J. A. 1938. *Confessions of an Economic Heretic*. London: George Allen & Unwin Ltd.

Hochschild, Adam. 2005. *Bury the Chains: Prophets and Rebels in the Fight to Free an Empire's Slaves*. New York: Houghton Mifflin.

Hochschild, Arlie. 2003. *The Managed Heart: The Commercialization of Human Feeling*. Berkeley: University of California Press.

Hochschild, Arlie, with Anne Machung. 1989. *The Second Shift*. New York: Viking Penguin.

Hodgson, Geoffrey. 2015. *Conceptualizing Capitalism*. Chicago: University of Chicago Press.

Hofstadter, Richard. 1955. *The Age of Reform*. New York: Vintage.

Holcomb, Julie. 2016. *Moral Commerce: Quakers and the Transatlantic Boycott of Slave Labor*. Ithaca, NY: Cornell University Press.

Horkheimer, Max, and Theodor Adorno. 2002 [1947]. *Dialectic of Enlightenment: Philosophical Fragments*. Stanford: Stanford University Press.

Horowitz, David. 1985. *The Morality of Spending: Attitudes Toward the Consumer Society in America, 1875-1940*. Baltimore: Johns Hopkins University Press.

Howe, Anthony. 1997. *Free Trade and Liberal England, 1846-1946*. New York: Oxford University Press.

Hudis, Peter. 2013. *Marx's Concept of the Alternative to Capitalism*. Chicago: Haymarket Books.

Hunt, Lynn. 2015. "Revolutionary Rights." In *Revisiting the Origins of Human Rights*, Pamela Slotte and Miia Halme, eds. New York: Cambridge University Press.

Huyssen, David. 2014. *Progressive Inequality: Rich and Poor in New York, 1890-1920*. Cambridge, MA: Harvard University Press.

Hyman, Louis, and Joseph Tohill. 2017. *Shopping for Change: Consumer Activism and the Possibilities of Purchasing Power*. Ithaca, NY: ILR Press.

Illouz, Eva. 2007. *Cold Intimacies: The Making of Emotional Capitalism*. New York: Polity Press.

Ingle, H. Larry. 1994. *First Among Friends: George Fox and the Creation of Quakerism*. New York: Oxford University Press.

Inikori, Joseph. 2002. *Africans and the Industrial Revolution*. New York: Cambridge University Press.

Jackson, Maurice. 2009. *Let This Voice Be Heard: Anthony Benezet, Father of Atlantic Abolitionism*. Philadelphia: University of Pennsylvania Press.

Jaeggi, Rahel. 2014. *Alienation*. New York: Columbia University Press.

Jasper, James. 1997. *The Art of Moral Protest: Culture, Biography, and Creativity in Social Movements*. Chicago: University of Chicago Press.

Jevons, William. 2013 [1871]. *The Theory of Political Economy*. Basingstoke: Palgrave Macmillan.

Johnson, Paul. 1983. "Credit and Thrift in the British Working Class, 1870-1939." In *The Working Class in Modern British History: Essays in Honor of Henry Pelling*, Jay Winter, ed. New York: Cambridge University Press.

Johnson, Walter. 2013. *River of Dark Dreams: Slavery and Empire in the Cotton Kingdom*. Cambridge, MA: Belknap Press.

Johnston, Josée, Alexandra Rodney, and Michelle Szabo. 2012. "Place, Ethics, and Everyday Eating: A Tale of Two Neighbourhoods." *Sociology* 46(6): 1091-1108.

Jones, Gareth Stedman. 1974. "Working-Class Culture and Working-Class Politics in London, 1870-1900: Notes on the Remaking of a Working Class." *Journal of Social History* 7(4): 460-508.

Jones, Peter d'Alroy. 1968. *The Christian Socialist Revival, 1877-1914*. Princeton: Princeton University Press.

Jordan, Jennifer. 2015. *Edible Memory: The Lure of Heirloom Tomatoes and Other Forgotten Foods*. Chicago: University of Chicago Press.

Joyce, Patrick. 1980. *Work, Society, and Politics: The Culture of the Factory in Late Victorian England.* New Brunswick, NJ: Rutgers University Press.

Joyce, Patrick. 1991. *Visions of the People: Industrial England and the Question of Class, 1848–1914.* New York: Cambridge University Press.

Kaplan, Cora, and J. R. Oldfield, eds. 2010. *Imagining Transatlantic Slavery.* New York: Palgrave Macmillan.

Karataşli, Şahan Savaş. 2020. "Capitalism and Nationalism in the Longue Durée: Hegemony, Crisis, and State-Seeking Nationalist Mobilization, 1492–2013." *International Journal of Comparative Sociology.* DOI: 10.1177/0020715220946473

Kelley, Florence. 1899. "Aims and Principles of the Consumers' League." *American Journal of Sociology* 5(3): 289–304.

Kelley, Florence. 1901. "The Committee of the General Federation of Women's Clubs on the Industrial Problem as It Affects Women and Children." *American Journal of Nursing* 1(11) (August): 813–815.

Kelley, Florence. 2009. *The Selected Letters of Florence Kelley, 1869–1931.* Kathryn Kish Sklar and Beverly Wilson Palmer, eds. Champaign: University of Illinois Press.

Kelley, Victoria. 1998. "The Equitable Consumer: Shopping at the Co-op in Manchester." *Journal of Design History* 11(4): 295–310.

Kelley, Victoria. 2016. "The Streets for the People: London's Street Markets, 1850–1939." *Urban History* 43(3): 391–411.

Konings, Martijn. 2015. *The Emotional Logic of Capitalism: What Progressives Have Missed.* Stanford: Stanford University Press.

Konings, Martijn. 2018. *Capital and Time: For a New Critique of Neoliberal Reason.* Stanford: Stanford University Press.

Krause, Monika. 2014. *The Good Project: Humanitarian Relief NGOs and the Fragmentation of Reason.* Chicago: University of Chicago Press.

Krippner, Greta. 2011. *Capitalizing on Crisis: The Political Origins of the Rise of Finance.* Cambridge, MA: Harvard University Press.

Kunze, Bonnelyn Young. 1994. *Margaret Fell and the Rise of Quakerism.* Stanford: Stanford University Press.

Kurasawa, Fuyuki. 2014. "The Long Shadow of History: The Paradoxes of Iconographic Reiteration in Anti-Slavery Advocacy." *American Journal of Cultural Sociology* 2(1): 3–32.

Lamont, Michele, and Laurent Thevenot, eds. 2000. *Rethinking Comparative Cultural Sociology: Repertoires of Evaluation in France and the United States.* New York: Cambridge University Press.

Lancaster, Bill. 1995. *The Department Store: A Social History.* Leicester: Leicester University Press.

Lasser, Carol. 2011. "Immediatism, Dissent, and Gender: Women and Sentimentalization of Transatlantic Anti-Slavery Appeals." In *Women, Dissent, and Anti-Slavery in Britain and America, 1790–1865,* Elizabeth Clapp and Julie Jeffrey, eds. New York: Oxford University Press.

Leach, William. 1993. *Land of Desire: Merchants, Power, and the Rise of a New American Culture*. New York: Vintage.

Lears, T. Jackson. 1981. *No Place of Grace: Antimodernism and the Transformation of American Culture, 1880–1920*. New York: Pantheon.

Lears, T. Jackson. 2009. *Rebirth of a Nation: The Making of Modern America, 1877–1920*. New York: HarperCollins.

Lechner, Frank, and John Boli. 2005. *World Culture: Origins and Consequences*. Malden, MA: Blackwell.

Lekakis, Eleftheria. 2013. *Coffee Activism and the Politics of Fair Trade and Ethical Consumption in the Global North: Political Consumerism and Cultural Citizenship*. Basingstoke: Palgrave Macmillan.

Lewis, Tania, and Emily Potter, eds. 2010. *Ethical Consumption: A Critical Introduction*. New York: Routledge.

Linebaugh, Peter, and Marcus Rediker. 2000. *The Many-Headed Hydra: Sailors, Slaves, Commoners, and the Hidden History of the Revolutionary Atlantic*. Boston: Beacon Press.

Livingston, James. 1997. *Pragmatism and the Political Economy of Cultural Revolution, 1850–1940*. Chapel Hill: University of North Carolina Press.

Lockley, Timothy. 2010. "Class and Slavery." In *The Oxford Handbook of Slavery in the Americas*, Robert Paquette and Mark Smith, eds. New York: Oxford University Press.

Loveman, Mara. 2014. *National Colors: Racial Classification and the State in Latin America*. Oxford: Oxford University Press.

Lukács, Georg. 1971. *History and Class Consciousness: Studies in Marxist Dialectics*. Cambridge, MA: MIT Press.

Luxemburg, Rosa. 2003. *The Accumulation of Capital*. New York: Routledge.

Lyon, Sarah. 2006. "Evaluating Fair Trade Consumption: Politics, Defetishization, and Producer Participation." *International Journal of Consumer Studies* 30(5): 452–464.

Mackey, John, and Rajendra Sisodia. 2013. *Conscious Capitalism: Liberating the Heroic Spirit of Business*. Boston: Harvard Business Review Press.

Maclachlan, Patricia. 2006. "Global Trends vs. Local Traditions: Genetically Modified Foods and Contemporary Consumerism in the United States, Japan, and Britain." In *The Ambivalent Consumer: Questioning Consumption in East Asia and the West*. Ithaca, NY: Cornell University Press.

Macpherson, C. B. 1962. *The Political Theory of Possessive Individualism: Hobbes to Locke*. Oxford: Clarendon Press.

Maddison, Angus. 2007. *Contours of the World Economy 1–2030 AD: Essays in Macro-Economic History*. New York: Oxford University Press.

Mahoney, James, and Dietrich Rueschemeyer, eds. 2003. *Comparative Historical Analysis in the Social Sciences*. New York: Cambridge University Press.

Malm, Andreas. 2016. *Fossil Capital: The Rise of Steam Power and the Roots of Global Warming*. New York: Verso Books.

Marshall, Alfred. 1961. *Principles of Economics*, 9th ed. New York: Macmillan.

Martin, John Levi. 1999. "The Myth of the Consumption-Oriented Economy and the Rise of the Desiring Subject." *Theory and Society* 28(3): 425–453.

Marx, Karl. 1935. *Wage-Labour and Capital; Value, Price, and Profit*. New York: International Publishers.

Marx, Karl. 1973. *Grundrisse*. New York: Penguin.

Marx, Karl. 1977 [1867]. *Capital. Vol. 1*. New York: Vintage.

Marx, Karl. 1991. *Capital. Vol. 3*. New York: Penguin.

Marx, Karl, and Friedrich Engels. 1978. "The Manifesto of the Communist Party." In *The Marx-Engels Reader*, Robert Tucker, ed. New York: Norton.

Massengill, Rebekah. 2013. *Wal-Mart Wars: Moral Populism in the Twenty-First Century*. New York: New York University Press.

McCloskey, Deirdre. 2006. *The Bourgeois Virtues: Ethics for an Age of Commerce*. Chicago: University of Chicago Press.

McCusker, John J., and Russell R. Menard. 2010. "The Origins of Slavery in the Americas." In *The Oxford Handbook of Slavery in the Americas*, Robert Paquette and Mark Smith, eds. New York: Oxford University Press.

McGerr, Michael. 2003. *A Fierce Discontent: The Rise and Fall of the Progressive Movement in America, 1870–1920*. New York: New Press.

McGovern, Charles. 2006. *Sold American: Consumption and Citizenship, 1890–1945*. Chapel Hill: University of North Carolina Press.

McKendrick, Neil. 1982. "George Packwood and the Commercialisation of Shaving: The Art of Eighteenth-Century Advertising." In *The Birth of a Consumer Society*, Neil McKendrick, John Brewer, and J. H. Plumb, eds. London: Hutchinson.

McKendrick, Neil, John Brewer, and J. H. Plumb. 1982. *The Birth of a Consumer Society: The Commercialization of Eighteenth Century England*. Bloomington: Indiana University Press.

Meng, Bo, M. Ye, and S.-J. Wei. 2017. "Value-Added Gains and Job Opportunities in Global Value Chains." IDE Discussion Paper No. 668, IDE–JETRO, Chiba City, Japan.

Mezzadra, Sandro, and Brett Neilson. 2019. *The Politics of Operations: Excavating Contemporary Capitalism*. Durham: Duke University Press.

Micheletti, Michele. 2003. *Political Virtue and Shopping: Individuals, Consumerism, and Collective Action*. New York: Palgrave Macmillan.

Midgley, Clare. 1992. *Women Against Slavery: The British Campaign, 1780–1870*. New York: Routledge.

Midgley, Clare. 2007. *Feminism and Empire: Women Activists in Imperial Britain, 1790–1865*. New York: Routledge.

Midgley, Clare. 2011. "The Dissenting Voice of Elizabeth Heyrick: An Exploration of the Links Between Gender, Religious Dissent, and Anti-Slavery Radicalism." In *Women, Dissent, and Anti-Slavery in Britain and America, 1790–1865*, Elizabeth Clapp and Julie Jeffrey, eds. New York: Oxford University Press.

Miller, Daniel. 1987. *Material Culture and Mass Consumption*. Malden, MA: Blackwell.

Miller, Daniel. 1997. "Could Shopping Ever Really Matter?" In *The Shopping Experience*, Pasi Falk and Colin Campbell, eds. London: Sage Publishers.

Miller, Laura. 2006. *Reluctant Capitalists: Bookselling and the Culture of Consumption*. Chicago: University of Chicago Press.

Miller, Michael. 1981. *The Bon Marché: Bourgeois Culture, and the Department Store, 1869–1920*. Princeton: Princeton University Press.

Mintz, Sidney. 1985. *Sweetness and Power: The Place of Sugar in Modern History*. New York: Penguin.

Mirowski, Philip, and Dieter Plehwe, eds. 2009. *The Road from Mont Pèlerin: The Making of the Neoliberal Thought Collective*. Cambridge, MA: Harvard University Press.

Mitchell, Ian. 2015. "Ethical Shopping in Late Victorian and Edwardian Britain." *Journal of Historical Research* 7(3): 310–329.

Mitchell, Timothy. 1989. "The World as Exhibition." *Comparative Studies in Society and History* 31(2): 217–236.

Mokyr, Joel. 1988. "Is There Still Life in the Pessimist Case? Consumption During the Industrial Revolution, 1790–1850." *Journal of Economic History* 48(1): 69–92.

Mokyr, Joel. 2018. *A Culture of Growth: The Origins of the Modern Economy*. Princeton: Princeton University Press.

Moore, Jr., Barrington. 1966. *Social Origins of Dictatorship and Democracy*. Boston: Beacon Press.

Morgan, Kenneth. 2007. *Slavery and the British Empire: From Africa to America*. New York: Oxford University Press.

Morgan, Philip D. 2010. "Ending the Slave Trade: A Caribbean and Atlantic Context." In *Abolitionism and Imperialism in Britain, Africa, and the Atlantic*, Derek R. Peterson, ed. Athens: Ohio University Press.

Mudge, Stephanie. 2018. *Leftism Reinvented: Western Parties from Socialism to Neoliberalism*. Cambridge, MA: Harvard University Press.

Muehlebach, Andrea. 2012. *The Moral Neoliberal: Welfare and Citizenship in Italy*. Chicago: University of Chicago Press.

Mukerji, Chandra. 1983. *From Graven Images: Patterns of Modern Materialism*. New York: Columbia University Press.

Nathan, Maud. 1926. *The Story of an Epoch-Making Movement*. New York: Doubleday.

Ngai, Sianne. 2012. *Our Aesthetic Categories: Zany, Cute, Interesting*. Cambridge, MA: Harvard University Press.

Nielsen, Kelly, and Tad Skotnicki. 2019. "Sociology Towards Death: Heidegger, Time, and Social Theory." *Journal of Classical Sociology* 19(2): 111–137.

Norman, Edward. 1987. *The Victorian Christian Socialists*. New York: Cambridge University Press.

O'Connell, Sean. 2009. *Credit and Community: Working-Class Debt in the UK Since 1880*. New York: Oxford University Press.

O'Day, Alan, ed. 1979. *The Edwardian Age: Conflict and Stability, 1900–1914*. Hamden, CT: Archon Books.

Ohmann, Richard. 1996. *Selling Culture: Magazines, Markets, and Class at the Turn of the Century*. New York: Verso Books.

Oldfield, Sybil. 1998. "Margaret Llewelyn Davies and Leonard Woolf." In *Women in the Milieu of Leonard and Virginia Woolf: Peace, Politics, and Education*, Wayne Chapman and Janet Manson, eds. New York: Pace University Press.

Olsen, Niklas. 2019. *The Sovereign Consumer: A New History of Neoliberalism*. New York: Palgrave Macmillan.

Opler, Daniel. 2018. "Retail Workers and Their Unions, 1850–2016." In *The Routledge Companion to the History of Retailing*, Jon Stobart and Vicki Howard, eds. New York: Routledge.

Osterhammel, Jürgen. 2014. *The Transformation of the World: A Global History of the Nineteenth Century*. Princeton: Princeton University Press.

Painter, Nell Irvin. 2008. *Standing at Armageddon: A Grassroots History of the Progressive Era*. New York: Norton.

Parker, Traci. 2019. *Department Stores and the Black Freedom Movement: Workers, Consumers, and Civil Rights from the 1930s to the 1980s*. Chapel Hill: University of North Carolina Press.

Paschel, Tianna. 2016. *Becoming Black Political Subjects: Movements and Ethno-Racial Rights in Colombia and Brazil*. Princeton: Princeton University Press.

Patel, Raj, and Jason Moore. 2017. *A History of the World in Seven Cheap Things: A Guide to Capitalism, Nature, and the Future of the Planet*. Berkeley: University of California Press.

Patterson, Orlando. 1982. *Slavery and Social Death: A Comparative Study*. Cambridge, MA: Harvard University Press.

Patterson, Orlando. 2014. "Making Sense of Culture." *Annual Review of Sociology* 40: 1–30.

Pearson, Susan. 2011. *The Rights of the Defenseless: Protecting Animals and Children in Gilded Age America*. Chicago: University of Chicago Press.

Pelling, Henry. 1968. *Popular Politics and Society in Late Victorian Britain*. New York: St. Martin's Press.

Pistor, Katharina. 2019. *The Code of Capital: How the Law Creates Wealth Inequality*. Princeton: Princeton University Press.

Pitkin, Hanna Fenichel. 1987. "Rethinking Reification." *Theory and Society* 16(2): 263–293.

Plumb, Milton M. 1951. "Records of the National Women's Trade Union League of America." *Quarterly Journal of Current Acquisitions* 8(4): 9–16.

Polanyi, Karl. 2001 [1944]. *The Great Transformation: The Political and Economic Origins of Our Time*. Boston: Beacon Press.

Porter, J. H. 1971. "The Development of the Provincial Department Store, 1870–1939." *Business History* 13(1): 64–71.

Postone, Moishe. 1993. *Time, Labor, and Social Domination: A Reinterpretation of Marx's Critical Theory*. New York: Cambridge University Press.

Powell, David. 1992. *British Politics and the Labour Question, 1868–1990*. New York: St. Martin's Press.

Pugh, Martin. 1999. *Britain Since 1789: A Concise History*. New York: St. Martin's Press.

Quirk, Joel, and David Richardson. 2010. "Religion, Urbanization, and Anti-Slavery Mobilization in Britain, 1787–1833." *European Journal of English Studies* 14(3): 263–279.

Rai, Amit. 2002. *Rule of Sympathy: Sentiment, Race, and Power, 1750–1850*. New York: Palgrave.

Ralph, Michael. 2015. *Forensics of Capital*. Chicago: University of Chicago Press.

Ralph, Michael, and Maya Singhal. 2019. "Racial Capitalism." *Theory and Society* 48(6): 851–881.

Rana, Aziz. 2010. *The Two Faces of American Freedom*. Cambridge, MA: Harvard University Press.

Rappaport, Erika. 1996. "'A Husband and His Wife's Dresses': Consumer Credit and the Debtor Family in England, 1864–1914." In *The Sex of Things: Gender and Consumption in Historical Perspective*, Victoria de Grazia and Ellen Furlough, eds. Berkeley: University of California Press.

Rappaport, Erika. 2000. *Shopping for Pleasure: Women in the Making of London's West End*. Princeton: Princeton University Press.

Rappaport, Erika. 2017. *A Thirst for Empire: How Tea Shaped the Modern World*. Princeton: Princeton University Press.

Redfern, Percy. 1913. *The Story of the C.W.S., 1863–1913: The Jubilee History of the Co-operative Wholesale Society Ltd*. Manchester: Co-operative Wholesale Society.

Redfern, Percy. 1920. *The Consumer's Place in Society*. Manchester: Co-operative Union.

Redfern, Percy. 1946. *Journey to Understanding*. London: George Allen & Unwin Ltd.

Rediker, Marcus. 2017. *The Fearless Benjamin Lay: The Quaker Dwarf Who Became the First Revolutionary Abolitionist*. Boston: Beacon Press.

Reed, Isaac Ariail. 2011. *Interpretation and Social Knowledge*. Chicago: University of Chicago Press.

Reed, Isaac Ariail. 2020. *Power in Modernity: Agency Relations and the Creative Destruction of the King's Two Bodies*. Chicago: University of Chicago Press.

Residents of Hull House. 1895. *Hull House Maps and Papers*. New York: T. Y. Crowell.

Ribas, Vanesa. 2015. *On the Line: Slaughterhouse Lives and the Making of the New South*. Berkeley: University of California Press.

Richards, Thomas. 1990. *The Commodity Culture of Victorian England: Advertising and Spectacle, 1851–1914*. Stanford: Stanford University Press.

Richardson, David. 1987. "The Slave Trade, Sugar, and British Economic Growth." In *British Capitalism and Caribbean Slavery: The Legacy of Eric Williams*, Barbara Solow and Stanley Engerman, eds. New York: Cambridge University Press.

Richardson, David. 2007. "The Ending of the British Slave Trade in 1807: The Economic Context." In *The British Slave Trade: Abolition, Parliament, and the People*, Stephen Farrell, Melanie Unwin, and James Walvin, eds. Edinburgh: University of Edinburgh Press.

Roberts, William Clare. 2017. *Marx's Inferno: The Political Theory of Capital*. Princeton: Princeton University Press.

Robins, Jonathan. 2012. "Slave Cocoa and Red Rubber: E. D. Morel and the Problem of Ethical Consumption." *Comparative Studies in Society and History* 54: 592–611.

Robinson, Cedric. 1983. *Black Marxism: The Making of the Black Radical Tradition*. London: Zed Press.

Rodgers, Daniel. 1978. *The Work Ethic in Industrial America, 1850–1920*. Chicago: University of Chicago Press.

Rodgers, Daniel. 1998. *Atlantic Crossings: Social Politics in a Progressive Age*. Cambridge, MA: Harvard University Press.

Rosa, Hartmut. 2003. "Social Acceleration: Ethical and Political Consequences of a Desynchronized High-Speed Society." *Constellations* 10(1): 3–32.

Rosa, Hartmut. 2013. *Social Acceleration: A New Theory of Modernity*. New York: Columbia University Press.

Rosa, Hartmut. 2019. *Resonance: A Sociology of Our Relationship to the World*. New York: Polity Press.

Rosenberg, Emily, ed. 2012. *A World Connecting: 1870–1945*. Cambridge, MA: Harvard University Press.

Rossignol, Marie-Jeanne, and Bertrand van Ruymbeke, eds. 2016. *The Atlantic World of Anthony Benezet (1713–1784): From French Reformation to North American Antislavery Activism*. Leiden: Brill.

Ruskin, John. 1903. *The Works of John Ruskin*. Vol. 17. New York: Longmans, Green, and Co.

Rutherford, Danilyn. 2018. *Living in the Stone Age: Reflections on the Origins of a Colonial Fantasy*. Chicago: University of Chicago Press.

Ryden, David Beck. 2012. "Eric Williams' Three Faces of West India Decline." *Review (Fernand Braudel Center)* 35(5): 117–133.

Schivelbusch, Wolfgang. 2014. *The Railway Journey: The Industrialization of Time and Space in the Nineteenth Century*. Berkeley: University of California Press.

Schneirov, Richard. 2006. "Thoughts on Periodizing the Gilded Age: Capital Accumulation, Society, and Politics, 1873–1898." *Journal of the Gilded Age and Progressive Era* 5(3): 189–224.

Schumpeter, Joseph. 1950. *Capitalism, Socialism, and Democracy*. New York: Harper.

Schwarzkopf, Stefan. 2015 "Consumer Communication as Commodity: British Advertising Agencies and the Global Market for Advertising, 1780–1980." In *Consuming Behaviors: Identity, Politics, and Pleasure Twentieth-Century Britain*, Erika Rappaport, Sandra Trudgen Dawson, and Mark J. Crowley, eds. New York: Bloomsbury Academic.

Scott, Gillian. 1998. *Feminism and the Politics of Working Women: The Women's Cooperative Guild, 1880s to the Second World War*. Bristol, PA: UCL Press.

Scott, Julius. 2019. *The Common Wind: Afro-American Currents in the Age of Revolution*. New York: Verso Books.

Semmel, Bernard. 1970. *The Rise of Free Trade Imperialism: Classical Political Economy, the Empire of Free Trade and Imperialism,* 1750–1850. Cambridge: Cambridge University Press.

Sewell, Jr., William H. 2005. *Logics of History: Social Theory and Social Transformation.* Chicago: University of Chicago Press.

Sewell, Jr., William H. 2008. "The Temporalities of Capitalism." *Socio-Economic Review* 8(6): 513–537.

Shaikh, Anwar. 2016. *Capitalism: Competition, Conflict, Crises.* New York: Oxford University Press.

Silva, Jennifer. 2013. *Coming Up Short: Working-Class Adulthood in an Age of Uncertainty.* New York: Oxford University Press.

Sisodia, Rajendra, Timothy Henry, and Thomas Eckschmidt. 2018 *Conscious Capitalism Field Guide: Tools for Transforming Your Organization.* Boston: Harvard Business Review Press.

Simmel, Georg. 1971. "The Metropolis and Mental Life." In *On Individuality and Social Forms: Selected Writings,* Don Levine, ed. Chicago: University of Chicago Press.

Sinha, Manisha. 2016. *The Slave's Cause: A History of Abolition.* New Haven: Yale University Press.

Sklar, Kathryn Kish. 1995a. *Florence Kelley and the Nation's Work: The Rise of Women's Political Culture,* 1830–1900. New Haven: Yale University Press.

Sklar, Kathryn Kish. 1995b. "Two Political Cultures in the Progressive Era: The National Consumers' League and the American Association for Labor Legislation." In *U.S. History as Women's History: New Feminist Essays,* Linda Kerber, Alice Kessler-Harris, and Kathryn Kish Sklar, eds. Chapel Hill: University of North Carolina Press.

Sklar, Kathryn Kish. 1998. "The Consumers' White Label Campaign of the National Consumers' League 1898–1919." In *Getting and Spending: European and American Consumer Societies in the Twentieth Century,* Susan Strasser, Charles McGovern, and Matthias Judt, eds. New York: Cambridge University Press.

Sklar, Martin. 1988. *The Corporate Reconstruction of American Capitalism,* 1890–1916. Cambridge: Cambridge University Press.

Skocpol, Theda. 1979. *States and Social Revolutions.* New York: Cambridge University Press.

Skocpol, Theda. 1992. *Protecting Soldiers and Mothers.* Cambridge, MA: Belknap Press.

Skocpol, Theda, and Margaret Somers. 1980. "The Uses of Comparative History in Macrosocial Inquiry." *Comparative Studies in Society and History* 22(2): 174–197.

Skotnicki, Tad. 2017. "Commodity Fetishism and Consumer Senses: Turn-of-the-Twentieth-Century Consumer Activism in the United States and England." *Journal of Historical Sociology* 30(3): 619–649.

Skotnicki, Tad. 2019. "Unseen Suffering: Slow Violence and the Phenomenological Structure of Social Problems." *Theory and Society* 48(2): 299–323.

Skotnicki, Tad. 2020. "Commodity Fetishism as Semblance." *Sociological Theory* 38(4): 314–330.

Slaughter, Thomas P. 2008. *The Beautiful Soul of John Woolman, Apostle of Abolition.* New York: Hill and Wang.

Sliwinski, Sharon. 2011. *Human Rights in Camera*. Chicago: University of Chicago Press.

Smith, Adam. 2003 [1776]. *The Wealth of Nations*. New York: Bantam Dell.

Sobering, Katherine. 2019. "The Relational Production of Workplace Equality: The Case of Worker-Recuperated Businesses in Argentina." *Qualitative Sociology* 42: 543–565.

Sombart, Werner. 1967. *The Quintessence of Capitalism: A Study of the History and Psychology of the Modern Business Man*. New York: H. Fertig.

Somers, Margaret and Fred Block. 2005. "From Poverty to Perversity: Ideas, Markets, and Institutions over 200 Years of Welfare Debate." *American Sociological Review* 70: 260–287.

Spillman, Lyn. 2012. *Solidarity in Strategy: Making Business Meaningful in American Trade Associations*. Chicago: University of Chicago Press.

Spillman, Lyn. 2019. *What Is Cultural Sociology?* New York: Polity Press.

Sraffa, Pierro. 1975. *Production of Commodities by Means of Commodities: A Prelude to a Critique of Economic Theory*. New York: Cambridge University Press.

Stamatov, Peter. 2013. *The Origins of Global Humanitarianism: Religion, Empires, and Advocacy*. New York: Cambridge University Press.

Stamatov, Peter. 2014. "Beyond and Against Capitalism: Abolitionism and the Moral Dimension of Humanitarian Practice." *International Social Science Journal* 65(215): 25–35.

Stapleford, Thomas. 2009. *The Cost of Living in America: A Political Historical of Economic Statistics, 1880–2000*. New York: Oxford University Press.

Stillerman, Joel. 2015. *The Sociology of Consumption: A Global Approach*. New York: Polity Press.

Stinchcombe, Arthur L. 1995. *Sugar Island Slavery in the Age of Enlightenment: The Political Economy of the Caribbean World*. Princeton: Princeton University Press.

Stobart, Jon. 2013. *Sugar and Spice: Grocers and Groceries in Provincial England, 1650–1830*. New York: Oxford University Press.

Stobart, Jon. 2017. "Cathedrals of Consumption? Provincial Department Stores in England, c. 1880–1930." *Enterprise & Society* 18(4): 810–845.

Stolle, Dietland, and Michele Micheletti. 2013. *Political Consumerism: Global Responsibility in Action*. New York: Cambridge University Press.

Storr, Virgil Henry. 2013. *Understanding the Culture of Markets*. New York: Routledge.

Storrs, Landon. 2000. *Civilizing Capitalism: The National Consumers' League, Women's Activism, and Labor Standards in the New Deal Era*. Chapel Hill: University of North Carolina Press.

Strasser, Susan, Charles McGovern, and Matthias Judt, eds. 1998. *Getting and Spending: European and American Consumer Societies in the Twentieth Century*. New York: Cambridge University Press.

Summers-Effler, Erika. 2010. *Laughing Saints and Righteous Sinners: Emotional Rhythms in Social Movement Groups*. Chicago: University of Chicago Press.

Sussman, Charlotte. 1994. "Women and the Politics of Sugar, 1792." *Representations* 48: 48–69.

Sussman, Charlotte. 2000. *Consuming Anxieties: Consumer Protest, Gender, and British Slavery, 1713–1833*. Stanford: Stanford University Press.

Sutherland, Keston. 2008. "Marx in Jargon." *World Picture* 1(Spring): 1–25.

Swaminathan, Srividhya. 2009. *Debating the Slave Trade: The Rhetoric of British National Identity, 1759–1815*. Burlington, VT: Ashgate.

Szasz, Andrew. 2007. *Shopping Our Way to Safety: How We Changed from Protecting the Environment to Protecting Ourselves*. Minneapolis: University of Minnesota Press.

Taussig, Michael. 1980. *The Devil and Commodity Fetishism in South America*. Chapel Hill: University of North Carolina Press.

Taylor, Arthur John. 1975. *The Standard of Living in Britain in the Industrial Revolution*. London: Methuen.

Thomas, Helen. 2000. *Romanticism and Slave Narratives: Transatlantic Testimonies*. New York: Cambridge University Press.

Thompson, E. P. 1971. "The Moral Economy of the English Crowd in the Eighteenth Century." *Past & Present* 50: 76–136.

Ticktin, Miriam. 2016. "Thinking Beyond Humanitarian Borders." *Social Research* 83(2): 255–271.

Tilly, Charles. 1990. *Coercion, Capital, and European States, AD 990–1990*. Cambridge, MA: Blackwell.

Tilly, Charles. 1995. *Popular Contention in Great Britain*. Cambridge, MA: Harvard University Press.

Tilly, Charles. 2006. *Regimes and Repertoires*. Chicago: University of Chicago Press.

Timmer, Marcel P., Bart Los, Robert Stehrer, and Gaaitzen J. de Vries. 2016. "An Anatomy of the Global Trade Slowdown Based on the WIOD 2016 Release." GGDC Research Memorandum GD-162. Groningen Growth and Development Centre, University of Groningen.

Topik, Stephen, and Allen Wells. 2012. "Commodity Chains in a Global Economy." In *A World Connecting, 1870–1945*, Emily Rosenberg, ed. Cambridge, MA: Harvard University Press.

Torrance, John. 1995. *Karl Marx's Theory of Ideas*. New York: Cambridge University Press.

Trentmann, Frank. 2001. "Bread, Milk, and Democracy: Consumption and Citizenship in Twentieth-Century Britain" In *The Politics of Consumption: Material Culture and Citizenship in Europe and America*, Martin Daunton and Matthew Hilton, eds. Oxford: Berg Publishers.

Trentmann, Frank. 2008. *Free Trade Nation: Commerce, Consumption, and Civil Society in Modern Britain*. New York: Oxford University Press.

Trentmann, Frank. 2016. *Empire of Things: How We Became a World of Consumers, from the Fifteenth Century to the Twenty-First*. New York: HarperCollins.

Trubek, Amy. 2008. *The Taste of Place: A Cultural Journey into Terroir*. Berkeley: University of California Press.

Turley, David. 1991. *The Culture of English Antislavery, 1780–1860*. New York: Routledge.

Turner, Jonathan, and Jan Stets. 2005. *The Sociology of Emotions*. New York: Cambridge University Press.

Twells, Alison. 2011. "'We Ought to Obey God Rather than Man': Women, Anti-Slavery, and Nonconformist Religious Cultures." In *Women, Dissent, and Anti-Slavery in Britain and America, 1790–1865*, Elizabeth Clapp and Julie Jeffrey, eds. New York: Oxford University Press.

Van Cleve, George. 2010. *A Slaveholders' Union: Slavery, Politics, and the Constitution in the Early American Republic*. Chicago: University of Chicago Press.

Veblen, Thorstein. 1994 [1899]. *The Theory of the Leisure Class*. New York: Penguin.

Vincent, Julien. 2006. "The Moral Expertise of the British Consumer, c. 1900: A Debate Between the Christian Social Union and the Webbs." In *The Expert Consumer: Associations and Professionals in Consumer Society*, Alain Chatriot, Marie-Emmanuelle Chessel, and Matthew Hilton, eds. Burlington, VT: Ashgate.

Wagner, Henry Raup, with Helen Rand Parish. 1967. *The Life and Writings of Bartolomé de las Casas*. Albuquerque: University of New Mexico Press.

Wallerstein, Immanuel. 1976. *The Modern World-System: Capitalist Agriculture and the Origins of the European World-Economy in the Sixteenth Century*. New York: Academic Press.

Wallerstein, Immanuel. 1983. *Historical Capitalism*. London: Verso Books.

Walker, R. B. 1973. "Advertising in London Newspapers, 1650–1750." *Business History* 15(2): 112–130.

Walsh, Claire. 1995. "Shop Design and the Display of Goods in Eighteenth-Century London." *Journal of Design History* 8(3): 157–176.

Walsh, Claire. 2014. "Stalls, Bulks, Shops and Long-Term Change in Seventeenth- and Eighteenth-Century England." In *The Landscape of Consumption: Shopping Streets and Cultures of Western Europe, 1600–1900*, Jan Hein Furnée and Clé Lesger, eds. Basingstoke: Palgrave Macmillan.

Walvin, James. 1986. *England, Slaves, and Freedom, 1776–1838*. Jackson: University of Mississippi Press.

Weatherill, Lorna. 1996. *Consumer Behavior and Material Culture in Britain, 1660–1760*. New York: Routledge.

Webb, Beatrice. 1930 [1891]. *The Co-operative Movement in Great Britain*. London: George Allen & Unwin Ltd.

Webb, Catherine. 1904. *Industrial Co-operation: The Story of a Peaceful Revolution*. Manchester: Co-operative Wholesale Society.

Webb, Catherine. 1927. *The Woman with the Basket: The History of the Women's Co-operative Guild, 1883–1927*. Manchester: C.W.S. Printing Works.

Weber, Max. 1930. *The Protestant Ethic and the Spirit of Capitalism*. London: George Allen & Unwin Ltd.

Weber, Max. 1946. "Religious Rejections of the World and Their Directions." In *From Max Weber: Essays in Sociology*, Hans Gerth and C. Wright Mills, eds. New York: Oxford University.

Whelan, Timothy. 2009. "William Fox, Martha Gurney, and Radical Discourse of the 1790s." *Eighteenth-Century Studies* 42(3): 397–411.

Whelan, Timothy. 2011. "Martha Gurney and the Anti-Slave Trade Movement, 1788–

94." In *Women, Dissent, and Anti-Slavery in Britain and America, 1790–1865*, Elizabeth Clapp and Julie Jeffrey, eds. New York: Oxford University Press.

Wherry, Frederick. 2006. "The Social Sources of Authenticity in Global Handicraft Markets: Evidence from Northern Thailand." *Journal of Consumer Culture* 6(1): 5–32.

Wherry, Frederick. 2012. *The Culture of Markets*. New York: Polity Press.

Wherry, Frederick. 2014. "Analyzing the Culture of Markets." *Theory and Society* 43(3–4): 421–436.

White, Jerry. 2013. *A Great and Monstrous Thing: London in the Eighteenth Century*. Cambridge, MA: Harvard University Press.

Wiebe, Robert. 1967. *The Search for Order, 1877–1920*. New York: Hill and Wang.

Wiedenhoft, Wendy. 2008. "An Analytical Framework for Studying the Politics of Consumption: The Case of the National Consumers' League." *Social Movement Studies* 7(3): 281–303.

Williams, Eric. 1994 [1944]. *Capitalism and Slavery*. Chapel Hill: University of North Carolina Press.

Williams, Rosalind. 1982. *Dream Worlds: Mass Consumption in Late Nineteenth Century France*. Berkeley: University of California Press.

Wilmers, Nathan. 2017. "Does Consumer Demand Reproduce Inequality? High-Income Consumers, Vertical Differentiation, and the Wage Structure." *American Journal of Sociology* 123(1): 178–231.

Wilson, J. F., Anthony Webster, and Rachael Vorberg-Rugh. 2013. *Building Co-operation: A Business History of the Co-operative Group, 1863–2013*. Oxford: Oxford University Press.

Wood, Ellen Meiksins. 1991. *The Pristine Culture of Capitalism: A Historical Essay on Old Regimes and Modern States*. New York: Verso Books.

Wright, Erik Olin, Andrew Levine, and Elliot Sober. 1992. *Reconstructing Marxism: Essays on Explanation and the Theory of History*. New York: Verso Books.

Wright, Gavin. 1990. "The Origins of American Industrial Success, 1879–1940." *American Economic Review* 80(4): 651–668.

Wyman-McCarthy, Matthew. 2018. "British Abolitionism and Global Empire in the Late 18th Century: A Historiographic Overview." *History Compass* 16(10): 1–12.

Yates, Joshua J., and James Davison Hunter, eds. 2011. *Thrift and Thriving in America: Capitalism and Moral Order from the Puritans to the Present*. New York: Oxford University Press.

Young, Michael. 2005. *Bearing Witness Against Sin: The Evangelical Birth of the American Social Movement*. Chicago: University of Chicago Press.

Zelizer, Viviana. 1994. *Pricing the Priceless Child: The Changing Social Value of Children*. Princeton: Princeton University Press.

Zelizer, Viviana. 2011. *Economic Lives: How Culture Shapes the Economy*. Princeton: Princeton University Press.

Žižek, Slavoj. 1989. *The Sublime Object of Ideology*. New York: Verso Books.

Žižek, Slavoj. 2009. *First as Tragedy, Then as Farce*. New York: Verso Books.

Zukin, Sharon. 2004. *Point of Purchase: How Shopping Changed American Culture and Business*. New York: Routledge.

Index

CULTURE AND ECONOMIC LIFE

Diverse sets of actors create meaning in markets: consumers and socially en-gaged actors from below; producers, suppliers, and distributors from above; and the gatekeepers and intermediaries that span these levels. Scholars have studied the interactions of people, objects, and technology; charted networks of innovation and diffusion among producers and consumers; and explored the categories that constrain and enable economic action. This series captures the many angles in which these phenomena have been investigated and serves as a high-profile forum for discussing the evolution, creation, and consequences of commerce and culture.

Reimagining Money: Kenya in the Digital Finance Revolution
Sibel Kusimba
2021

Black Privilege: Modern Middle-Class Blacks
with Credentials and Cash to Spend
Cassi Pittman Claytor
2020

Global Borderlands: Fantasy, Violence, and Empire in Subic Bay, Philippines
Victoria Reyes
2019

The Costs of Connection: How Data Is Colonizing Human
Life and Appropriating It for Capitalism
Nick Couldry and Ulises A. Mejias
2019

The Moral Power of Money: Morality and Economy in the Life of the Poor
Ariel Wilkis
2018

The authorized representative in the EU for product safety and compliance is:
Mare Nostrum Group
B.V Doelen 72
4831 GR Breda
The Netherlands

www.ingramcontent.com/pod-product-compliance
Lightning Source LLC
Chambersburg PA
CBHW030349270326
41926CB00009B/1026